Eat Out at Home

Neven Maguire has spent his life entertaining, first at his parents' restaurant and guesthouse and now at his multi-award-winning MacNean House and Restaurant. Neven has sold over a quarter of a million cookbooks in Ireland and has won a number of awards, including two Irish Book Awards. A regular on RTÉ radio and television, Neven lives in Blacklion, Co. Cavan with his wife Amelda and twins Connor and Lucia.

Eat Out at Home

THE ART OF
COOKING FOR
FRIENDS AND FAMILY

Neven Maguire

GILL BOOKS

Gill Books
Hume Avenue
Park West
Dublin 12
www.gillbooks.ie

Gill Books is an imprint of M.H. Gill and Co.
© Neven Maguire 2024
978 18045 8171 1

Compiled by Orla Broderick
Designed by www.grahamthew.com
Photography by Gillian Buckley
Food styling by Sally Dunne, assisted by Tilly Brennan
Index by Eileen O'Neill
Edited by Sylvia Tombesi-Walton
Proofread by Emma Dunne
Printed and bound by L.E.G.O. SpA, Italy
This book is typeset in Swear text 10pt

The paper used in this book comes from the wood pulp of sustainably managed forests.

All rights reserved.

No part of this publication may be copied, reproduced or transmitted in any form or by any means, without written permission of the publishers.

A CIP catalogue record for this book is available from the British Library.

5 4 3 2 1

I'm dedicating this book to my wife Amelda and my twins Connor and Lucia. Thank you for all the love and support, I love cooking for you, and I enjoy sharing the love of good food with you all!

Contents

SMALL PLATES 4
Caponata with Burrata.. 6
Crispy Squid with Smoked Paprika Mayonnaise 8
Carlingford Oysters with Shallot & Tarragon Dressing 11
Mussels in Spiced Cream 12
Two Bruschettas: Tomato & Basil, Broad Bean 15
Beetroot & Hazelnut Salad with Whipped Goat's Cheese 16
Spanakopita 18
Spiced Cauliflower Bites 21
Crispy Duck Confit Salad.. 23
Ham Hock Terrine 24
Celeriac Remoulade with Smoked Trout 26
Chicken Potstickers... 28
Mushroom Risotto 31
Sweet Potato & Cáis Óir Fritters................................ 32
Crab Gratin.. 35
Smoked Salmon Wreath... 37
Baba Ghanoush Sala.. 39
Artichoke & Parma Ham Salad 40
Tunisian Carrot Salad... 42
Spanish Tapas 45
Sizzling Garlic & Chilli Prawns 46
Fully Loaded Nachos 49
Bubbling Cheese with Roasted Grapes 50
Pickled Mixed Vegetables....................................... 53
Crispy Lamb-Stuffed Flatbreads 54

BIG PLATES 56
Sticky Damson Ham with Star Anise 58
Crispy Spatchcock Chicken with Lemon & Herbs 61
One-Pot Fish Pie 62
Beef Ragu Lasagne 64
Italian Stuffed Conchiglioni 67
Fragrant Butterflied Lamb 69
Cottage Pie 71
Roast Picanha & Chargrilled Pepper Salad 72
Tacos with Chicken Tinga 74
Aubergines Stuffed with Onions, Tomato, Chilli & Parsley 76
Greek Beef & Macaroni Pie 79
Crispy Porchetta with Fennel & Herbs 80
Aromatic Poached Salmon with Avocado & Cucumber Salad ... 83
Butter Chicken 85
Slow-Cooked Onion & Goat's Cheese Tart 86
Chicken Shawarma 88
Iberico Pork with Red Gooseberry Relish 92
Macaroni Cheese with 'Nduja Crumbs 95
Chateaubriand with Béarnaise Sauce 96
Turkey Roulade with Maple Glaze 98
Large Plaice with Garlic Butter Sauce 101
Stuffed Beef Rolls with Tomato Ragu 102
Hake with Red Pepper Sauce 104
Spiced Roast Cauliflower 106
Beef & Medjool Date Tagine 108

SIDE PLATES 110
Focaccia with Rosemary & Sea Salt 112
Homemade Flatbreads 114
Chargrilled Tenderstem Broccoli with Caesar Dressing 117
Green Couscous 118
Chargrilled Aubergine with Tahini Dressing 120
Frites 123
Smashed Roast Potatoes 124
Grilled Corn Salad 127
Pilau Rice 131
House Salad with Amelda's Dressing 132
Green Beans with Goat's Cheese 134
Lemon Roast Potato Wedges 137
Braised Petits Pois with Bacon 138
Pickled Red Onions 140
Potato Gratin 143
Grilled Courgettes with Green Chimichurri Sauce 144
Warm Potato Salad 146
Slow-Roast Tomatoes with Puy Lentils 148
Creamy Butter Beans with Leeks 153
Chargrilled Cabbage with Kimchi Dressing 155
Steamed Asparagus with Hollandaise 156
Tomato & Cucumber Salad with Whipped Feta 158
Honey-Glazed Spiced Carrots with Pistachio & Dill 160
Summer Slaw 163
Apple & Fennel Salad 164

Introduction

The place where MacNean Restaurant is today was our family home when I was a youngster. It was also a restaurant and guesthouse run by my parents, Joe and Vera. So, for as long as I can remember, there were conversations about food, ingredients, recipes, hospitality, guests, teams in the kitchen, and front of house. Good food and hospitality were at the centre of our lives and that is the tradition my family, team and I have inherited and aim to live up to.

A restaurant is as much about company, atmosphere and enjoyment as it is about food, and where better to combine those elements than in your own home with family and friends? It is with that in mind that I am excited to share some of what I have learned over the years in *Eat Out at Home*.

The recipes are designed for you to mix and match according to your tastes and the occasion. One of the things I know from my years in the kitchen is that when it comes to what we like to eat, there are no hard and fast rules. So be as creative as you like with these recipes. It is all about enjoyment. You can be as simple or as adventurous as you feel comfortable with. I look forward to hearing what combinations of Small Plates, Big Plates, Side Plates and Sweet Things work best for you. We have tried out many of these recipes with success in the Cookery School over the years. I hope you will agree that this is a doable way to plan a whole range of interesting and sophisticated meals.

Whether you are planning a meal by the number of guests, or by season, or by what can be prepared in advance, there are lots of suggestions at the back of the book. From 'throw it together' meals to big family celebrations, from dinner parties to an intimate date night table for two, from party drinks and canapés to summer al fresco meals, and whether you are an experienced host or a novice entertainer, you will find lots of ideas and practical tips to help you entertain with confidence and flair, creating memorable times for family and friends.

One of my very first television programmes was called *Cook with Love*. That was how I thought about cooking then, and I still do today. For me, food has always been more than just nourishment. It is about people being together. I hope that these recipes and ideas enable you to make your special occasions that bit more special, and just as much fun, to make your everyday meals, well, less *everyday*.

SWEET THINGS	166
Affogato	168
Moroccan Orange Salad with Pomegranate	170
Aperol Spritz Sorbet	173
Hot Chocolate with Cinnamon Churros	175
Summer Blush	176
Mango with Lime, Chilli & Star Anise	178
Lemon Posset with Passion Fruit	180
Vanilla Panna Cotta with Clarke's Strawberries	182
Apple Mojito	185
Lemon Curd Cheesecake	187
Basque Cheesecake with Cherry Compote	188
Cinnamon Swirl Apple Cake	190
Coconut Crème Brûlée	193
Coole Swan Chocolate Truffles	194
Chocolate Mousse Cups	197
Warm Blondies with Sea Salt Toffee Sauce	198
Walnut & Espresso Slice	200
Summer Fruit Trifle	203
Brown Butter Madeleines	205
Tiramisu	206
Victoria Sponge with Rhubarb, Lemon Curd & Cream	208
Pavlova Wreath with Exotic Fruit	211
Peanut Butter Fudge with Goji Berries & Pistachios	212
Red Velvet Cake	215
Cookies & Cream Birthday Cake	216
Cooking by numbers	218
Cooking by season	224
Cooking by timings	228
Vegetarian listing	234
Acknowledgements	236
Index	238

Small Plates

Caponata with Burrata

This classic Sicilian appetiser can be bought in the supermarket, but this is a versatile recipe so you can make it your own. I throw in salty capers, the best-quality olives I can find (often it's worth stoning them yourself) and some sweet, plump golden raisins. It makes for a vibrant centrepiece more than substantial enough to serve on its own, but the rich, creamy burrata takes it to another level.

—

Serves 6–8
2 red peppers
6 celery sticks, finely diced
100ml olive oil
2 aubergines, cut into 2cm dice
1 white onion, finely chopped
20g caster sugar
150g tomato purée
100ml white-wine vinegar
20g fresh flat-leaf parsley, leaves stripped and chopped
40g small capers, well rinsed
4 anchovies, finely chopped
75g good-quality stoned green or black olives
50g golden raisins
4 burrata cheeses
extra virgin olive oil for drizzling
sea salt and freshly ground black pepper

Preheat the oven to 200°C (400°F/Gas Mark 6). Place the peppers in a parchment-lined baking tray and bake for about 30 minutes, until the skins are blackened and blistered. Transfer to a large bowl and cover with cling film. Once cooled, take off the skins and remove the seeds, then cut the flesh into dice and put in a large bowl. Set aside.

Blanch the celery in a pan of boiling water for 2 minutes. Drain, refresh under cold running water and gently fold into the peppers.

Pour the olive oil into a shallow heavy-based casserole or pan, and put over a medium heat. Sauté the aubergines for 15–20 minutes, until they are soft. Scoop out of the pan and add to the pepper and celery mixture – you should be left with oil in the pan.

Add the onion to the pan and sauté until well softened but not coloured. Sprinkle in the sugar and stir in the tomato purée, then cook to reduce until it has taken on a darkened colour. Pour in the vinegar and simmer for a few minutes. Season generously and fold the parsley (reserving a little for the garnish), capers, anchovies, olives and raisins into the vegetable mixture. Leave at room temperature.

To serve, spoon the caponata on to a large platter. Nestle in the balls of burrata; then, just before sitting down at the table, roughly tear them open with your fingers. Drizzle with the extra virgin olive oil and sprinkle with the rest of the parsley.

SERVE WITH …

Artichoke & Parma Ham Salad (p.40) and **Focaccia with Rosemary & Sea Salt** (p.112) as part of an antipasti spread in the late summer. The caponata can literally be served with anything in this book, but it is particularly delicious with **Fragrant Butterflied Lamb** (p.69) or some pan-fried hake. A glass of **Summer Blush** (p.176) will get the party started.

AND FOR DESSERT …

Finish with a platter of fresh seasonal fruit – the best you can find – piled high on crushed ice.

Crispy Squid with Smoked Paprika Mayonnaise

I could have filled half this book with all the little plates I have tasted in the tapas bars in San Sebastián, Spain. This is one of the dishes I cannot resist when I visit. In Spain there is a flour specially milled for frying – harina de trigo; *finely ground semolina is a good substitute. Sheridans sells smoked pimentón paprika in small tins, and the flavour really elevates the mayonnaise.*

—

Serves 4–6
For the mayonnaise
2 garlic cloves, crushed
200g mayonnaise
1 tsp smoked paprika
2 tbsp extra virgin olive oil

For the squid
450g cleaned medium-sized squid
olive oil, for shallow-frying
semolina, for dusting
sea salt and freshly ground black pepper
lemon wedges, to serve

To make the mayonnaise, beat the garlic into the mayonnaise with the paprika and the extra virgin olive oil. Season to taste and leave for the flavours to develop.

Cut the squid pouches across into thin rings and separate the tentacles into pairs. Spread on to a tray and season with salt and pepper.

Pour the olive oil into a large deep-frying pan to a depth of 1cm, and heat to 190°C (375°F) over a medium-high heat. Toss the squid in enough of the semolina to lightly coat, shaking off any excess, and leave for 1–2 minutes so the semolina becomes slightly damp. Shallow-fry in small batches for 1 minute until crisp and lightly golden. Drain quickly on kitchen paper and put into a warm serving dish; repeat with the rest of the squid.

Serve the crispy squid hot, with bowls of the smoked paprika mayonnaise and lemon wedges.

SERVE WITH …
I would happily eat this on any occasion. For an early summer meal, it would work brilliantly as a starter before **Iberico Pork with Red Gooseberry Relish** (p.92), perhaps with some **Creamy Butter Beans with Leeks** (p.153), since it provides a deliciously tart contrast to the over-the-top creaminess of the beans.

AND FOR DESSERT …
In summer, try fresh raspberries with a generous helping of **Lemon Curd Cheesecake** (p.187) or a wobbly **Summer Fruit Trifle** (p.203).

Carlingford Oysters with Shallot & Tarragon Dressing

We have some of the best oysters in the world in Ireland, and they are wonderful examples of nature's bounty. Many of you will be familiar with Carlingford oysters, which have a sweet, nutty flavour and a slight tannic, lingering aftertaste. The success of this dish lies entirely on shucking the oysters immediately before serving. The dressing elevates the oysters' unique taste and brings another high note.

—

Serves 4
20 Carlingford oysters
2 small shallots, very finely chopped
2 tsp chopped fresh tarragon
2 tsp chopped fresh flat-leaf parsley
6 tbsp seasoned rice vinegar
lime wedges, to garnish

To open the oysters, wrap one hand in a clean tea towel and hold the oyster in it with the flat shell uppermost. Push the point of an oyster knife into the hinge, located at the narrowest point, and wiggle the knife back and forth until the seal of the hinge breaks and you can get the knife between the two shells. Twist the point of the knife upwards to lever up the top shell, cut through the ligament attaching the oyster to the top of the shell and lift the shell off. Gently release the oyster meat from the bottom shell, pick out any little bits of shell and then pour away the juices. Arrange the oysters in their bottom shells on a platter or small plates.

To make the dressing, mix the shallots, tarragon, parsley and seasoned rice vinegar. Spoon a little of the dressing on to each oyster. Garnish with the lime wedges and serve straight away.

SERVE WITH ...
Allow 4–6 oysters per person for an appetiser, though it can be fun to start a larger meal – at Christmas, for example – with just a couple each. They make a lovely light meal when followed by the **Aromatic Poached Salmon with Avocado & Cucumber Salad** (p.83) and boiled new potatoes.

AND FOR DESSERT ...
Clean your palate with **Mango with Lime, Chilli & Star Anise** (p.178) – with or without the tequila, depending on the day of the week!

Mussels in Spiced Cream

Turn your kitchen into a French bistro with this twist on moules frites, which you can serve with a lovely glass of crisp white wine. The amounts of this recipe can be easily altered depending on how many guests you have. When I am making this for a main course I tend to buy 500g per person.

—

Serves 4–6
1kg fresh mussels
knob of butter
2 small shallots, finely chopped
2 garlic cloves, thinly sliced
1 tsp mild curry seasoning
120ml dry white wine
1 lemon
150ml cream
20g flat-leaf parsley, leaves stripped and finely chopped
sea salt and freshly ground black pepper

Scrub the mussels in a large bowl of cold water, and swish them around with your hands to wash them thoroughly. Use a small sharp knife to scrape off any barnacles attached to the shells, discarding any mussels with broken shells. Pull off the beards using a knife to help you – they just need a good tug. If any mussels are open, tap them sharply against the side of the sink – if they do not close, discard them as they are not edible. Rinse again and put in a colander.

Heat a large pan with a tight-fitting lid over a high heat. Add the butter, then, when it starts to sizzle, add the shallots, garlic and curry seasoning. Sauté for 1 minute, then pour in the wine. Pare a good strip of rind from the lemon and add to the pot with a good squeeze of juice, catching the pips with your fingers. Tip in the mussels and cover with the lid. The pan should not be more than half full – the mussels need plenty of space to move around so that they cook evenly. Bring to a fast boil and cook for 3–4 minutes until they start to open, shaking the pan occasionally. Add the cream, season and quickly fold in the parsley.

Remove the pan from the heat to stop the mussels cooking any further. Discard any mussels that have stayed close. Spoon into warmed bowls and pour over the pan juices, leaving behind the very end, which may have a little grit in it.

SERVE WITH …
Focaccia with Rosemary & Sea Salt (p.112) is great to soak up all the juices. You can also serve this as a big pot in the middle of the table with a pile of **Frites** (p.123) and a bowl of **House Salad with Amelda's Dressing** (p.132), allowing everyone to dip in.

AND FOR DESSERT …
There is no better way to finish this meal than with some **Brown Butter Madeleines** (p.205) and good coffee.

Two Bruschettas: Tomato & Basil, Broad Bean

Bruschetta made with warm sourdough is a great way to start a meal. You need to taste the flame in the bread; the easiest way to achieve this is with a well-seasoned cast-iron griddle pan, but you also get fantastic results over a barbecue or an open fire. Make this when you can get hold of Irish tomatoes grown for flavour, which – with very little work – can transport you to the Mediterranean.

—

Serves 6–8
For the broad bean bruschetta
500g frozen broad beans
extra virgin olive oil, for drizzling
3 tbsp freshly grated Parmesan
1 fresh mint sprig, leaves stripped and finely chopped
pinch of dried chilli flakes

For the tomato and basil bruschetta
300g vine-ripened Irish tomatoes
1 fresh basil sprig

1 small sourdough loaf
1 garlic clove, halved
sea salt and freshly ground black pepper

To make the broad bean topping, cook the beans in a pan of boiling salted water for 4–5 minutes until tender. Drain and refresh under cold running water and slip the beans out of their skins. Put in a bowl and drizzle with a little olive oil, then roughly mash and fold in the Parmesan, mint and chilli flakes. Season to taste. This can be done a few hours in advance and kept covered with cling film at room temperature.

For the tomato topping, cut the tomatoes into chunky pieces and season to taste. Tear in the basil and add another drizzle of olive oil.

Heat a griddle pan over a high heat until smoking. Meanwhile, cut the sourdough loaf into thick slices, approximately 1.5cm, discarding the ends. Add the slices of bread to the pan in batches and cook for 1–2 minutes on each side until lightly charred. As soon as they are done, rub with the garlic and drizzle lightly with olive oil.

Spoon the two different toppings on the bruschetta when ready to serve and arrange on a platter – the two different colours will look fantastic.

SERVE WITH ...
This is the perfect starter before a sumptuous **Beef Ragu Lasagne** (p.64) or, as a meat-free option, **Italian Stuffed Conchiglioni** (p.67), alongside a nice crisp green salad.

AND FOR DESSERT ...
The first time I had **Affogato** (p.168), I couldn't believe how just a few ingredients could taste so good. This five-minute treat is right up there with the great Italian desserts, and a perfect way to end a meal.

Beetroot & Hazelnut Salad with Whipped Goat's Cheese

A classic combination that looks sophisticated but is so easy to make, this is perfect for anyone who is growing their own herbs – there's something incredibly satisfying about being able to say they came from your own garden.

—

Serves 6

200g soft goat's cheese
75g cream cheese
finely grated rind of 1 lemon
4 tbsp extra virgin olive oil
100g whole hazelnuts
100g raw baby beetroots (a striped variety, if possible)
4 cooked beetroots
50g mixed soft herbs, such as parsley, chives, dill, mint, basil or chervil
3 tbsp white-wine vinegar
1 tbsp raw Irish honey
sea salt and freshly ground black pepper

Put the goat's cheese, cream cheese and lemon rind in a bowl with one tablespoon of the olive oil and a pinch of salt. Beat with an electric whisk until light and fluffy. Cover and chill for up to 24 hours.

Heat a non-stick frying pan over a medium heat and toast the hazelnuts for a few minutes, tossing occasionally to ensure they cook evenly. Tip out, leave to cool and then rub off the skins and roughly chop.

Peel the raw beetroots and cut into wafer-thin slices – a mandolin is perfect if you have one. Put the beetroots in a bowl with another tablespoon of oil and a little seasoning.

Cut the cooked beetroot into 1cm cubes. Pick the leaves from the herbs; if using chives, cut into 3cm lengths and add to the beetroot. Whisk the rest of the olive oil with the vinegar and honey, and season to taste.

Arrange the raw beetroot slices overlapping on small plates and add a quenelle of the goat's cheese mixture to each one. Toss the cooked beetroot and herbs in the dressing and scatter around the plates. Finish with the hazelnuts to serve.

SERVE WITH ...
This highly visual dish works almost year-round as our climate suits this earthy vegetable. For a spring or early summer lunch, serve with **Large Plaice with Garlic Butter Sauce** (p.101) and **Steamed Asparagus with Hollandaise** (p.156). Come winter, opt for **Stuffed Beef Rolls with Tomato Ragu** (p.102) and **House Salad with Amelda's Dressing** (p.132).

AND FOR DESSERT ...
Victoria Sponge with Rhubarb, Lemon Curd & Cream (p.208) in spring, when rhubarb season has just started. In winter, I'd treat myself and guests to **Walnut & Espresso Slice** (p.200) with a bowl of softly whipped cream to round off the meal nicely.

Spanakopita

This dish will remind many of you of holidays on the Greek Islands. The earthy flavour of spinach works perfectly with salty feta, all balanced out by the sweetness of the red onion and scallions. These parcels can be prepared a day ahead, then baked just before you are ready to serve.

—

Makes 24

1 tbsp olive oil
1 red onion, finely chopped
6 scallions, trimmed and finely chopped
350g spinach, thick stalks removed
100g feta cheese
1 large egg
1 tbsp freshly grated Parmesan cheese
pinch of freshly grated nutmeg
1 tbsp chopped fresh mint, plus extra to garnish, or use pea shoots
100g butter
275g packet filo pastry, thawed if frozen (about 6 sheets in total)
2 tbsp sesame seeds
sea salt and freshly ground black pepper

Preheat the oven to 180°C (350°F/Gas Mark 4). Meanwhile, heat the oil in a large pan and add the onion and scallions, then cook gently for 2–3 minutes until softened but not browned. Add the spinach a handful at a time, until it has all wilted down, stirring constantly. Tip into a large sieve and drain well, pressing out all the excess liquid with a wooden spoon. Leave to cool.

Crumble the feta cheese into a bowl, then mix in the egg, Parmesan, cooled spinach mixture, nutmeg and mint. Season to taste.

Melt the butter in a small pan and leave to cool a little. Unroll the sheets of pastry and cut the stack lengthways into strips about 6cm wide. Brush the top layer with melted butter. Place a heaped spoonful of the filling in the centre of one strip, at the nearest end to you, and fold one bottom corner of the pastry diagonally over the filling, so that the corner touches the opposite side to make a triangle. Fold over the filled triangular corner and continue folding it along the whole strip into a triangular parcel. Repeat until you have 24 parcels in total.

Brush the undersides of each parcel with a little butter and place on a baking sheet lined with non-stick parchment paper. Brush the tops with the rest of the butter and sprinkle with the sesame seeds. Bake for 20–25 minutes until crisp and golden brown. Leave to cool for a few minutes before arranging on plates or a platter to serve. Garnish with torn mint leaves or pea shoots.

SERVE WITH…
Delicious hot or cold, these vegetarian morsels are great for a garden picnic, alongside a **Tomato & Cucumber Salad with Whipped Feta** (p.158), some decent shop-bought hummus and a tray of **Lemon Roast Potato Wedges** (p.137).

AND FOR DESSERT…
Keep the grazing theme going and opt for the **Peanut Butter Fudge with Goji Berries & Pistachios** (p.212), cut up into bite-sized pieces that will shine tantalisingly like jewels on the plate.

Spiced Cauliflower Bites

There's a bit of fun here – a veggie take on the American classic of buffalo chicken wings. These bites strike the perfect balance of crisp, tender and spicy, which makes them addictively delicious. Served alongside a tangy buttermilk ranch dressing, they always prove irresistible, even to those who think they are not keen on cauliflower!

Serves 4
1 cauliflower
1 tbsp paprika
1 tsp ground cumin
1 tsp garlic granules
100g plain flour
200ml kefir or buttermilk
6 tbsp hot chilli sauce
2 tbsp maple syrup
25g butter
sea salt and freshly ground black pepper
shop-bought buttermilk ranch dressing, to serve

Preheat the oven to 220°C (425°F/Gas Mark 7). Break the cauliflower into even-sized florets, trimming them down as necessary. Mix the paprika, cumin, garlic and flour in a large bowl. Season generously with salt and pepper. Make a well in the centre and whisk in the kefir or buttermilk.

Tip the cauliflower into the batter and toss to coat, then spread out on to a parchment-lined baking tray and bake for 20–25 minutes until it begins to crisp at the edges.

Heat the hot chilli sauce, maple syrup and butter in a small pan over a low heat. Brush generously all over the cauliflower bites and return to the oven for another 8–10 minutes until sizzling and nicely charred on the edges.

Arrange the spiced cauliflower bites on a large platter with a small bowl of the buttermilk ranch for dipping.

SERVE WITH ...
Go all-American and tuck into my killer **Macaroni Cheese with 'Nduja Crumbs** (p.95). These cauliflower bites will balance out some of the richness and help to get some veggies into your meal.

AND FOR DESSERT ...
An important aspect of a meal is time to let the food settle, and waiting for dessert is a good excuse to linger at the table. My **Warm Blondies with Sea Salt Toffee Sauce** (p.198) are made in advance, so all you have to do after a leisurely break is bring them out and enjoy the reaction they evoke!

Crispy Duck Confit Salad

A beautiful, fragrant salad with plenty of punchy flavours and chunks of succulent duck confit. Happily, these days you don't have to make your own duck confit – all you need to do is pop it in the oven to melt away the fat before forking the meat off the bone.

—

Serves 4

2 confit duck legs
250g spinach, watercress and rocket salad
4 scallions, trimmed and thinly sliced
2 baby cucumbers, thinly sliced
1 small, firm ripe mango, peeled and cut into slivers
15g fresh coriander, leaves stripped
15g fresh mint leaves, torn
2 tbsp chilli jam
1 tbsp lime juice
1 tbsp olive oil
1 tbsp sesame oil

Preheat the oven to 220°C (425°F/Gas Mark 7). Cook the duck in a baking tin according to packet instructions until crispy.

While the duck is cooking, put the salad leaves in a bowl with the scallions, cucumbers, mango, coriander and mint leaves, tossing lightly to combine. Make the dressing by putting the chilli jam in a screw-topped jar with the lime juice and oils; shake vigorously to combine.

When the duck is cooked, leave to rest for a few minutes, then shred the meat and crispy skin, discarding the bones and any fatty bits.

Divide the prepared salad among the plates and scatter over the duck, then drizzle over the dressing to serve.

SERVE WITH …

Light but satisfying, this salad works all year round – and especially in winter. Part of its charm is that it needs nothing to go with it. However, if you're making it for a big dinner party, serve it with **Smashed Roast Potatoes** (p.124) and sprinkled with **Pickled Red Onions** (p.140).

AND FOR DESSERT …

Forget about pudding! Instead, make a round of **Apple Mojitos** (p.185), and before you know it you'll have a table full of laughter and chatter – with the odd person looking for seconds …

Ham Hock Terrine

This ham hock terrine tastes delicious cut into slices, and it is perfect if you are catering for big numbers as you can have one course done and completely forgotten about until your guests arrive. It is also a classic starter for the Large Plaice with Garlic Butter Sauce (p.101) alongside a simple bowl of boiled potatoes.

—

Serves 8–10
2 unsmoked ham hocks, soaked overnight (each about 1.5kg)
1 large onion, roughly chopped
2 carrots, roughly chopped
2 celery sticks, roughly chopped
2 bay leaves
20g fresh flat-leaf parsley, leaves chopped and stalks reserved
10 black peppercorns
3 tbsp apple cider vinegar
lamb's lettuce, crusty bread and mustard & gherkin relish, to serve

Put the hams hocks in a large pan with the vegetables, bay leaves, parsley sprigs and peppercorns, then pour over enough water to cover. Bring to a simmer, then reduce the heat and cover partially with a lid. Simmer very gently for 3–4 hours, skimming off any impurities if necessary, until the ham hocks are very tender. Transfer to a chopping board and leave until cool enough to handle, reserving 150ml of the liquid.

Take the meat off the bone and shred into another bowl, discarding any skin, fat and cartilage. Add the reserved stock and vinegar, then mix everything together thoroughly. Layer pieces of cling film to the size of an A3 piece of paper on a clean work surface. Pile the mixture along the bottom length of the cling film, leaving about 10cm free on each side. Roll into a large, tight sausage shape, piercing with a skewer a couple of times to release any air, then put in the fridge overnight. This can be made up to 4 days in advance.

To serve, carve the ham hock terrine into slices about 2cm thick. Peel off the cling film and put on to plates. Serve with a little lamb's lettuce, some crusty bread and a dollop of the mustard & gherkin relish, if liked.

SERVE WITH ...
If you are after a Christmas classic with a twist, this ham hock is a modern make-ahead starter that eats beautifully with my **Apple & Fennel Salad** (p.164), the **Celeriac Remoulade** (p.26) without the smoked trout and perhaps some **Focaccia with Rosemary & Sea Salt** (p.112).

AND FOR DESSERT ...
A delicious, light and moreish **Red Velvet Cake** (p.215) filled and topped with cream-cheese frosting – cake heaven! This is a truly beautiful cake, perfect for a real celebration.

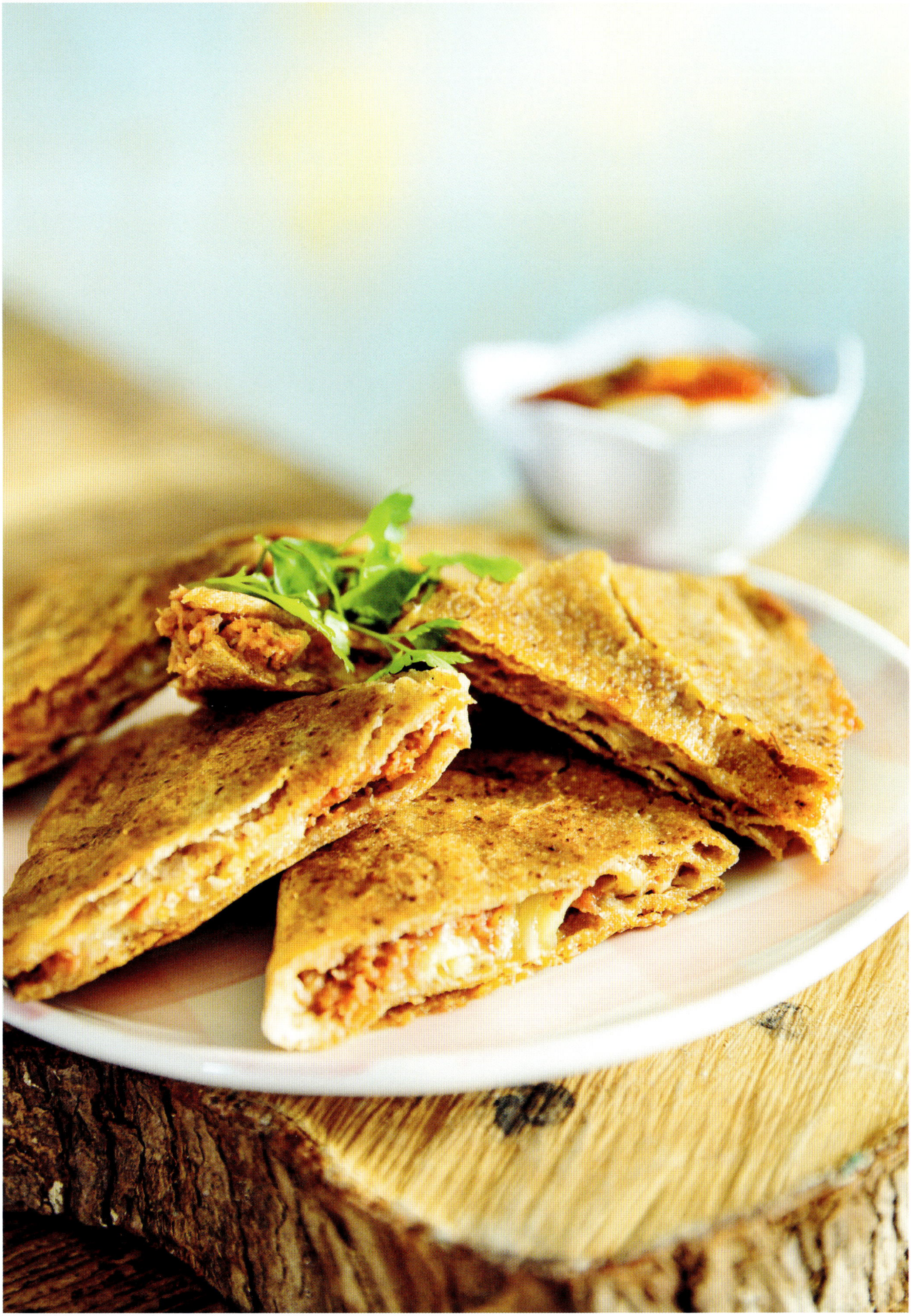

Big Plates

Sticky Damson Ham with Star Anise

I cannot overstate how good this is – and I speak as someone who has spent a lifetime experimenting with glazes for ham. If I have large numbers to cater for, it is a go-to in our house. Initially I'd serve it hot, and then use any leftovers the following day, either as part of breakfast with some poached eggs or for sandwiches.

—

Serves 8–10
2kg unsmoked gammon joint
1 onion, sliced
2 celery sticks, roughly chopped
1 tbsp black peppercorns
8 star anise
175g damson plum jam or conserve
juice of 1 orange
100g light brown sugar

Rinse the gammon with fresh water and put in a pan of boiling water. Add the onion, celery, peppercorns and 2 of the star anise. Bring to a simmer over a low heat and cook for 1½ hours. Leave to cool in the liquid.

Meanwhile, make the glaze. Put the damson jam or conserve in a small pan with the orange juice, sugar and the rest of the star anise. Heat gently until the sugar has dissolved, then simmer for 3–4 minutes or until reduced to a thick glaze, stirring to ensure it doesn't catch at the bottom. Leave to cool slightly.

Preheat the oven to 220°C (425°F/Gas Mark 7). Remove the gammon from the pan and put into a baking tin. Using a sharp knife, cut off the rind, leaving the fat on top and score diagonally into a diamond pattern. Pour around 500ml of the cooking liquid, which will help to keep the joint moist.

Smear the damson glaze all over the ham, reserving 2 tablespoons, making sure the star anise are sitting on top of the joint. Roast for 20–30 minutes until cooked through. Remove from the oven and drizzle over the remaining glaze. Leave to rest for at least 15 minutes or up to 1 hour, covered loosely with tin foil.

Carve slices from the ham and arrange on plates to serve.

SERVE WITH …
For an Irish menu with a twist, start with **Carlingford Oysters with Shallot & Tarragon Dressing** (p.11), then serve the ham with **Chargrilled Cabbage with Kimchi Dressing** (p.155) and **Potato Gratin** (p.143).

AND FOR DESSERT …
I regularly wheel out my **Red Velvet Cake** (p.215). If you're hopeless with a piping bag and don't feel up to making the cream-cheese-frosting kisses, you can decorate it with heaps of fresh flowers or berries; cherries are also perfect.

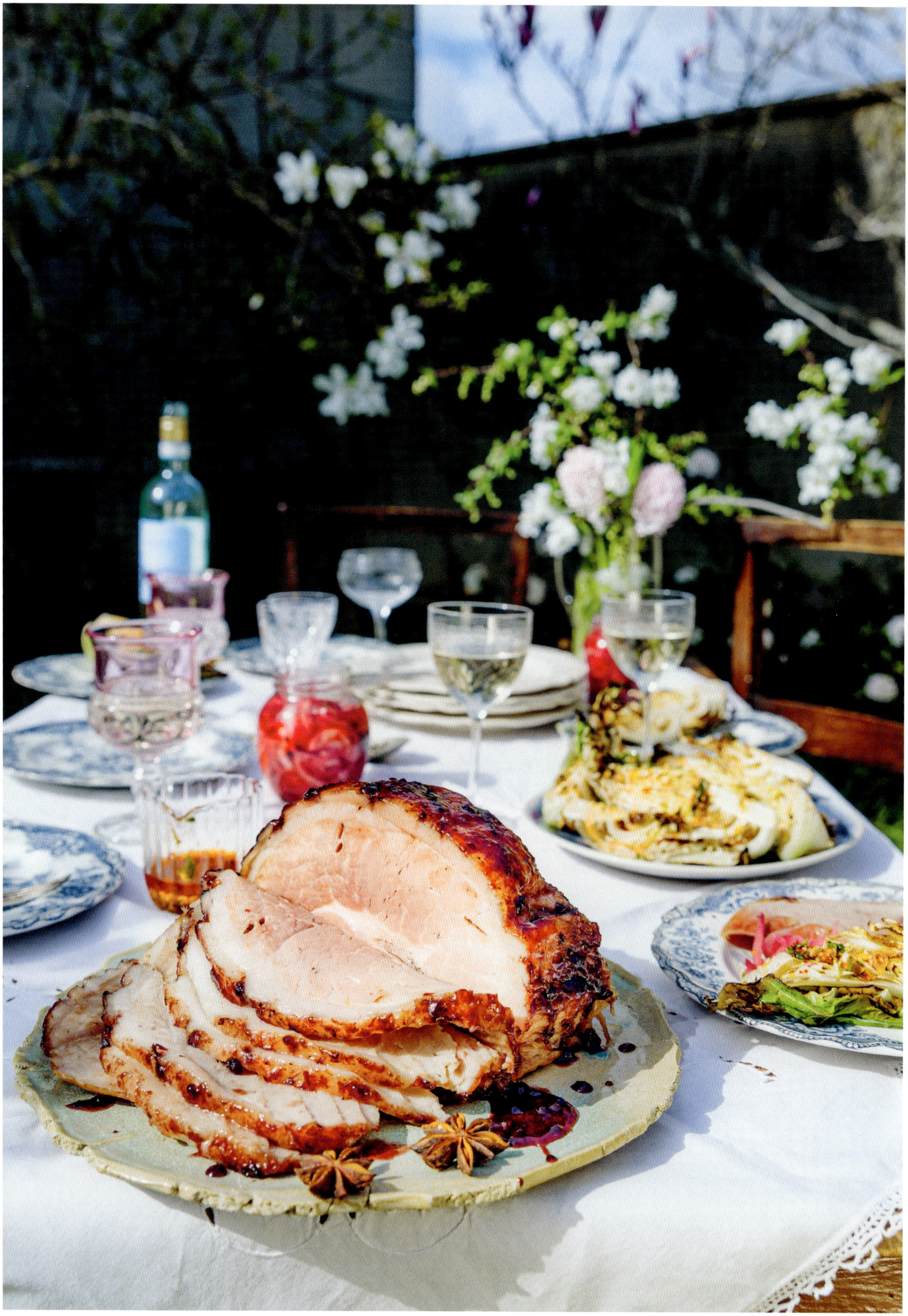

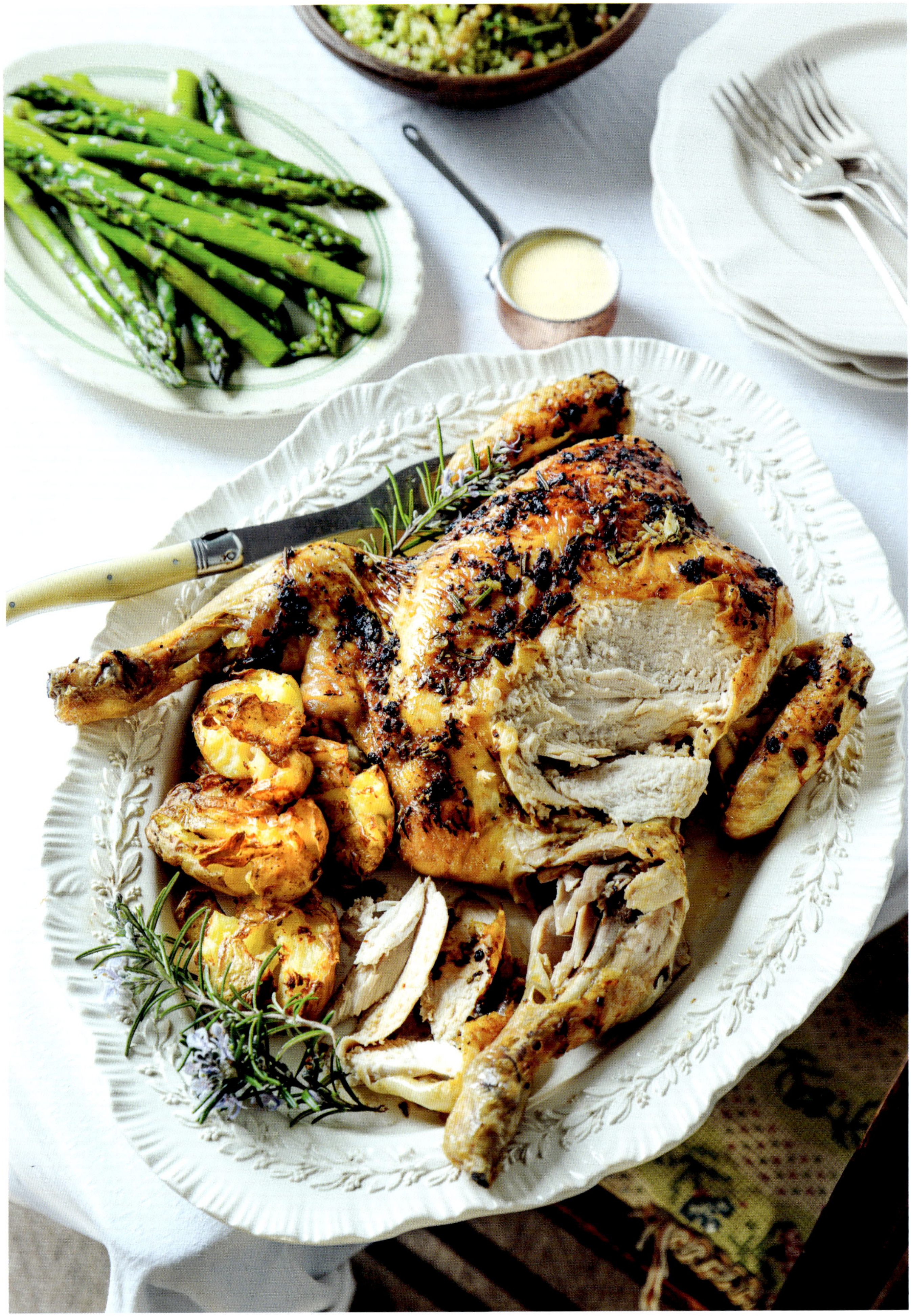

Crispy Spatchcock Chicken with Lemon & Herbs

This is a fail-safe, a dish that everyone loves and that can be dressed up or down with sides and a dessert. The speediest, easiest way to roast a whole chicken is to spatchcock (or butterfly) it first. This technique exposes lots of skin directly to the heat, guaranteeing thorough browning and crisping. It's a perfect recipe for the summer, and it will also cook brilliantly on the barbecue.

—

Serves 4

1.2kg whole chicken (preferably free-range or organic)
6 garlic cloves, crushed
a few sprigs each of thyme and rosemary, leaves picked and chopped
a few bay leaves, torn
finely grated rind and juice of 1 lemon, plus 1 extra, sliced
5 tbsp olive oil
1 packet of fresh rosemary
sea salt and freshly ground black pepper

Spatchcock the chicken by placing it breast-side down with the legs towards you. Use a kitchen scissors or sharp knife to cut along the backbone and through the ribs. Flip it over and press down the backbone so that the chicken flattens out.

In a dish large enough to hold the chicken, combine the garlic, herbs, and lemon rind, juice and slices with the oil. Season with salt and pepper, give it a good mix and rub the mixture all over the chicken. Cover and set aside at room temperature for 1 hour.

Preheat the oven to 220°C (425°F/Gas Mark 7). Put the chicken in a shallow baking tin, skin side up, spread all the marinade back over the bird and arrange the slices of lemon on top. Roast for 45 minutes until cooked through and tender. Remove from the oven and leave to rest for 15 minutes, then carve into portions (and the breasts into slices). Garnish with the extra herb sprigs to serve.

SERVE WITH ...
This goes beautifully with **Smashed Roast Potatoes** (p.124). When cooking for more than four people, roast two chickens and have platters alongside filled with **Steamed Asparagus with Hollandaise** (p.156) and **Green Couscous** (p.118), or **Grilled Corn Salad** (p.127) and **Warm Potato Salad** (p.146).

AND FOR DESSERT ...
Something classic and comforting, such as **Summer Fruit Trifle** (p.203), is especially good if you think people might go for seconds.

One-Pot Fish Pie

This pie is a simple concoction, but I just love it. I usually assemble it in advance, keep it in the fridge for up to two days and then glaze it – allowing a few extra minutes in the oven to account for it coming straight from the fridge.

—

Serves 6–8

400g packet all-butter puff pastry, thawed
50g plain flour, plus extra for dusting
50g butter
2 shallots, finely chopped
2 leeks, finely chopped
2 large potatoes, peeled and cut into chunks
500ml fresh chicken stock
100ml cream
750g mixture undyed smoked haddock, fresh salmon and hake or cod, all skinned, boned and cut into large chunks
2 tbsp chopped fresh dill, plus extra to serve
1 egg, beaten with 1 tbsp water (egg wash)
lemon wedges, to serve
sea salt and freshly ground black pepper

Preheat the oven to 180°C (350°F/Gas Mark 4). Roll out the pastry on a lightly floured board and make a 30cm circle, trimming down the edges as necessary. Use the trimmings to make some decorations for the pie. Place the circle and decorations on a parchment-lined baking sheet and chill until needed.

Melt the butter over a medium heat in a shallow casserole or skillet pan. Tip in the shallots, leeks and potatoes, and sauté for 4–5 minutes until the shallots and leeks are softened. Sprinkle over the flour and cook for another minute, stirring constantly. Gradually add the chicken stock, whisking until smooth after each addition. Pour in the cream and season to taste, then bring to a simmer.

Stir the fish chunks into the sauce and simmer for another 1–2 minutes until the fish is just tender, then fold in the dill. Wipe around the edges of the casserole, then cover the pie filling with the chilled pastry lid, tucking down the edges to form a double rim. Brush with the egg wash and prick lightly with a fork, then decorate with the pastry shapes and brush them with egg wash. Bake the fish pie for 30 minutes until the pastry is well risen and golden. Garnish with a little dill and lemon wedges. Serve immediately.

SERVE WITH...

All this requires is a crisp salad with a sharp dressing. Another dish that would go very well with it is **Braised Petits Pois with Bacon** (p.138), but there's no need to overgild an already magnificent lily ...

AND FOR DESSERT...

When rhubarb is in season, I can't resist a glorious **Victoria Sponge with Rhubarb, Lemon Curd & Cream** (p.208), which leaves nothing for me to do last minute.

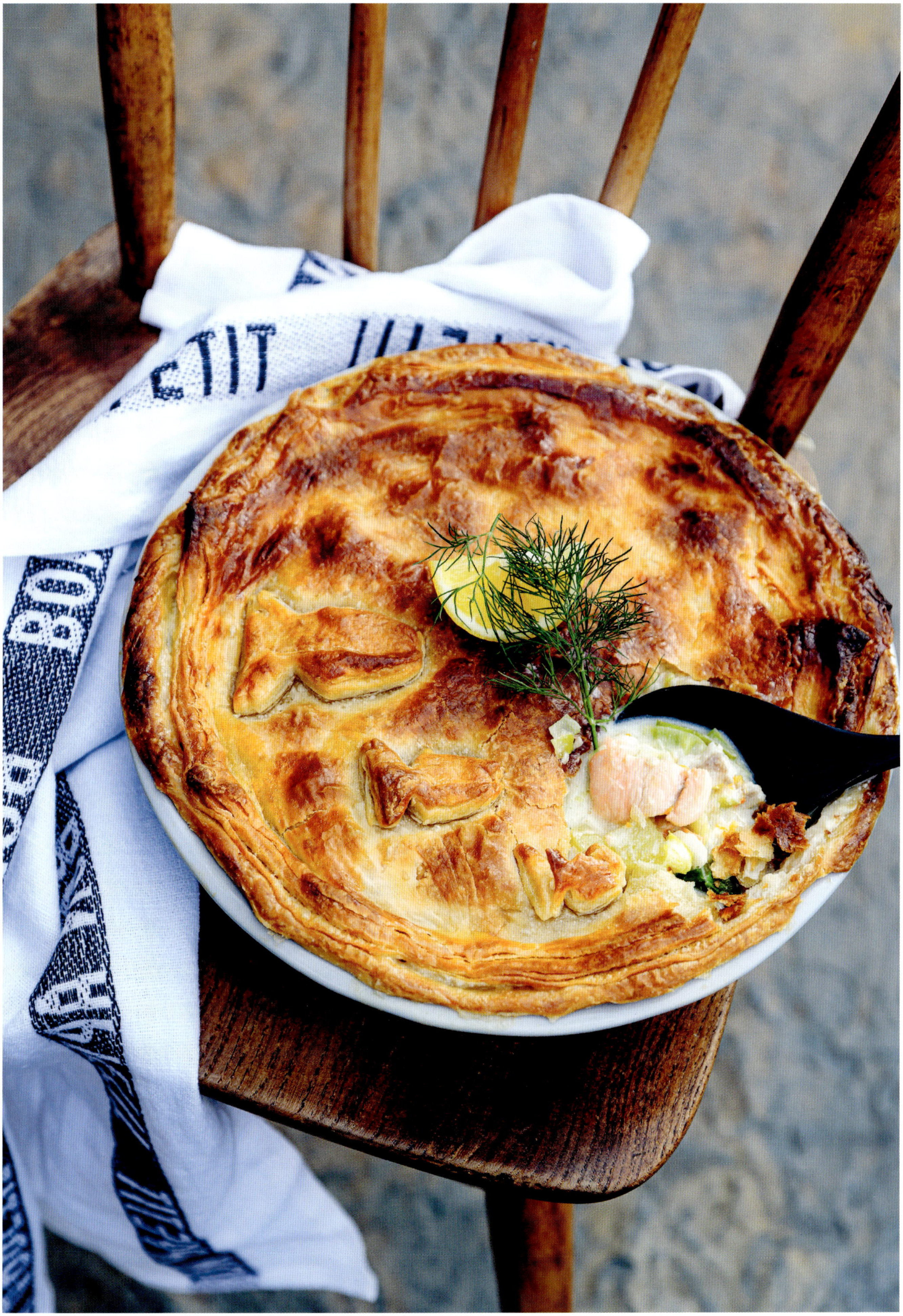

Beef Ragu Lasagne

Once you've tried this way of cooking lasagne, you'll be hooked. The rich ragu is first roasted gently in the oven giving the beef a delicious melt-in-the-mouth texture. The acidity of the tomatoes complements the fatty richness of the meat; both are balanced out by the creamy, oozing layers of the béchamel sauce.

—

Serves 4
2 tbsp olive oil
500g casserole beef slices
1 onion, finely chopped
2 celery sticks, finely chopped
1 tsp fresh thyme leaves
500g jar passata (Italian sieved tomatoes)
25g butter
2 tbsp plain flour
400ml milk
50g freshly grated Parmesan, plus a little extra
1 packet fresh egg lasagne sheets
1 buffalo burrata cheese
sea salt and freshly ground black pepper

Preheat the oven to 170°C (325°F/Gas Mark 3). Heat a shallow casserole or skillet pan over a high heat, then add 1 tablespoon of the oil. Season the beef and sauté for 2–3 minutes until lightly browned, then transfer to a plate. Add the rest of the olive oil and sauté the onion, celery and thyme until softened. Stir in the passata, add in the beef, then cover with a lid. Cook for 2 hours, then leave to relax for 15 minutes, before using two forks to shred the beef into small pieces.

Meanwhile, make the béchamel sauce by melting the butter in a small pan over a medium heat. Whisk in the flour and then, gradually add the milk until you have a smooth sauce. Season generously and stir in the Parmesan.

Spread a couple of spoons of the beef ragu in the bottom of an ovenproof dish. Cover with a layer of the lasagne sheets, cutting to fit with scissors. Cover with half of the remaining ragu, then add half of the béchamel sauce in dollops, spreading with a palette knife for an even layer.

Add another layer of the lasagne sheets and cover with the rest of the beef ragu. Add a final layer of the lasagne sheets, then spread the remaining béchamel sauce on top. Tear over the burrata and scatter a little more Parmesan on top. Bake for 30 minutes until lightly golden and bubbling. Rest for 10 minutes before cutting into slices to serve.

SERVE WITH ...
The simplest platter of **Two Bruschettas** (p.15) would be hard to match for a starter. And alongside, I'd always have a bowl of **Summer Slaw** (p.163) or **House Salad with Amelda's Dressing** (p.132).

AND FOR DESSERT ...
Tiramisu (p.206) served with a pot of strong Italian coffee.

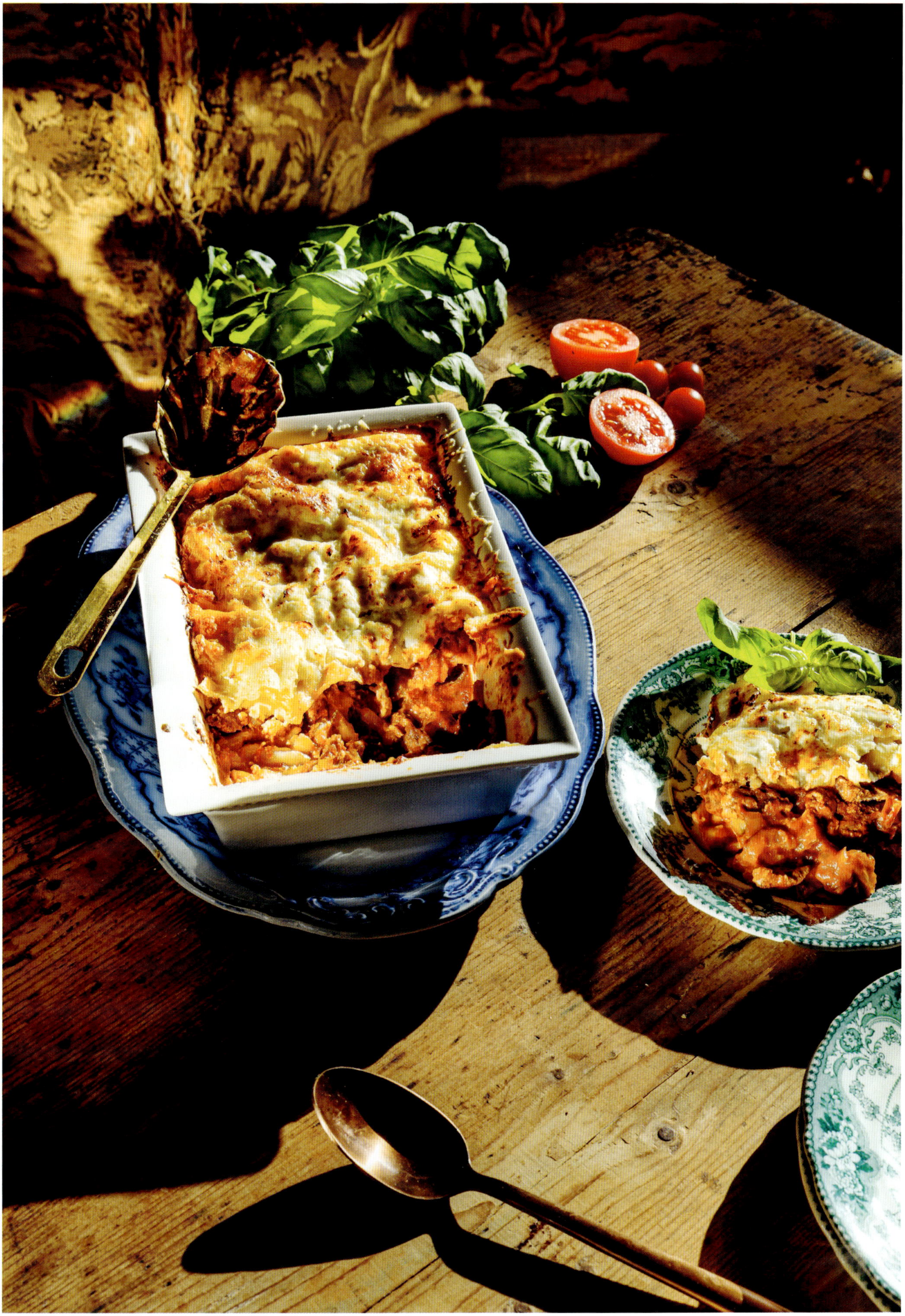

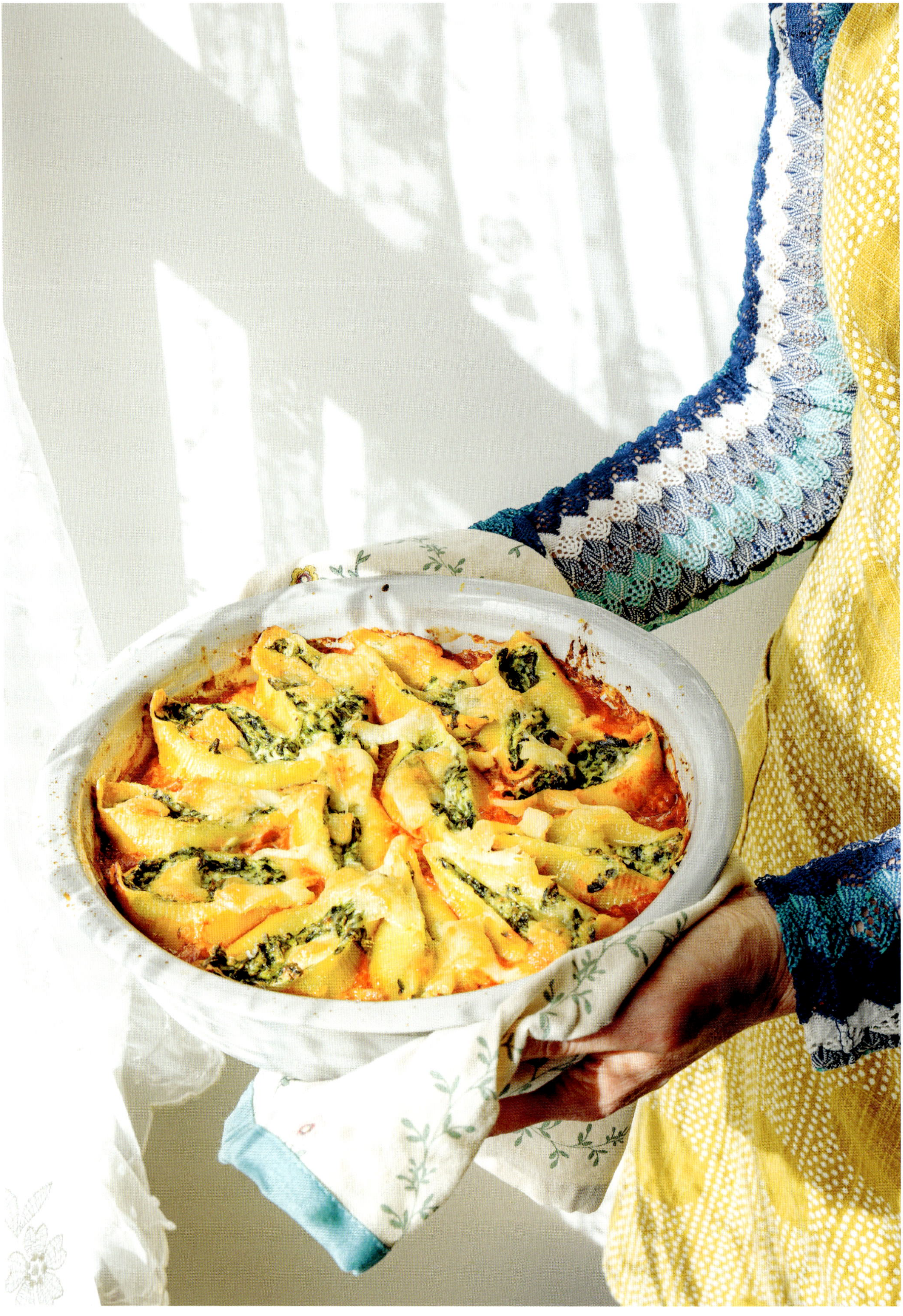

Italian Stuffed Conchiglioni

Like most baked pasta dishes, this lends itself wonderfully well to a large gathering. It's the kind of dish everyone loves, including vegetarians, and it can be made a day or two in advance. Just cover it and keep it in the fridge, then simply warm it in the oven until bubbling and golden.

—

Serves 4
1 tbsp olive oil
1 white onion, finely chopped
4 garlic cloves, crushed
1 tsp dried chilli flakes
500g passata (Italian sieved tomatoes)
pinch of sugar
350g baby spinach leaves
250g ricotta
4 tbsp freshly grated Parmesan, plus extra to garnish
1 large egg
large pinch of grated nutmeg
50g conchiglioni (giant pasta shells)
200g Buffalo mozzarella, cut into cubes
sea salt and freshly ground black pepper

Preheat the oven to 180°C (350°F/Gas Mark 4). Heat a large non-stick frying pan over a medium to high heat. Add the oil, then tip in the onion, half the garlic and chilli flakes, and sauté for 3–4 minutes until softened. Add the passata, season to taste and add the sugar, then blend to a smooth sauce. Set aside until needed.

Meanwhile, pour a kettle of boiling water over the spinach in a colander in the sink. Leave to cool a little, then squeeze out all the excess moisture and finely chop. Put the spinach in a bowl with the ricotta, Parmesan and egg. Add the rest of the garlic with the nutmeg and season generously, mixing well to combine.

Put the pasta shells into a large pan of boiling salted water and return to the boil. Simmer for 3 minutes, then drain into a colander in the sink.

Pour the tomato sauce into a shallow baking dish (about 1.5 litres in capacity). Fill the pasta shells with the spinach and ricotta mixture, and put into the sauce, making sure they are spaced well apart, then scatter over the mozzarella and garnish with Parmesan. If not eating right away, this can be covered with cling film and kept in the fridge. Otherwise, bake for 25–30 minutes until bubbling and golden brown. Serve straight to the table.

SERVE WITH …
A glistening **Artichoke & Parma Ham Salad** (p.40) should stop any grumbles from those who like to see some meat on the table. I'd probably have a bowl of crusty bread or perhaps some **Focaccia with Rosemary & Sea Salt** (p.112) to mop up all the delicious juices.

AND FOR DESSERT …
Despite **Affogato** (p.168) being strictly for grown-ups, it has a childlike quality that delights everyone. It suits a supper party more than a family meal, although you could always fill some waffle cones with a scoop of ice cream if you have little ones around.

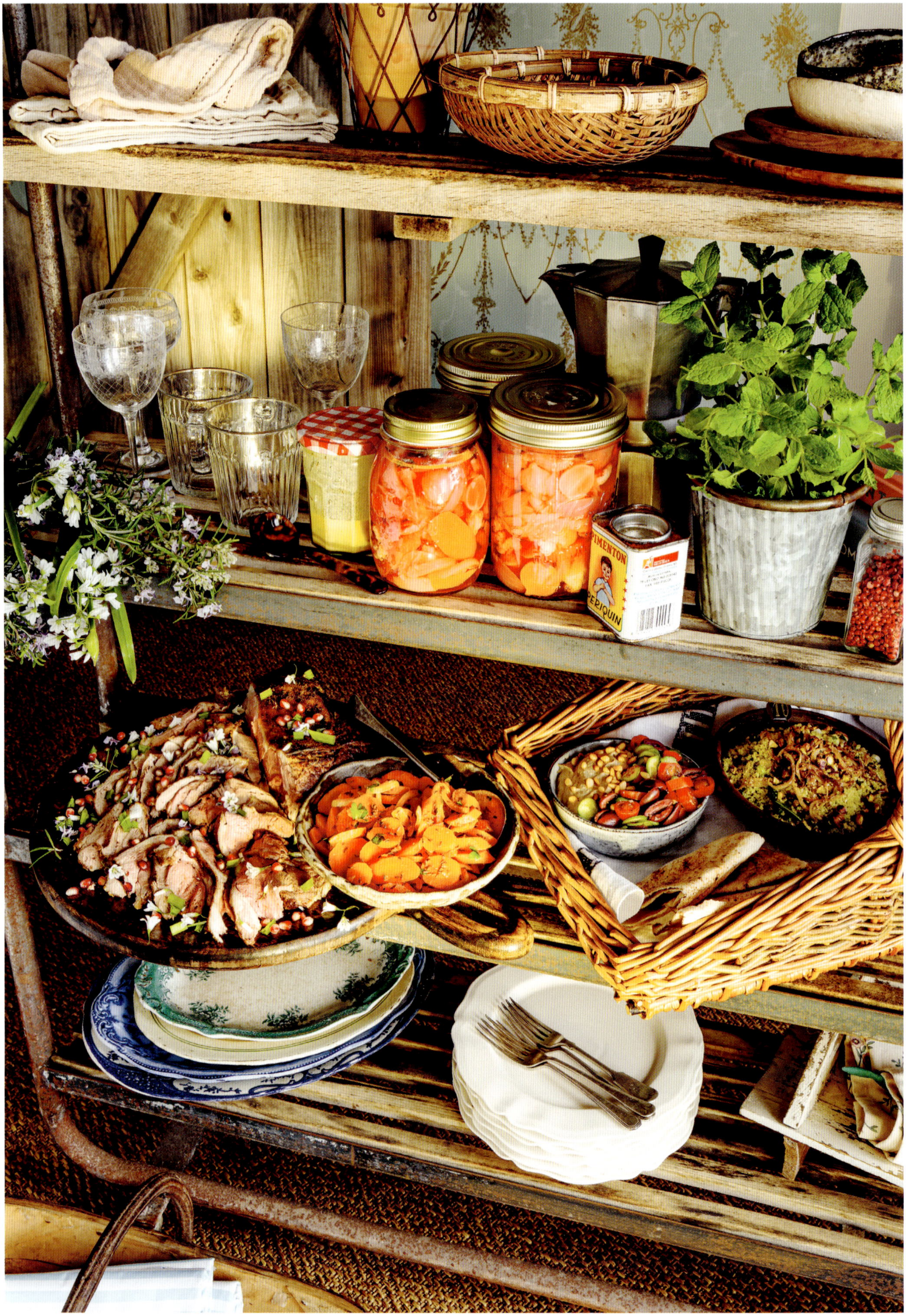
PIMENTON
PERIQUIN

Fragrant Butterflied Lamb

This is one of my favourite ways to serve lamb – it is very easy to cook and can be carved in seconds. Get your butcher to do the hard work of cutting out the bone, and ask him to remove the parchment-like covering on the skin, too. I like lamb slightly undercooked and served pink; if it's overdone, you can call it slow-cooked, and no one will be any the wiser!

—

Serves 4

2–2.5kg leg of lamb, boned and well trimmed, roughly 4–5cm thick
25g chopped fresh mint, plus extra to garnish
finely grated rind and juice of 2 lemons
4 garlic cloves, crushed
2 tbsp ground coriander
2 tsp paprika
2 tsp ground cumin
2 tsp coarsely ground black pepper
1 tsp cayenne pepper
4 tbsp extra virgin olive oil
2 tbsp pomegranate seeds (optional)
1 sprig fresh rosemary (optional)
good pinch of sea salt

Place the lamb in a shallow non-metallic dish. Mix the remaining ingredients, except the salt and pomegranate seeds, and rub over the meat. Cover with cling film and chill overnight or, if time is short, leave to stand at room temperature for 2–3 hours, turning the lamb over from time to time.

When you are ready to cook, if the lamb has been chilled overnight, bring it back to room temperature. Preheat the oven to 240°C (475°F/Gas Mark 9) or light a barbecue; if using a charcoal barbecue, light it 45 minutes before you want to start cooking; if using a gas barbecue, light it 10 minutes beforehand.

If cooking in the oven, place the lamb, cut-side up, on a rack in a large roasting tin and season with salt. For rare meat, roast for 25–30 minutes. For medium-rare meat, roast for 35–40 minutes, turning over halfway through. If barbecuing, cook the lamb over medium-hot coals for about 50 minutes for medium-rare lamb, turning occasionally.

Remove the lamb from the oven or barbecue, and leave it to rest in a warm place for 10 minutes. If you don't like your lamb too pink, you can cover it with foil at this point, and it will continue to cook. Carve into slices and arrange on plates, drizzling any juices from the tin. Scatter over some mint to garnish, then add the pomegranate seeds and fresh rosemary, if using.

SERVE WITH ...

The subtle smokiness of **Baba Ghanoush Salad** (p.39) with plenty of **Homemade Flatbreads** (p.114) is perfect to get your appetite going while the lamb cooks. When you've a piece of meat as good as this, you only need a platter of something colourful, like **Tunisian Carrot Salad** (p.42) and perhaps some **Green Couscous** (p.118).

AND FOR DESSERT ...

Finish with something creamy, like a **Coconut Crème Brûlée** (p.193) or **Vanilla Panna Cotta** (p.182) served with the nicest fresh fruit you can lay your hands on.

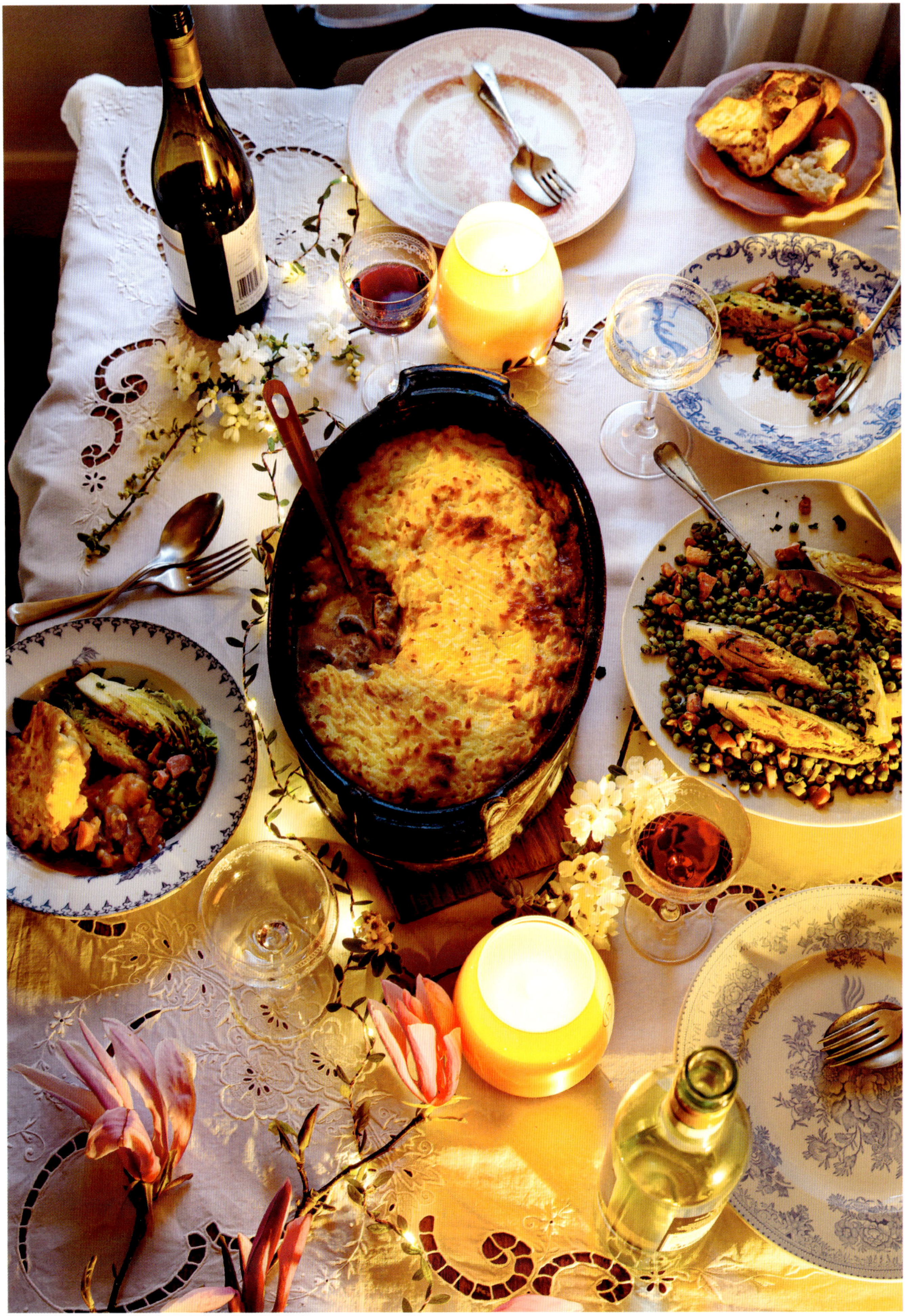

Cottage Pie

When it's freezing outside, all I crave is comfort food, particularly this delicious cottage pie. Simple ingredients – but put them together, and it's a showstopper. To get the fluffiest potato topping, I use a ricer when mashing potatoes. The egg yolks make it puff up and set. Once it's spread over the top and sprinkled with cheese, a quick fluff with a fork will create the perfect peaks and valleys.

—

Serves 6
900g Irish casserole beef pieces
2 tbsp olive oil
1 large onion, very finely chopped
1 large carrot, very finely chopped
1 celery stick, very finely chopped
1 garlic clove, crushed
1 tsp fresh thyme leaves
1 tbsp tomato purée
250ml red wine
500ml beef stock (fresh or from a cube)
2 tbsp Worcestershire sauce
1.25kg potatoes (such as Rooster)
50g butter, cut into cubes
4 tbsp cream
100g mature Cheddar, finely grated
2 egg yolks
sea salt and freshly ground black pepper

Dry the casserole beef pieces with kitchen paper. Leave on a plate for 30 minutes to return to room temperature.

Preheat the oven to 170°C (325°F/Gas Mark 3). Meanwhile, season the beef and heat a shallow casserole dish over a high heat. Add half the oil and sauté the beef for about 3 minutes until lightly browned. Transfer to a plate.

Reduce the heat to medium, then add the rest of the oil and sauté all the vegetables, garlic and thyme for 4–5 minutes until they have picked up a bit of colour. Stir in the tomato purée and cook for 1–2 minutes, stirring. Pour in the wine and allow it to bubble down a little, then stir in the stock and season with the Worcestershire sauce. Stir the beef pieces back in, then bring to a simmer, cover with a lid, pop in the oven and bake for 2 hours until the meat is meltingly tender.

Meanwhile, put the potatoes in a large pan of salted water, bring to the boil, then cover and cook for 20–25 minutes until completely tender when pierced with a knife. Drain and return to the pan for a few minutes to dry out. Mash until smooth, then season and mash in the butter. Beat in the cream with most of the cheese and the egg yolks. Spoon dollops of the potato mixture all over the beef and smooth into an even layer with a spatula. Sprinkle over the rest of the cheese and fluff up with a fork. Bake for another 30–40 minutes until bubbling and golden brown. Serve straight to the table.

SERVE WITH …
Elevate this dish to dinner-party status by serving a platter of **Carlingford Oysters with Shallot & Tarragon Dressing** (p.11) as your guests arrive. If you want an extra vegetable, the **Braised Petits Pois with Bacon** (p.138) are a classic.

AND FOR DESSERT …
Go for gold and serve the **Warm Blondies with Sea Salt Toffee Sauce** (p.198) or the **Cinnamon Swirl Apple Cake** (p.190), warm from the oven with lashings of custard.

Roast Picanha & Chargrilled Pepper Salad

This cut is such a firm favourite in our house that when I'm down in Dublin I often pick one up from Dunnes, since they always have it in stock. It's what I made for Amelda on Mother's Day this year – by special request!

—

Serves 6–8

1.2kg Irish Angus Picanha
1 tbsp olive oil
½ tsp dried thyme
3 large red peppers
3 large yellow peppers
2 tbsp extra virgin olive oil
2 tsp balsamic glaze
small handful fresh basil leaves
sea salt and freshly ground black pepper

Preheat the oven to 200°C (400°F/Gas Mark 6). Allow the Picanha to return to room temperature; then, using a sharp knife, score the fat cap in a criss-cross pattern. Heat the olive oil in a large frying pan over a medium-high heat. Once the oil begins to shimmer and is just starting to smoke, place the meat in the pan and sear for 2–3 minutes on each side.

Put the seared Picanha on a wire rack in a roasting tin, then season generously and sprinkle with the thyme. Arrange the peppers around the joint and roast for 40 minutes (for medium-rare). Remove from the oven and transfer the meat to a platter, then cover loosely with foil and leave to rest for 20 minutes.

Meanwhile, transfer the peppers to a large bowl with tongs and cover with cling film. Leave for 10 minutes to help the skins steam off, then strip off the skins and discard the cores and seeds. Cut the flesh, which will be nicely blackened in places, into strips and arrange on a platter. Drizzle over the extra virgin olive oil and balsamic glaze, then tear the basil on top. Season to taste.

Carve the rested roast Picanha into thin slices and add to the separate platter to serve.

SERVE WITH …

Get your taste buds tingling with **Apple Mojitos** (p.185) and small bowls of **Pickled Mixed Vegetables** (p.53). This juicy Brazilian roast dinner is just as good served at room temperature, with **Warm Potato Salad** (p.146) and the smoky flavours of **Grilled Courgettes with Green Chimichurri Sauce** (p.144). It would also be delicious with a bowl of **Frites** (p.123).

AND FOR DESSERT …

A devilishly nice **Summer Fruit Trifle** (p.203) – nothing else needed.

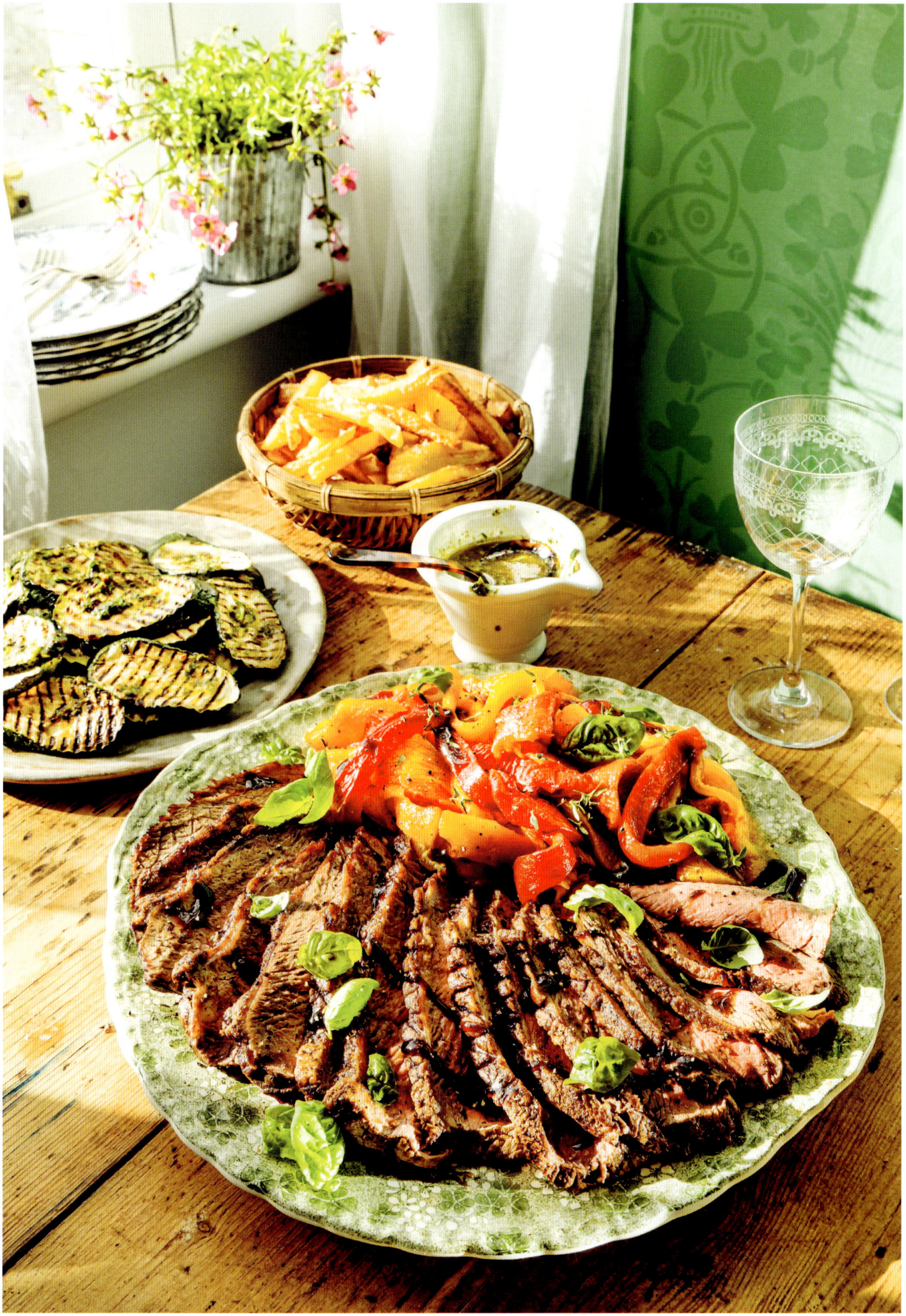

Tacos with Chicken Tinga

The night I was introduced to proper Mexican food, in the trendy 777 on South Great George's Street, the Mexican ambassador was in attendance, and it was a full-blown party. This street-food classic was one of the most memorable things I tasted. It's a delicious shredded-chicken stew with a touch of chipotle. Here is a simplified version of that recipe that you can make at home.

—

Serves 4

4 tbsp olive oil
500g skinless and boneless chicken thighs, sliced
1 onion, finely chopped
1 red pepper, seeded and finely chopped
2 garlic cloves, crushed
½ tsp dried thyme
1 tbsp tomato purée
2 tbsp chipotle paste
175ml chicken stock (fresh or from a cube)
3 ripe tomatoes, roughly chopped
12 small soft corn tortillas
sea salt and freshly ground black pepper
soured cream, fresh coriander and lime wedges, to serve

Preheat the oven to 150°C (300°F/Gas mark 2). Heat half the oil in a casserole dish or skillet pan over a medium to high heat. Season the chicken and sauté for 6–8 minutes until golden brown. Transfer to a bowl.

Add the rest of the oil to the casserole, reduce the heat to low and sauté the onion and pepper for 10 minutes until softened but not coloured. Stir in the garlic and thyme, then cook for another 2 minutes. Stir in the tomato purée and chipotle paste, and cook for 1–2 minutes.

Return the chicken and any juices to the casserole, stirring well to coat. Pour in the stock and add the tomatoes. Season generously and bring to a gentle simmer, then cover with a lid and roast for 2 hours until the chicken is meltingly tender, stirring after 1 hour to make sure that everything is cooking evenly.

When the chicken is ready, shred it up using two forks. Turn off the oven and put the tortillas inside for a few minutes to warm. Serve the chicken straight to the table with the warm tortillas, soured cream, coriander and lime wedges on the side, letting everyone construct their own tacos.

SERVE WITH …
For me, **Pickled Red Onions** (p.140) make this dish complete, while the **Summer Slaw** (p.163) would be a bonus. If you're making a night of it, go all in and start with the **Fully Loaded Nachos** (p.49), followed by a **Grilled Corn Salad** (p.127).

AND FOR DESSERT …
It can only be **Mango with Lime, Chilli and Star Anise** (p.178), maybe drizzled around a **Vanilla Panna Cotta** (p.182). And tequila shots for anyone who is in a boozy mood.

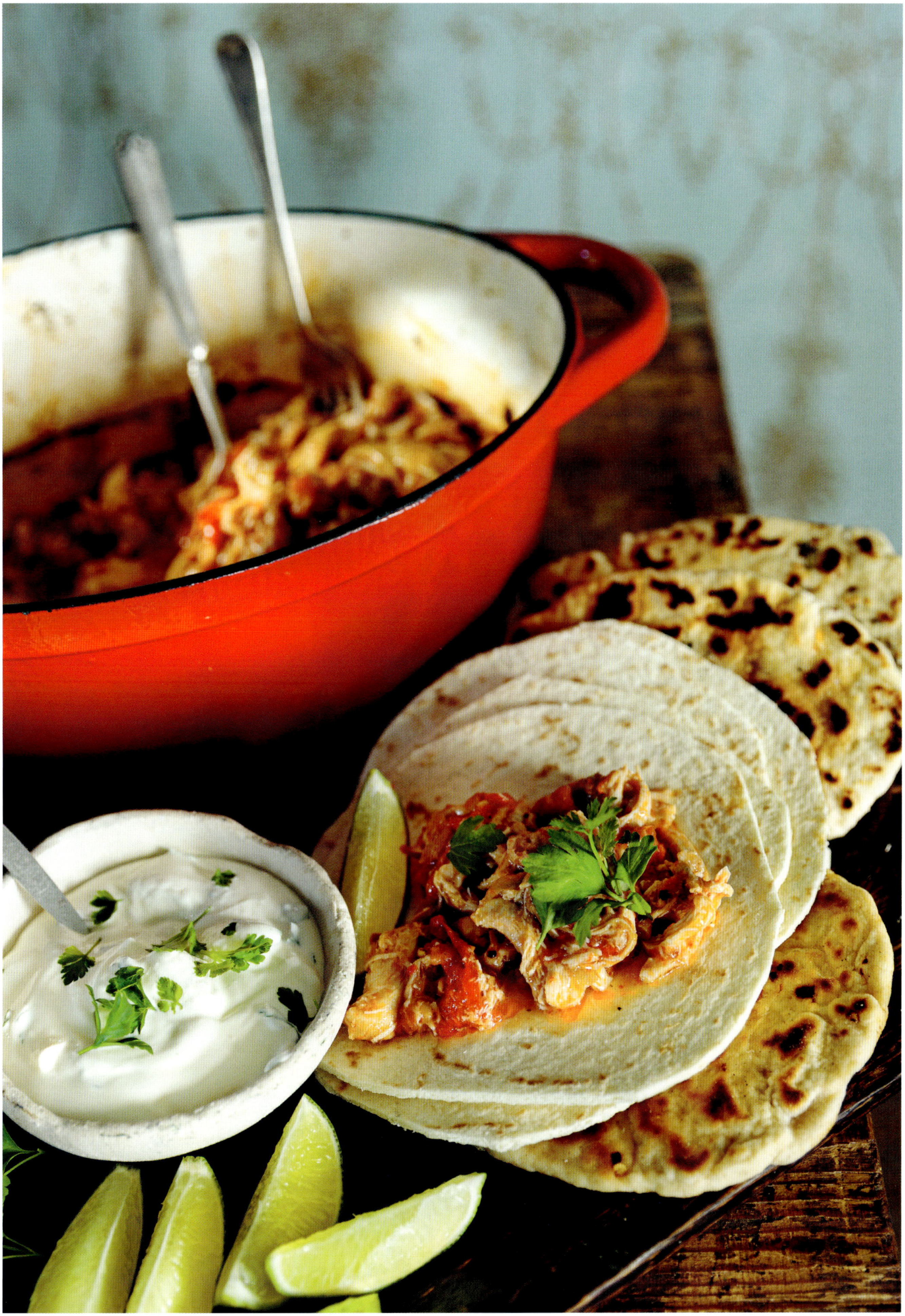

Aubergines Stuffed with Onions, Tomato, Chilli & Parsley

This is Imam Bayildi, a traditional Turkish recipe with its roots in the country's Ottoman past. I've been told that the name translates as 'the Imam fainted' – either because he found this simple dish cooked by his wife incredibly delicious, or because he was shocked by the expense of the large amount of olive oil used in the cooking of it!

—

Serves 6

6 small aubergines (about 250g each)
200ml extra virgin olive oil
2 onions, thinly sliced
4 garlic cloves, crushed
1 tsp dried chilli flakes
4 ripe tomatoes, chopped
20g fresh flat-leaf parsley, leaves stripped and finely chopped
400g passata (Italian sieved tomatoes)
1 tsp caster sugar
fresh basil (to serve)
sea salt and freshly ground black pepper

Using a swivel peeler, cut 1cm strips off the aubergine skin working lengthways. Heat 4 tablespoons of the olive oil in a casserole dish or skillet pan over a medium heat. Sauté the aubergines for 8–10 minutes until they start to soften but still have firmness, turning occasionally. Transfer to a plate and wipe out the pan.

Add another 4 tablespoons of oil to the dish. Sauté the onions for about 10 minutes until softened but not coloured. Stir in the garlic and chilli, and sauté for another minute. Add the chopped fresh tomatoes and season generously, then simmer for another 5 minutes until the sauce has thickened. Remove from the heat and stir in the parsley. Transfer to a bowl and wipe out the pan.

Preheat the oven to 180°C (350°F/Gas Mark 4). Meanwhile, use a small sharp knife to make an incision lengthways in each aubergine to form a deep pocket, being careful not to cut through to the other side and leaving about 2cm at each end. Put the aubergines back into the pan and spoon in as much of the onion mixture as possible, piling them up with any excess.

To make the sauce, mix the passata with the sugar and season generously. Pour over the aubergines, then drizzle the rest of the olive oil on top. Cover with a lid or some tin foil, and bake for about 40 minutes until the aubergines are completely tender and the sauce has reduced and thickened.

Leave the aubergines to cool a little, then garnish with the basil. For me this is a dish best served at room temperature.

SERVE WITH …
Add a **Spiced Roast Cauliflower** (p.106), a **Tunisian Carrot Salad** (p.42) and a pile of **Homemade Flatbreads** (p.114) for a weeknight vegan meal.

AND FOR DESSERT …
Either **Peanut Butter Fudge with Goji Berries & Pistachios** (p.212) or **Moroccan Orange Salad with Pomegranate** (p.170) would be perfect.

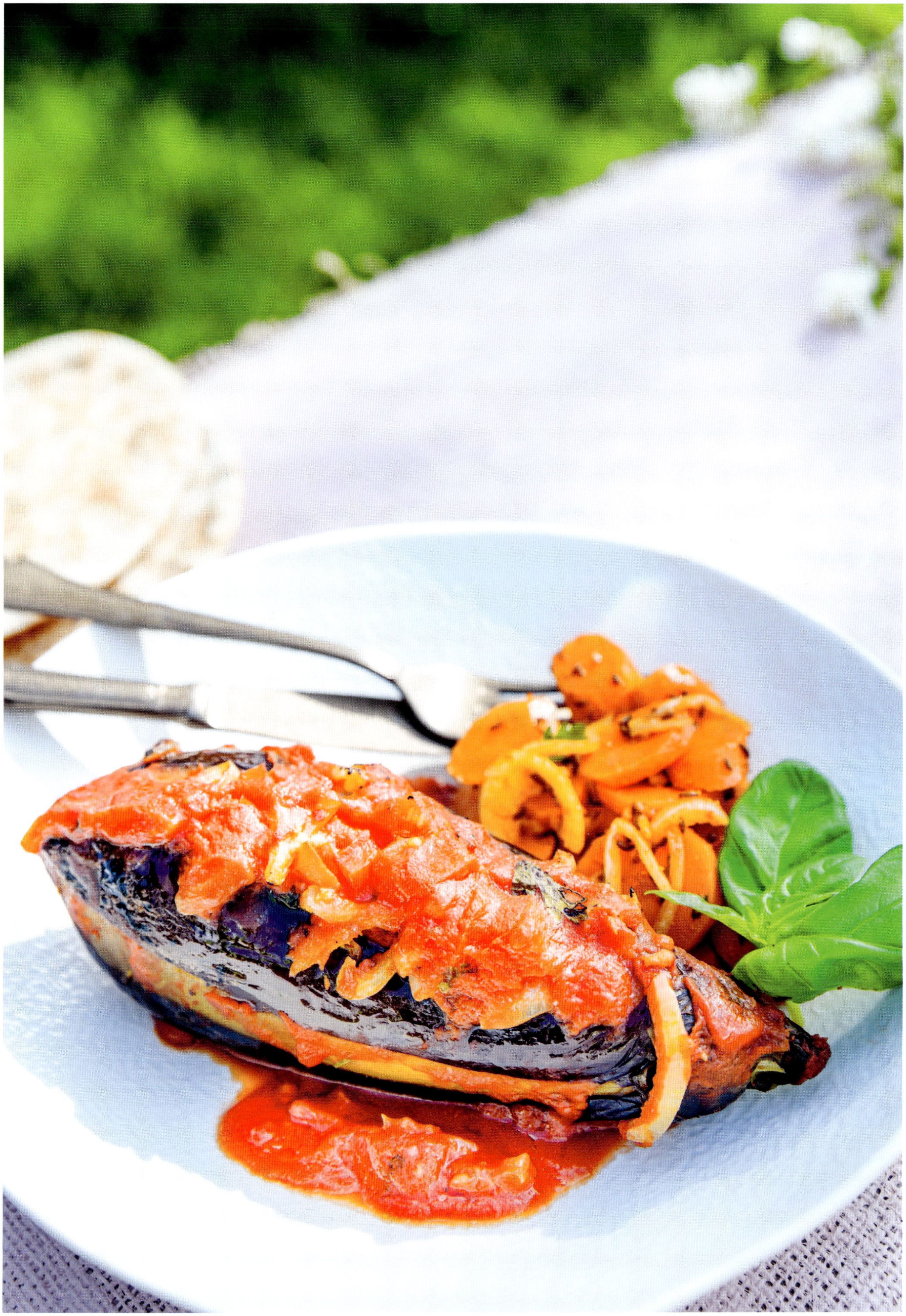

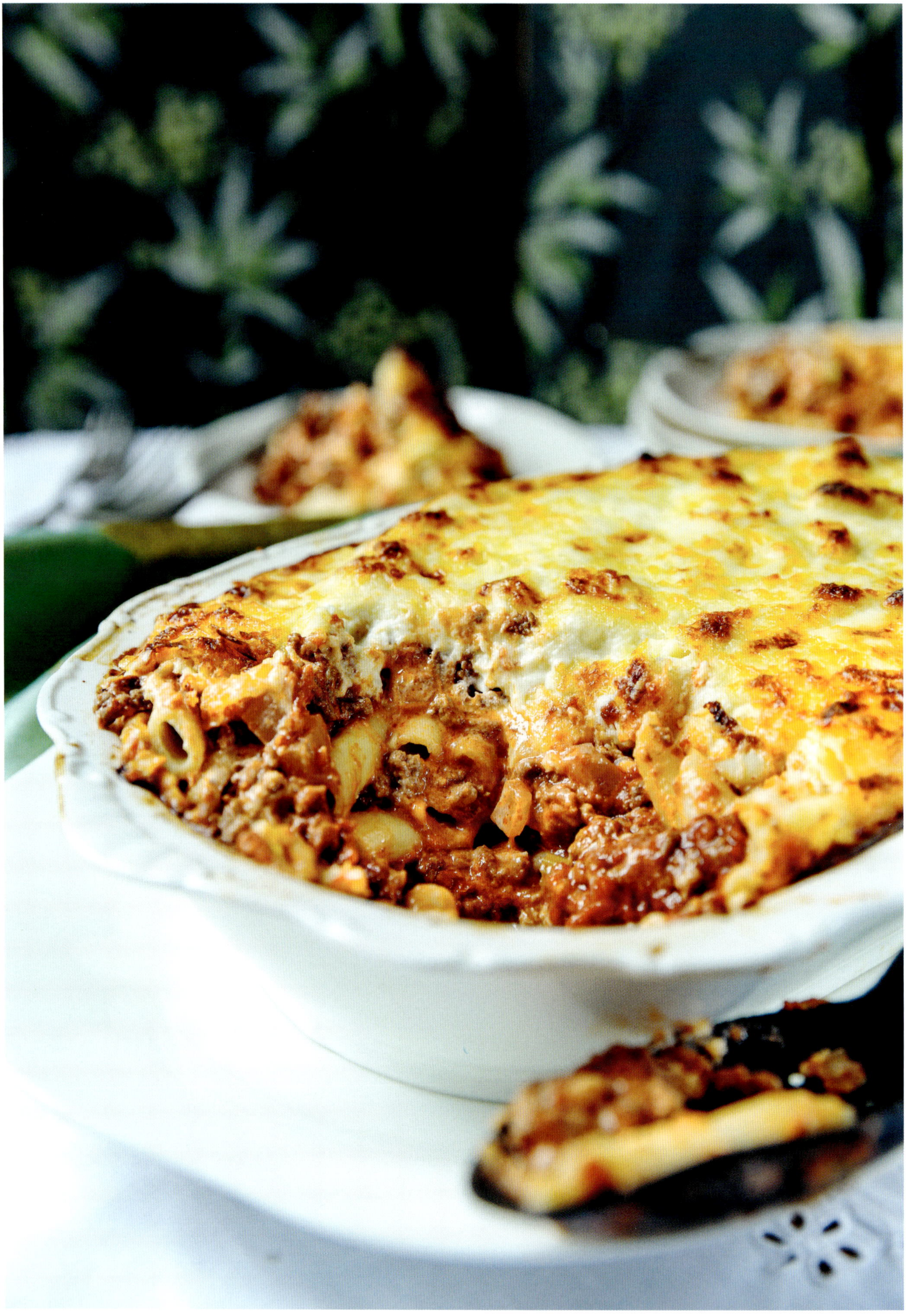

Greek Beef & Macaroni Pie

If you fancy a change from your regular lasagne, this might just be the recipe for you. Known as pastitsio in Greece, this is a great all-in-one dish that everyone will be happy to eat. Traditionally, it is made with long, hollow pasta tubes like De Cecco's Zita n.18, but if you cannot find them just use rigatoni or tortiglioni.

—

Serves 6–8
2 tbsp olive oil
675g lean minced beef
1 large onion, finely chopped
2 celery sticks, finely chopped
4 garlic cloves, finely chopped
1 heaped tsp ground cinnamon
2 tsp dried oregano
140g tin tomato purée
300ml red wine
400g tin chopped tomatoes
500g pasta tubes (zita, rigatoni or tortiglioni)
100g butter, plus extra for greasing
100g plain flour
1 litre milk
good pinch of grated nutmeg
2 eggs, lightly beaten
200g Irish Cáis Óir grilling cheese, coarsely grated (or use halloumi)
sea salt and freshly ground black pepper

Heat the oil in a large sauté pan over a high heat and brown the minced beef for about 5 minutes, breaking up any lumps with a potato masher. Stir in the onion, celery and garlic, and sauté for another few minutes until softened. Sprinkle over the cinnamon and oregano, then stir in the tomato purée and cook for another minute or so. Pour in the wine and allow to bubble down. Add the tomatoes, season with salt and pepper and bring to the boil. Reduce the heat and simmer for 40 minutes until the sauce has thickened.

Preheat the oven to 180°C (350°F/Gas Mark 4). Bring a large pan of salted water to a rolling boil and cook the pasta according to packet instructions until al dente. Drain and put in a large bowl.

Meanwhile, make the sauce. Melt the butter in a pan over a medium heat. Add the flour and cook for 1 minute, stirring. Gradually add the milk, then bring to the boil, stirring. Reduce the heat and simmer gently for 5–6 minutes until thickened, stirring occasionally. Add the nutmeg and season with salt and pepper.

Stir a quarter of the sauce into the pasta with the eggs and half of the cheese. Butter a large shallow ovenproof dish, spread half of the pasta mixture on the bottom and cover with half of the ragu. Repeat with the remaining pasta mixture and ragu. Spoon the rest of the sauce on top and scatter over the remaining cheese. Bake for about 40 minutes until bubbling and golden brown. Leave to stand for 30 minutes before slicing and serving on plates.

SERVE WITH ...
A green salad, some crusty bread and a decent red wine are all you are going to need with this for a relaxed family gathering. If you want to extend the meal, serve it with my sublime **Spanakopita** (p.18), which are crispy parcels of spinach, mint and feta.

AND FOR DESSERT ...
Break up a slab of your favourite chocolate and scatter over bowls of ice cream, perhaps alongside pitted cherries.

Crispy Porchetta with Fennel & Herbs

The irresistible crunch hints at just how good this porchetta recipe is. It is perfect for feeding a crowd, and it will really make it feel like a special occasion without breaking the bank. Ask your butcher to take the pork from the thinner end if possible, because it will be much easier to roll. This method takes three days, but it's relatively easy once you've mastered the rolling technique.

—

Serves 10–12

2½ kg piece boneless pork belly, skin on and scored

4 tsp sea salt flakes

2 tbsp fennel seeds

2 tsp black peppercorns

4 fresh rosemary sprigs, leaves stripped off

3 fresh sage sprigs, leaves stripped off

3 fresh thyme sprigs, leaves stripped off

6 garlic cloves, peeled

3 tbsp extra virgin olive oil

finely grated rind of 1 lemon

½ tsp dried chilli flakes

250ml dry white wine

Season the pork all over with a tablespoon of salt, then cover with cling film on a tray and chill. Toast the fennel and peppercorns in a frying pan for 1–2 minutes, then bash in a pestle and mortar. Roughly chop the herbs with the garlic, add to the pestle and mortar and pound to a rough paste. Mix in 2 tablespoons of oil, the lemon rind and chilli flakes.

Put the pork joint skin-side down on a chopping board. Using a sharp knife, score the flesh in a criss-cross pattern, then cut away a 4cm strip of the meat along the long side closest to you, leaving the skin exposed. This will make it easier to roll up. Massage the fennel mix into the slashed meat, then place the strip of meat you've cut away along the middle.

Starting from the longest side that hasn't been cut, roll up the belly as tightly as you can to enclose the filling. Tie the joint with butcher's string at 2cm intervals. This is best done 24 hours in advance.

When ready to cook, preheat the oven to 170°C (325°F/Gas Mark 3). Put the joint on a roasting tin with a trivet, rub the remaining tablespoon of oil into the skin and season with the rest of the salt. Roast for 3 hours, basting every 30 minutes for the first hour. Increase the oven temperature to 230°C (450°F/Gas Mark 8) and roast for another 20–30 minutes, checking regularly, until the skin is crackled and the meat tender. Rest for a good 30 minutes – porchetta is best served warm.

Meanwhile, pour the excess fat off the juices in the pan. Add the wine to the juices and place the pan directly on the hob. Cook for a few minutes until reduced, scraping the bottom of the pan with a wooden spoon to remove the sediment.

Carve the porchetta into slices and arrange on warmed plates with the gravy.

SERVE WITH ...
Smashed Roast Potatoes (p.124), steamed broccoli and **Pickled Red Onions** (p.140) would be perfect.

AND FOR DESSERT ...
Tiramisu (p.206) – jiggly and just set, but fabulously rich.

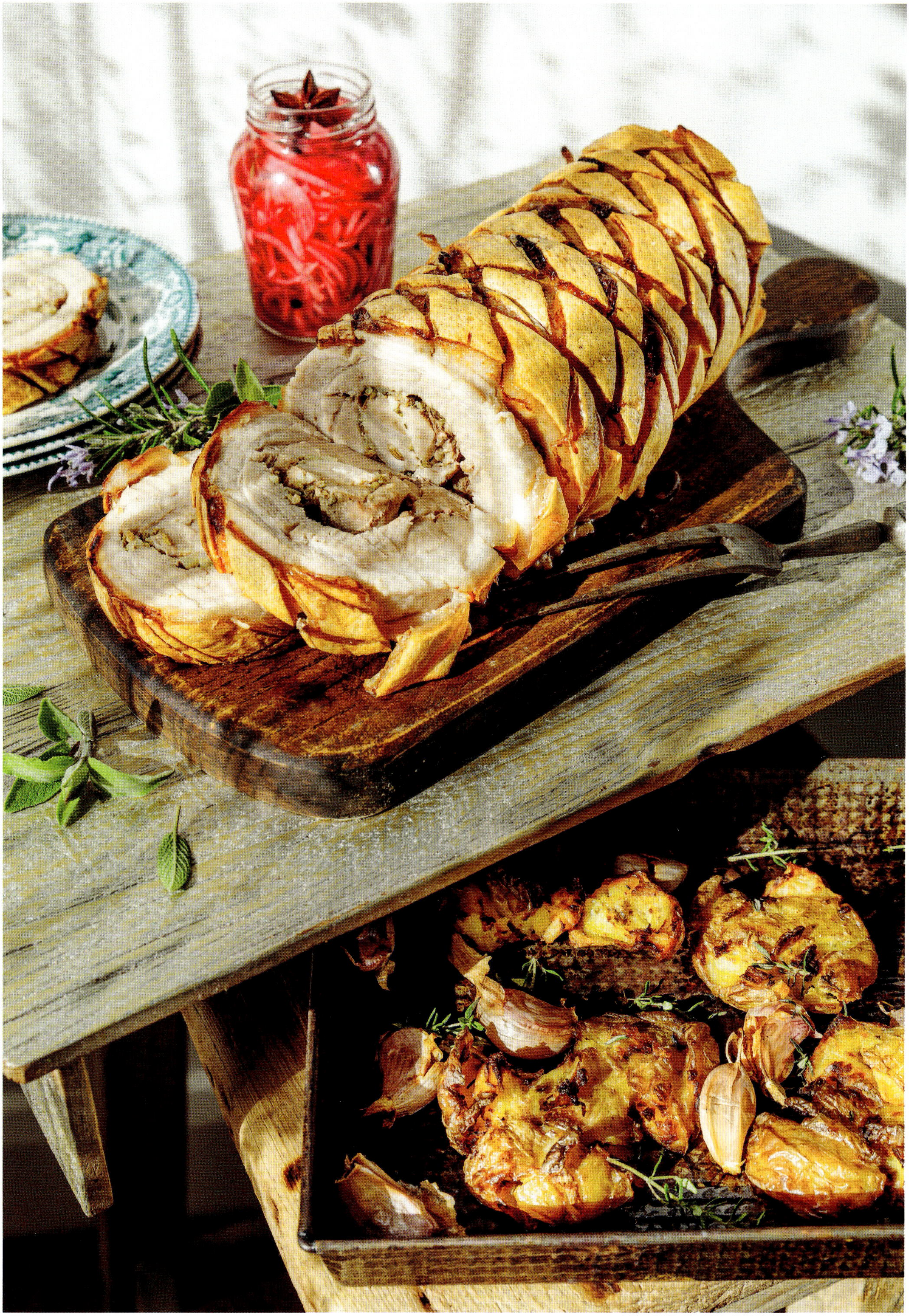

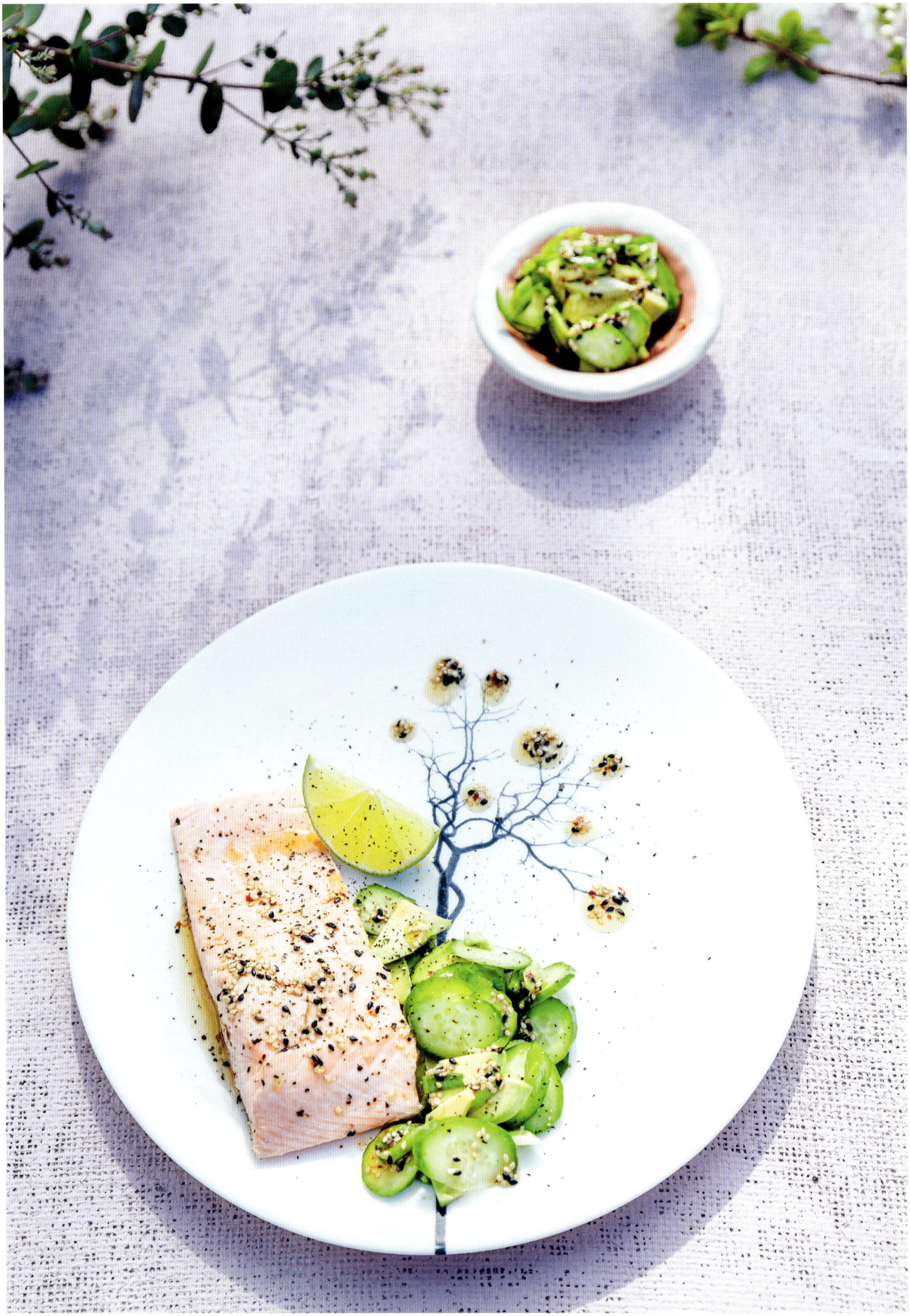

Aromatic Poached Salmon with Avocado & Cucumber Salad

Light, delicate salmon, crunchy cucumber and creamy avocado perform a graceful dance with the powerful notes of sesame in this most simple of dishes. Baby cucumbers work best because they are almost seedless, with a robust flesh that stays crisp.

—

Serves 4
300ml chicken stock (from a cube is fine)
1 tbsp Thai fish sauce (nam pla)
2 tbsp soy sauce
4 x 150g boneless and skinless salmon fillets (preferably organic)
2 tbsp rice vinegar
1 tbsp caster sugar
½ tsp dried chilli flakes
2 tbsp toasted sesame oil
1 tbsp toasted sesame seeds, plus extra to garnish
2 firm ripe avocados
100g baby cucumbers, trimmed and thinly sliced
2 scallions, trimmed and thinly sliced
lime wedges, to serve

Put the stock into a pan that will fit the fish fillets comfortably in one layer, and add the Thai fish sauce and 1 tablespoon of the soy sauce. Bring to a gentle simmer, then, using a fish slice, lower the salmon fillets into the liquid. Return to a gentle simmer and cook for 5 minutes, then switch off the heat. Set aside for 15 minutes until the fish is nicely poached and just opaque all the way through.

Meanwhile, make the dressing. Put the rice vinegar in a screw-topped jar with the sugar and the rest of the soy sauce. Add the chilli flakes and shake well, then add the sesame oil with the sesame seeds and shake again.

Cut the avocados in half, remove the stones and peel off the skin, then cut into chunks. Put in a bowl and fold in the cucumbers, scallions and the dressing.

Arrange the poached salmon on plates and add some of the avocado and cucumber salad. Garnish with the rest of the sesame seeds and the lime wedges to serve.

SERVE WITH ...
This wonderfully simple dish takes a matter of minutes to prepare, and the elegant salad can be dressed up according to your mood. It is a satisfying meal on its own, but it can also be served alongside cold soba noodles or **Pilau Rice** (p.131). If you want to extend the meal, start with the **Chicken Potstickers** (p.28) that you could have tucked away in the freezer ...

AND FOR DESSERT ...
With such a light meal, you could go lavish and impress your guests with a **Pavlova Wreath** (p.211) glistening with exotic fruit.

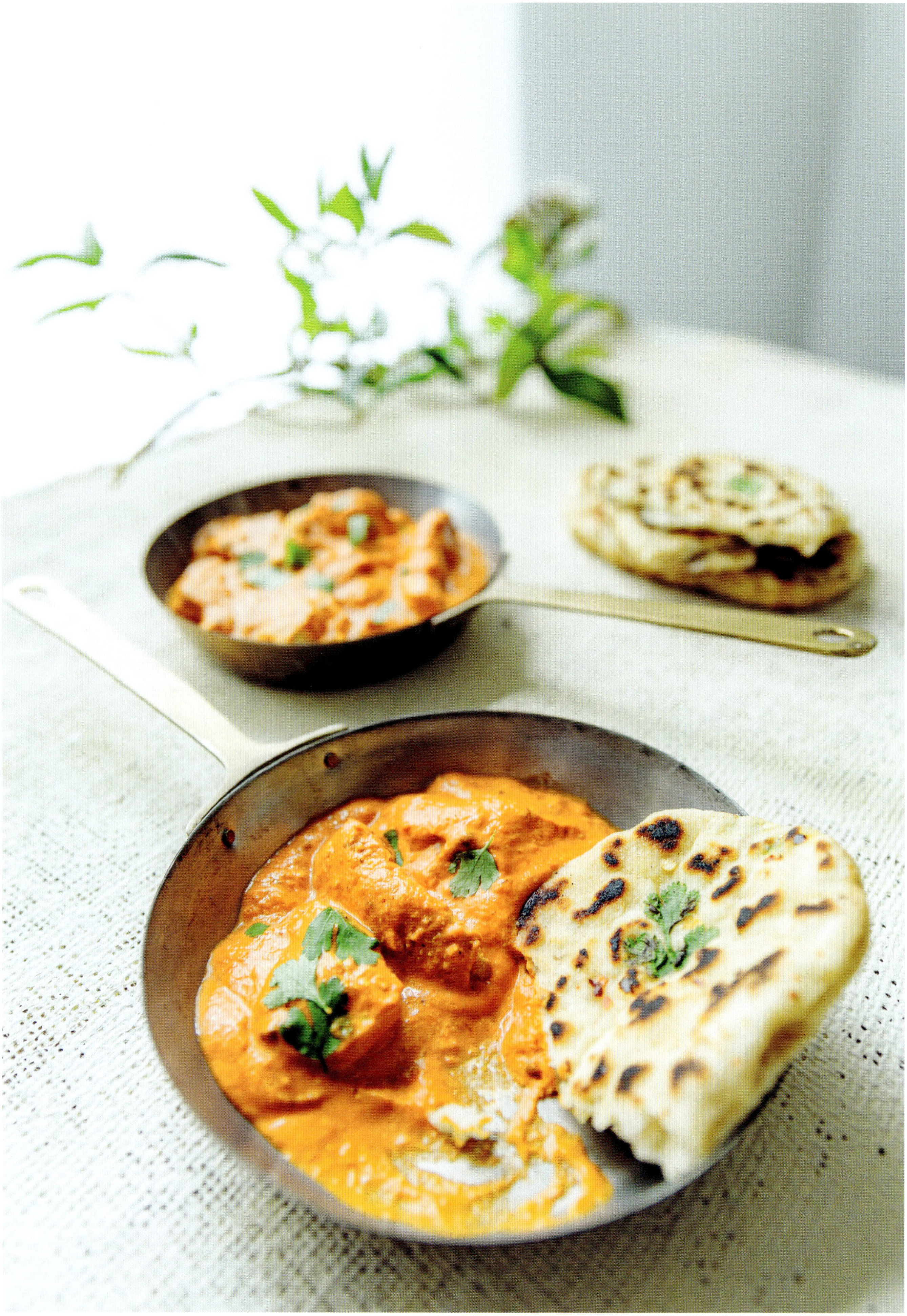

Butter Chicken

Swap your usual takeaway curry for this homemade chicken makhana, which combines marinated chicken with a rich, buttery sauce. This is an authentic Indian curry with its origins in Delhi, where it was first made to use up pieces of leftover tandoori chicken.

—

Serves 4–6

500g skinless and boneless chicken breasts or thighs
juice and finely grated rind of 1 lemon
3 tbsp mild curry seasoning
4 tbsp natural yogurt
3 tbsp sunflower oil
30g butter
2 red onions, thinly sliced
2 garlic cloves, sliced
1 red chilli, seeded
3cm piece fresh root ginger, peeled and sliced
20g fresh coriander
400ml passata (Italian sieved tomatoes)
120ml cream
sea salt and freshly ground black pepper

Trim the chicken and cut into bite-sized pieces. Put in a bowl and stir in half the lemon juice with a good pinch of salt. Add 2 tablespoons of the curry seasoning, the yogurt and 1 tablespoon of the oil. Mix to combine, then season generously with pepper. Cover and leave to marinate for at least 1 hour or up to 3 days in the fridge.

Heat the rest of the oil and a knob of the butter in a wok or skillet over a high heat, and quickly sear the marinated chicken in batches until golden brown, transferring with a slotted spoon to a clean bowl as you go.

Add the onions to the pan and sauté for 4–5 minutes until they start to caramelise. Tip in the garlic, chilli and ginger, then add another knob of the butter and sauté for 1–2 minutes.

Chop the stalks from the coriander and add them to the pan with the rest of the curry seasoning and another knob of the butter. Toast for a few minutes until very fragrant.

Pour the passata into the pan and bring to a simmer, then add the cream and the rest of the lemon juice. Transfer to a blender and blend until you have a very smooth sauce. Return to the pan and add the chicken with any juices and reheat gently for about 5 minutes until the chicken is cooked through and tender. Season to taste, then fold in the lemon rind with the rest of the butter and the coriander leaves, reserving a few sprigs to garnish. Transfer to bowls and garnish with the coriander sprigs.

SERVE WITH...

This mild and creamy curry is sure to please all tastes. Make some **Homemade Flatbreads** (p.114), perhaps brushing them with a little melted butter and sprinkling with black onion seeds. A bowl of **Pilau Rice** (p.131) completes the meal, alongside some spiced mango chutney, mint raita and lime pickle.

AND FOR DESSERT...

Lemon Posset with Passion Fruit (p.180) is not unlike a traditional Indian dessert, so it would finish the meal off beautifully.

Slow-Cooked Onion & Goat's Cheese Tart

This tart is laden with anchovies, their saltiness offset by the sweetness of the well-cooked onions and the slightly bitter taste of the olives ... Then you have the creaminess of the goat's cheese and the richness of the puff pastry underneath. The onions do take some time to cook properly, but for the tart to be at its most delicious, it needs super-soft onions with no crunch.

—

Serves 4–6

4 large red onions, finely sliced
15g butter
400g packet all-butter puff pastry, thawed
plain flour, for dusting
1 heaped tsp chopped fresh thyme
2 x 50g tins anchovies, drained
200g goat's cheese log, sliced
60g pitted black olives
1 beaten egg mixed with 1 tbsp water, to glaze
a few sprigs of sage, to serve
freshly ground black pepper

Preheat the oven to 200°C (400°F/Gas Mark 6). Put the red onions in a frying pan with the butter, and cook over a very low heat for 20–30 minutes until they are super soft, stirring regularly.

While the onions are cooking, roll out the puff pastry on a floured surface to a 36cm x 26cm rectangle. Mark a border about 2cm wide around the pastry, then score all the way around the border in a criss-cross pattern. Prick the inside with a fork – this will stop the pastry from puffing up too much when it cooks. Put the puff pastry in the fridge for 30 minutes to firm up.

Once the onions are soft, add the thyme and cook for another minute, then remove them from the heat and leave to cool a little. Get the pastry from the fridge, then spoon the onions on to the rested pastry and spread into an even layer inside the border. Arrange the anchovies on top in a criss-cross pattern, then stud with the slices of goat's cheese and olives. Season with black pepper and glaze the border with egg wash. Bake for 20–25 minutes or until the pastry is puffed up and golden brown. Remove from the oven and leave to cool a little. Scatter over the sage, then cut into squares and serve warm or cold.

SERVE WITH ...
This is the kind of tart that seamlessly stretches a meal out. It lends itself well to picnics, so pack it up in a basket, perhaps with some **Grilled Corn Salad** (p.127) and pick up a rotisserie chicken on the way.

AND FOR DESSERT ...
For picnics, grab some meringues while you are in the shop, and serve with a punnet of Clarke's king strawberries, which are a favourite of mine.

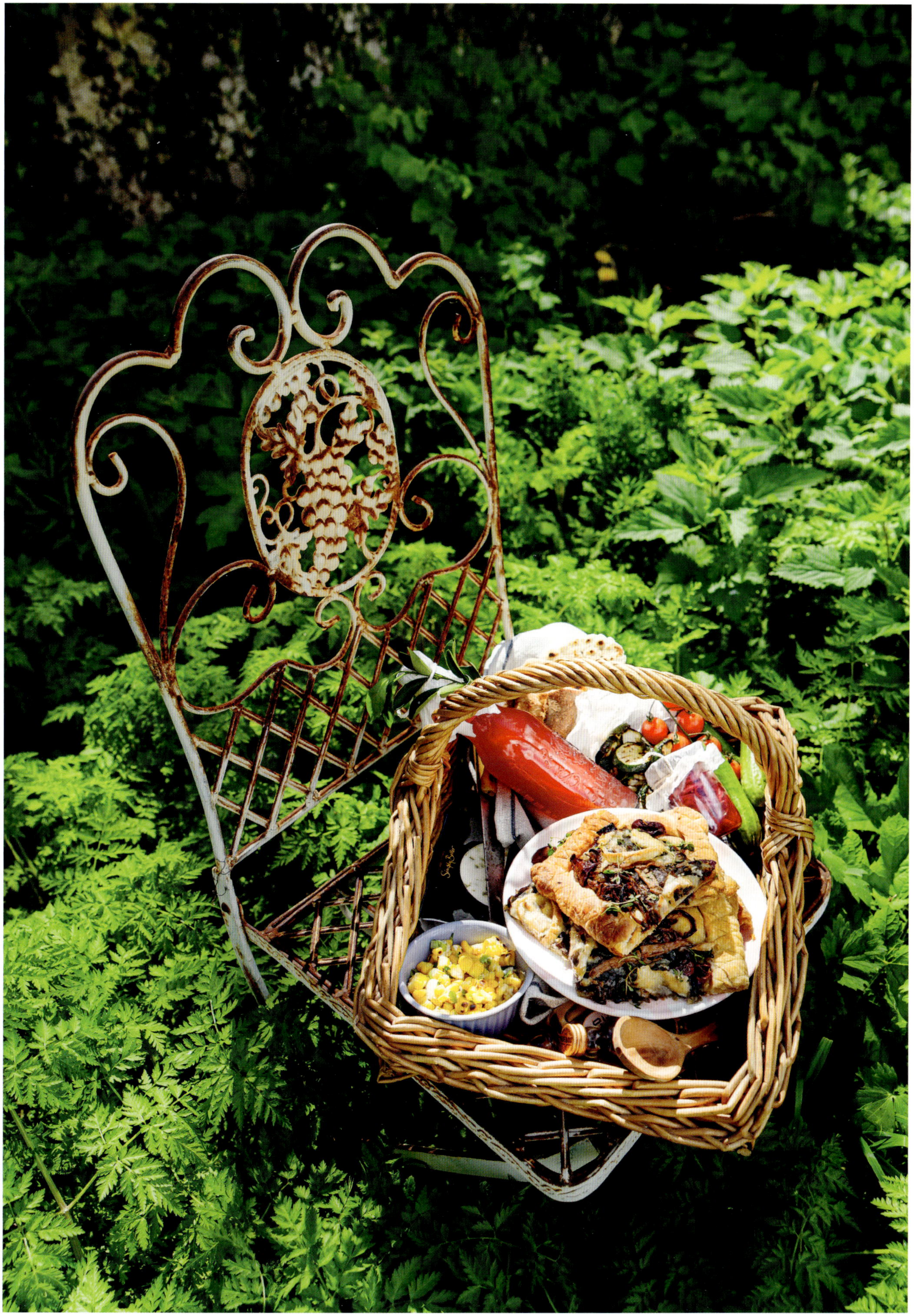

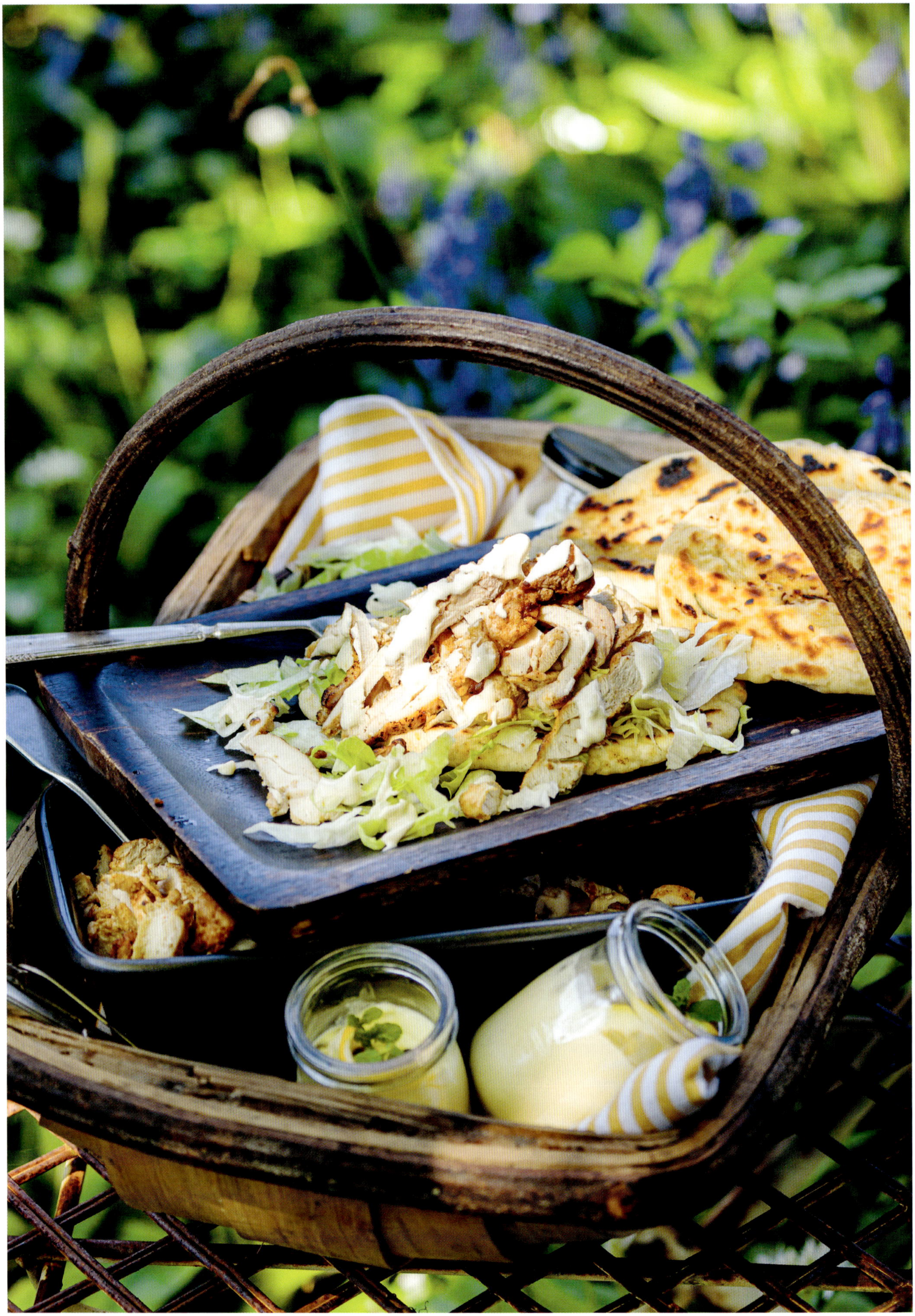

Chicken Shawarma

Anyone who has tasted genuine chicken shawarma – spiced meat cooked on a spit, then stuffed into a flatbread with pickles, various sauces, tomato and salad – will know it's right up there with the top food combinations. In this version, more practical for the home cook, you layer the marinated chicken up in a loaf tin, so you retain all the succulence. It will beat your local kebab shop version hands down.

—

Serves 6–8

100ml olive oil
finely grated rind and juice of 2 lemons
2 tsp ground cumin
2 tsp paprika
1 tsp ground coriander
½ tsp ground cinnamon
4 garlic cloves, crushed
750g skinless and boneless chicken thighs, well trimmed
250ml natural yogurt
6–8 tbsp tahini
4 large Homemade Flatbreads (p.114), or use shop-bought
1 Irish iceberg lettuce, shredded
fresh mint sprigs, to garnish (optional)
sea salt and freshly ground black pepper

Put the oil into a large bowl and add half of the lemon juice and rind, with two teaspoons of salt and plenty of pepper. Tip in all the spices and garlic, then stir until evenly combined. Fold in the chicken and cover with cling film. Chill for at least 6 hours or up to 3 days – the longer, the better!

When ready to cook, preheat the oven to 180°C (350°F/Gas Mark 4). Layer up the marinated pieces of chicken in a 900g non-stick loaf tin and press down firmly, then roast for 40 minutes until the chicken is cooked through and tender. When the shawarma is ready, leave it in the tin for 10 minutes so that all the juices settle back into the chicken.

Meanwhile, make the sauce. Put the yogurt into a bowl, then stir in the tahini and the rest of the lemon juice and rind. Season with salt and pepper.

Turn out the loaf tin onto a platter and slice the chicken shawarma. Heat the flatbreads and scatter with lettuce before piling high with the spiced meat and drizzling over the sauce. Garnish with mint sprigs, if liked, to serve.

SERVE WITH …

For a lavish spread, serve this with **Pickled Mixed Vegetables** (p.53) or **Pickled Red Onions** (p.140), **Slow Roast Tomatoes with Puy Lentils** (p.148), **Baba Ghanoush** (p.39), **Tunisian Carrot Salad** (p.42), **Crispy Lamb-Stuffed Flatbreads** (p.54), **Chargrilled Aubergine with Tahini Dressing** (p.120), **Spiced Roast Cauliflower** (p.106) and **Summer Slaw** (p.163).

AND FOR DESSERT …

After all that, there might not be much room for dessert! I'd probably just add a **Moroccan Orange Salad with Pomegranate** (p.170) or a **Lemon Posset** (p.180) to my display and leave it at that.

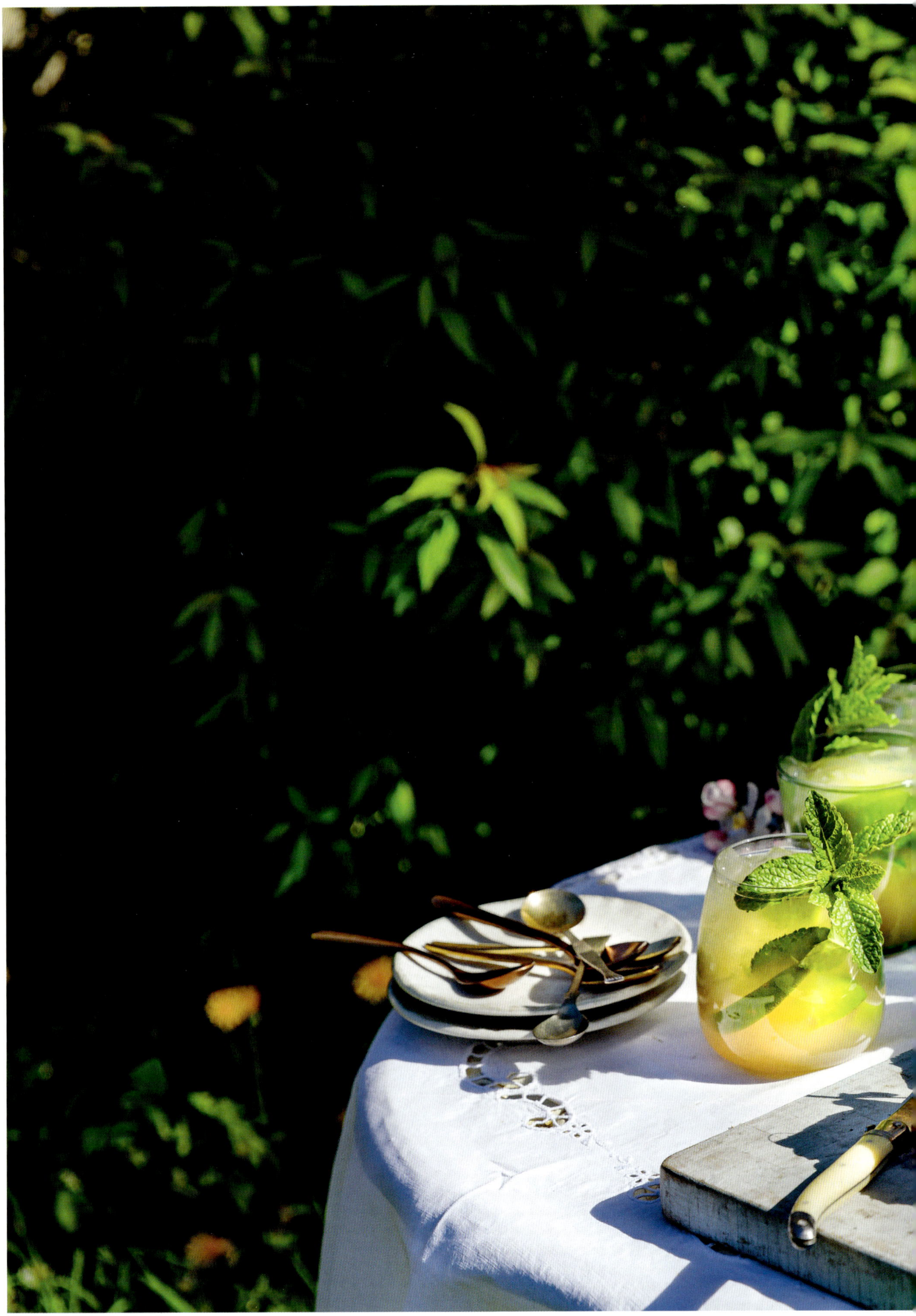

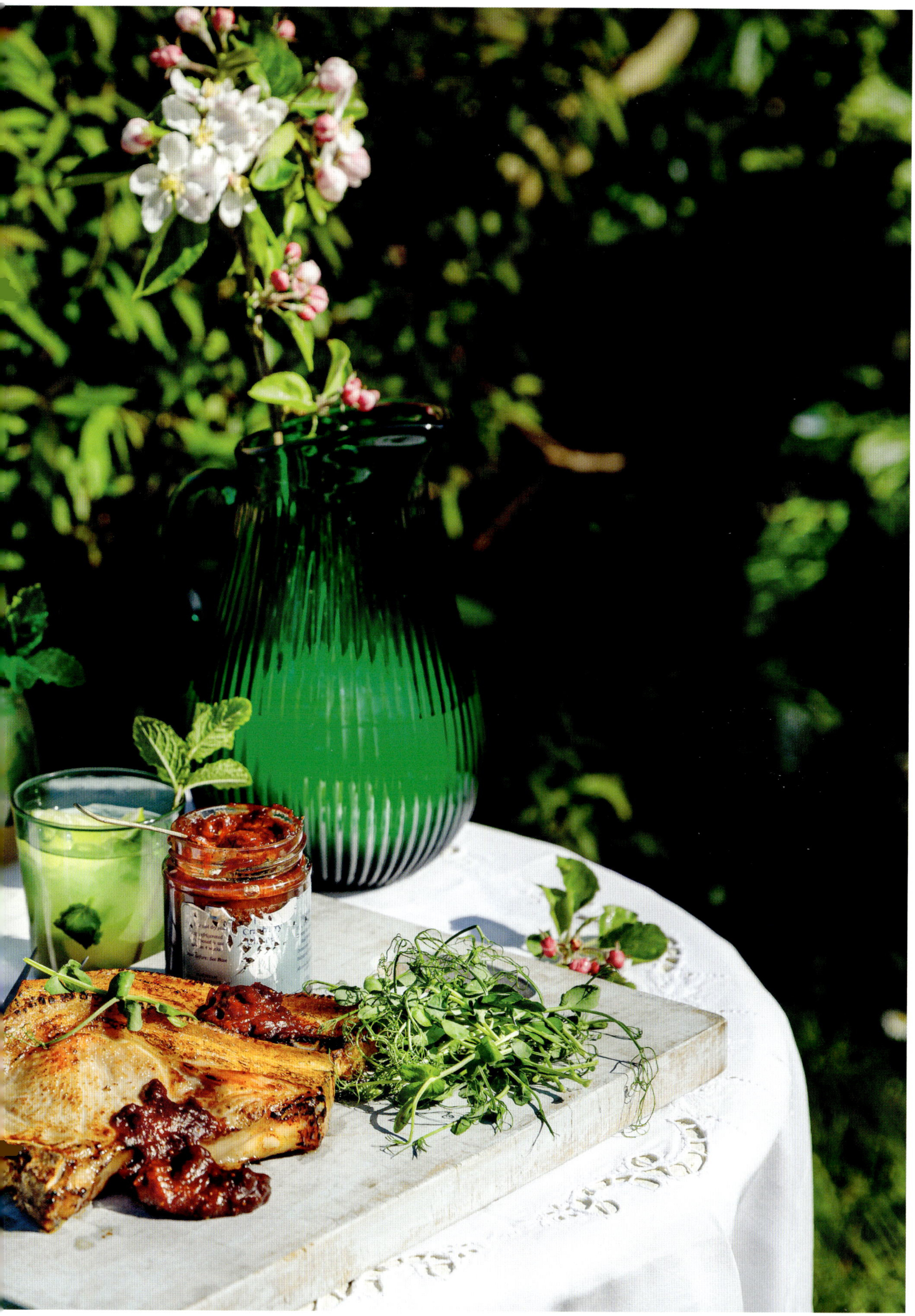

Iberico Pork with Red Gooseberry Relish

Whenever I see gooseberries, I grab them before I even know what I'm going to do with them. Alternatively, for this recipe you can use figs or plums – both have a lovely affinity with Iberico pork. This Spanish breed is blessed with naturally marbled meat, rendering it buttery and tender. Serving them on the pan lets that marbling break down and melt into the muscle.

—

Serves 2–4
For the relish
½ tsp fennel seeds
½ cinnamon stick
1 tsp green peppercorns
300g red gooseberries, topped and tailed
1 large red onion, thinly sliced
100ml balsamic vinegar
50g caster sugar
2 tsp black mustard seeds

2 Iberico pork chops
1 tbsp olive oil
20g butter, diced and chilled
2 fresh thyme sprigs
sea salt and freshly ground black pepper

First, make the gooseberry relish. Put the fennel seeds, cinnamon and green peppercorns in a hot frying pan and toast for 30 seconds until fragrant. Tip into a pestle and mortar, and bash until finely ground. Put the gooseberries in a large pan with the ground spices, red onion, balsamic, sugar and mustard seeds. Slowly bring to the boil, stirring to dissolve the sugar. Reduce the heat until very low, and simmer gently for 15–20 minutes, stirring occasionally, until the mixture becomes thick and the gooseberries are completely soft. Transfer to a sterilised clean jar and chill until needed. Properly sealed, this relish will keep for a couple of months in the fridge.

Take the pork chops out of their packaging and leave on a tray to come back to room temperature, then pat dry with kitchen paper and season all over. Heat a large non-stick frying pan until smoking hot. Swirl in the oil and add the chops. Cook for 1 minute, then add the butter and thyme, and cook for 3–4 minutes until golden brown. Turn the chops over, baste with the butter and cook for another 2–3 minutes. Remove from the heat, transfer to a warm platter and leave to rest for 10 minutes.

These chops are quite large, and the meat is wonderfully rich, so you'll find that they go further than you'd expect. Carve into slices and serve with a bowl of gooseberry relish and a steamed green vegetable, if liked.

SERVE WITH ...
These free-range pork chops are perfect for a barbecue or if you are having friends over. Add a side of **Chargrilled Tenderstem Broccoli with Caesar Dressing** (p.117) and a bowl of boiled new potatoes, and you've a dinner fit for kings!

AND FOR DESSERT ...
If gooseberries are in season, you should also be able to get some decent cherries to serve with big, thick slices of luxurious **Basque Cheesecake** (p.188) or **Chocolate Mousse Cups** (p.197).

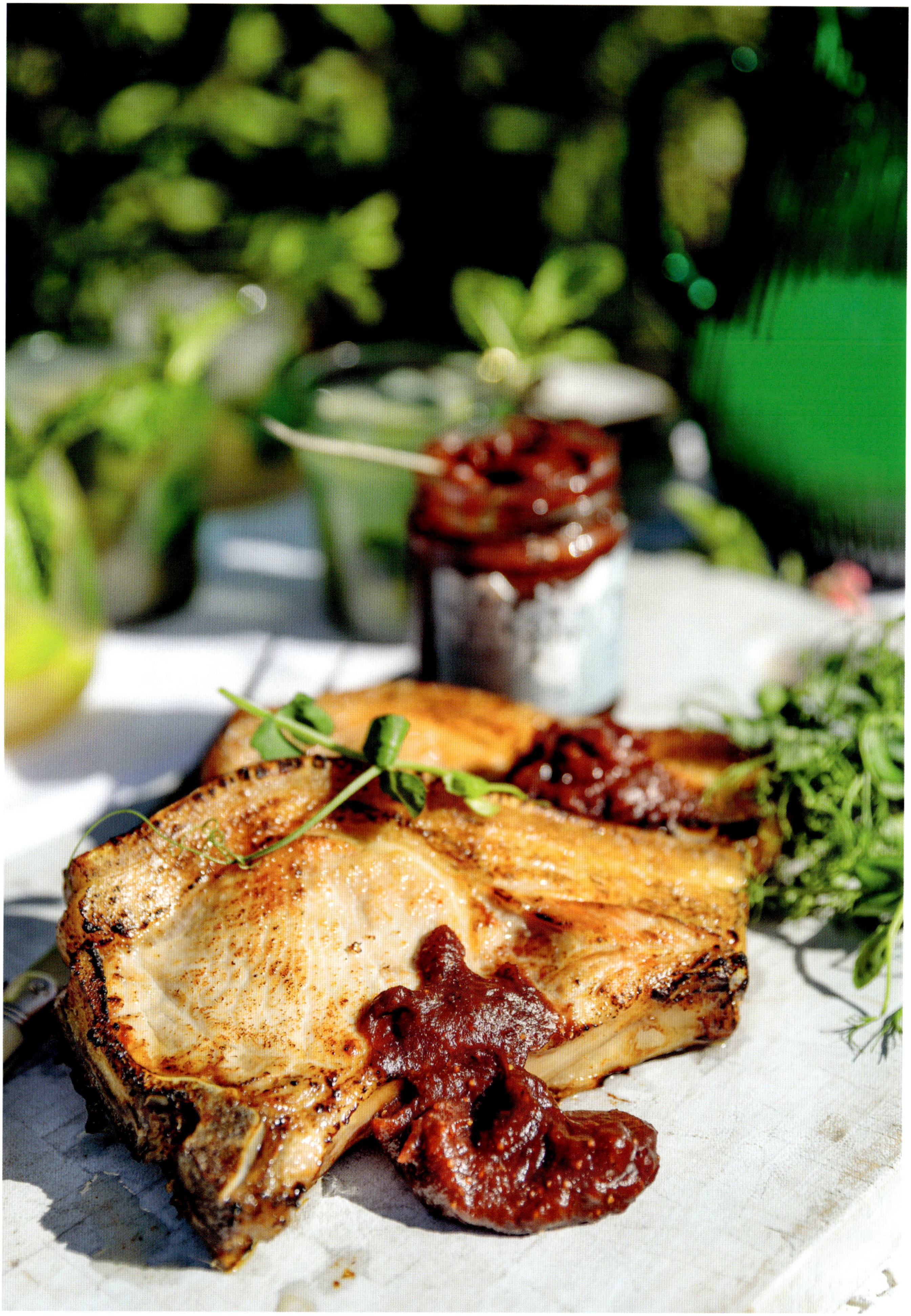

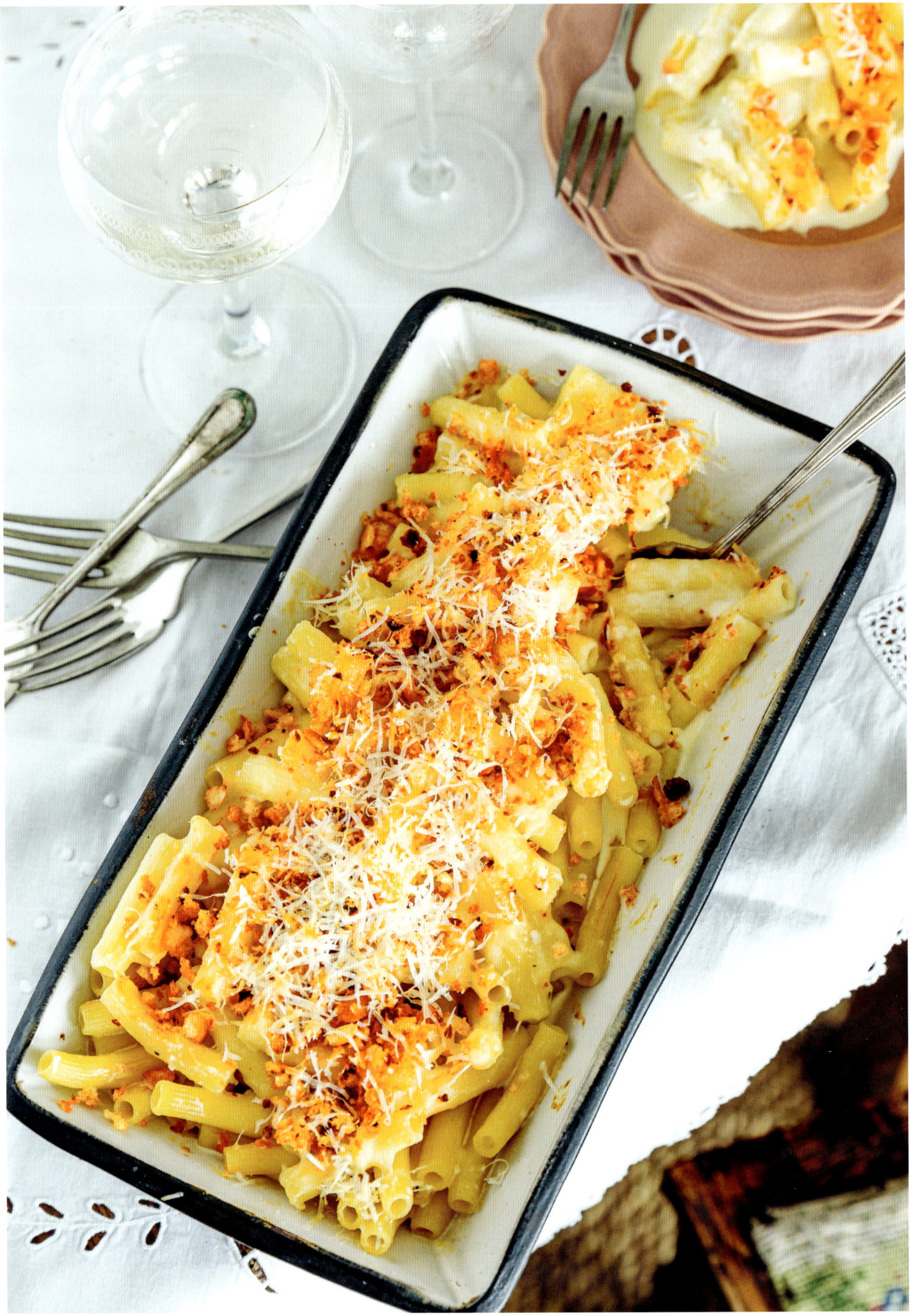

Macaroni Cheese with 'Nduja Crumbs

I've noticed a resurgence in the popularity of macaroni cheese, which I have spotted as a side on the menu in the smartest of restaurants. Deliciously rich and gooey, creamy and comforting, this mac and cheese should please even the fussiest of eaters. It also freezes brilliantly, and it can be left overnight to defrost in the fridge.

—

Serves 4
350g macaroni (try to find the long variety)
1 tbsp 'nduja
40g fresh ciabatta breadcrumbs
25g butter
1 garlic clove, crushed
3 tbsp plain flour
500ml milk
50g mature Cheddar or Gruyère, finely grated
50g freshy grated Parmesan
sea salt and freshly ground black pepper

Preheat the oven to 180°C (350°F/Gas Mark 4). Cook the macaroni in a large pan of boiling salted water for 7–8 minutes until al dente.

Meanwhile, heat the 'nduja in a non-stick frying pan over a low heat, pushing it down with a wooden spoon so that it starts to melt. Stir in the breadcrumbs and a pinch of salt, then fry for 1–2 minutes until the breadcrumbs have absorbed the 'nduja. Set aside.

Next, heat a sauté pan over a medium heat. Add the butter and allow it to sizzle, then sauté the garlic for 1 minute. Sprinkle over the flour and cook for another minute, stirring. Gradually add the milk, whisking continuously until the sauce is smooth. Simmer for 2–3 minutes until thickened. Season with salt and pepper, then remove from the heat and stir in the Cheddar (or the Gruyère) and half of the Parmesan.

Take a small cupful of water from the macaroni, then drain into a colander in the sink. Tip the pasta into the sauce, stirring until evenly combined; add a little of the cooking water if you think it needs it. Transfer to a buttered ovenproof dish and scatter with the rest of the Parmesan and the 'nduja crumbs. Bake for 25–30 minutes until crisp and golden.

SERVE WITH …
For me, this is a dish that embraces simplicity. As such, it needs nothing else, though the gooey richness of the cheese pairs perfectly with the **House Salad with Amelda's Dressing** (p.132).

AND FOR DESSERT …
If anyone has room – although, after a hefty portion of macaroni cheese, that is doubtful – I'd opt for **Warm Blondies with Sea Salt Toffee Sauce** (p.198). Incidentally, this menu works particularly well for a gang of teenagers.

Chateaubriand with Béarnaise Sauce

This is my dream meal! All-year-round heaven, but perfectly suited for a special Sunday lunch or if you are out to impress someone. Making a Béarnaise is not as difficult as you think, and once you've mastered the technique, you'll realise there's nothing much to it.

—

Serves 6

675g beef fillet (the thick end, known as chateaubriand), at room temperature
1 tbsp olive oil
250g unsalted butter
2 tbsp dry white wine
2 tbsp vinegar
2 tbsp chopped fresh tarragon
1 shallot, finely chopped
2 egg yolks
½ lemon
1 tbsp chopped fresh flat-leaf parsley
pinch of cayenne pepper
sea salt and freshly ground white pepper
fresh watercress and rosemary sprigs to garnish

Preheat the oven to 240°C (475°F/Gas Mark 9). Rub the chateaubriand with olive oil, then sprinkle with salt and pepper.

Seal the chateaubriand in a heavy-based ovenproof frying pan over a high heat for about 6 minutes, turning regularly, until golden brown on all sides. Transfer the pan to the oven and roast for about 12 minutes for medium-rare, or to your liking. Remove and rest in a warm place for 10 minutes.

Meanwhile, for the Béarnaise, melt the butter in a small pan or in the microwave. Combine the white wine, vinegar, 1 tablespoon of the tarragon, the shallot and half a teaspoon of pepper in a pan. Bring to a simmer and reduce until about 1 tablespoon of liquid remains. Strain into a liquidiser or mini blender, pushing down the tarragon leaves to extract the liquid.

Add 1 tablespoon of warm water to the liquidiser together with the egg yolks and turn on the machine. Pour the hot butter into a jug and start to pour the butter very slowly on to the egg yolks in the liquidiser. As the sauce emulsifies, increase the butter flow to a thin, steady stream.

As the Béarnaise sauce thickens, you will notice a change in the sound of the machine. If the sauce is too thick, add a little warm water or lemon juice to taste. Add the remaining tarragon leaves, the parsley and cayenne pepper, and blend briefly. Season with salt. Keep warm in a bowl or jug set in a pan of hot but not boiling water.

Carve the chateaubriand into 12–16 slices, divide between warmed plates, garnish with watercress and rosemary and serve with Béarnaise sauce on the side and a big bowl of frites.

SERVE WITH …
If you don't like the idea of **Frites** (p.123) for a dinner party, serve with **Lemon Roast Potato Wedges** (p.137) instead.

AND FOR DESSERT …
A dramatic plate of **Basque Cheesecake with Cherry Compote** (p.188), or a dish of **Coole Swan Chocolate Truffles** (p.194).

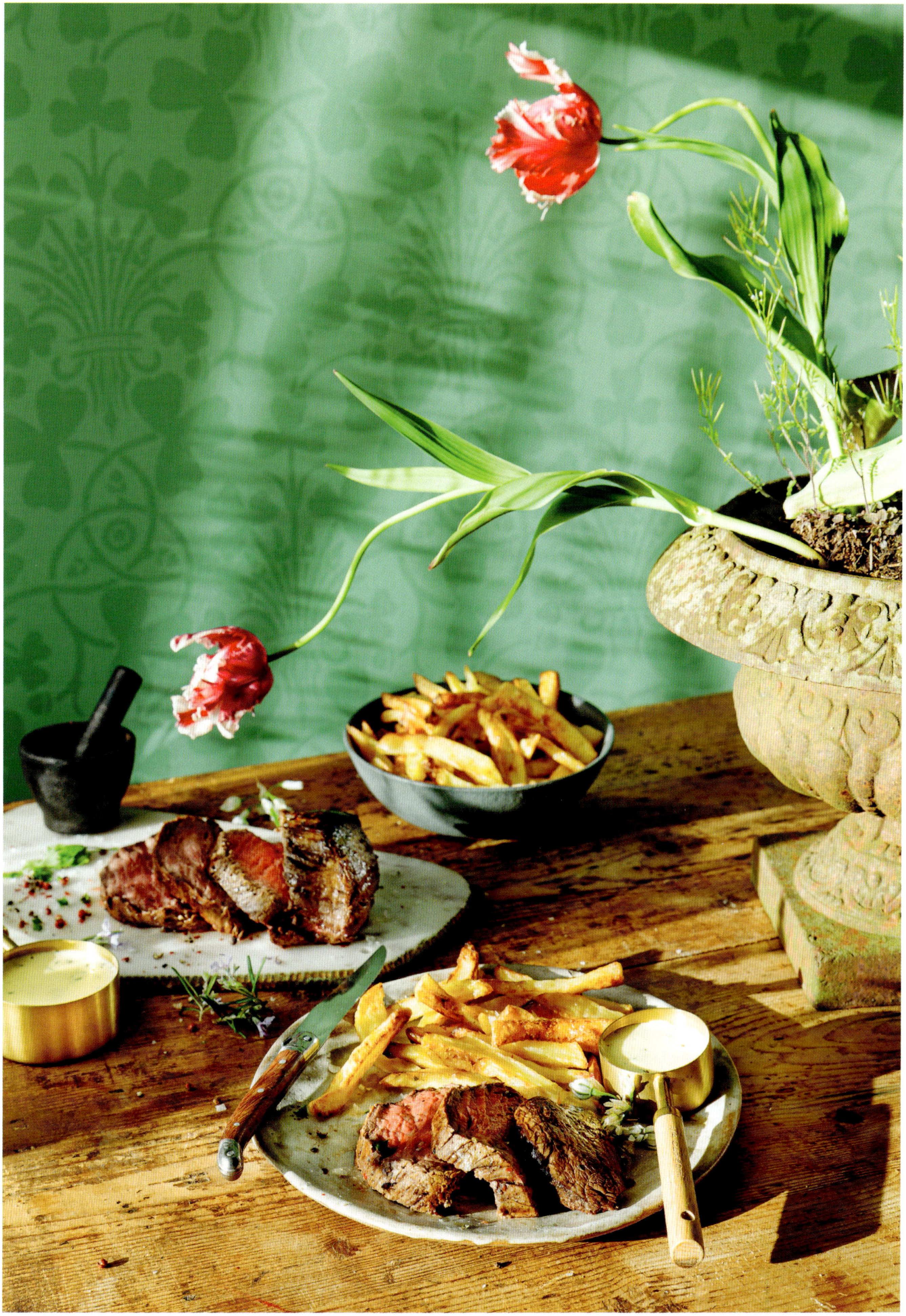

Turkey Roulade with Maple Glaze

There is no need for impressive carving skills with this easy-to-serve turkey recipe with gravy. It is so easy to prepare and great if you want to get ahead. Then, all you have to do is put it in the oven before carving into neat, spiralled slices studded with cranberries and pistachios.

—

Serves 6–8

75g butter
1 large onion, finely chopped
100g fresh ciabatta breadcrumbs
2 tsp chopped fresh mixed herbs (sage, rosemary and thyme)
20g fresh flat-leaf parsley, leaves stripped off
1.75–2kg boneless turkey breast, skin on
50g dried cranberries or chopped apricots
2 tbsp maple syrup
200ml carton poultry gravy
sea salt and freshly ground black pepper

Preheat the oven to 200°C (400°F/Gas Mark 6). Heat a sauté pan over a medium heat, melt half of the butter and gently sauté the onion for 8–10 minutes until softened but not coloured. Season well. Put the breadcrumbs and herbs into a food processor and blitz to fine crumbs, then add the sautéed onions and pulse to make a paste.

Put the turkey breast skin-side down on a chopping board, then butterfly it by cutting partway into the thickest side. Open the turkey breast out and cover with parchment paper, then use a rolling pin to gently bash it out to an even 2cm thickness. Remove the parchment and season, then spread over the breadcrumb paste, leaving a border around the edges.

Scatter the cranberries or apricots on top, then press down so that they form part of the stuffing. Starting from one of the short sides, roll the turkey breast into a tight log shape, then tie at even intervals with kitchen string. Melt the rest of the butter in a small pan with the maple syrup, and use this to glaze the joint, reserving any that is left over. This will keep in the fridge for 2 days, or it can be frozen and defrosted.

Put the turkey roulade on a rack in a roasting tin and roast for 40 minutes, basting halfway through with the rest of the glaze, until the turkey is cooked through. A thermometer should read 70°C. Transfer the roulade to a platter, cover loosely with foil and leave to rest for 15 minutes. Meanwhile, put the roasting tin on the hob and stir in the gravy with a splash of boiling water, scraping the bottom of the tin to remove any sediment.

Carve the turkey into slices and arrange on plates, then pour over some of the gravy to serve.

SERVE WITH ...
For Christmas made easy, serve with **Smashed Roast Potatoes** (p.124) or **Potato Gratin** (p.143).

AND FOR DESSERT ...
Choose a classic like the **Pavlova Wreath with Exotic Fruit** (p.211).

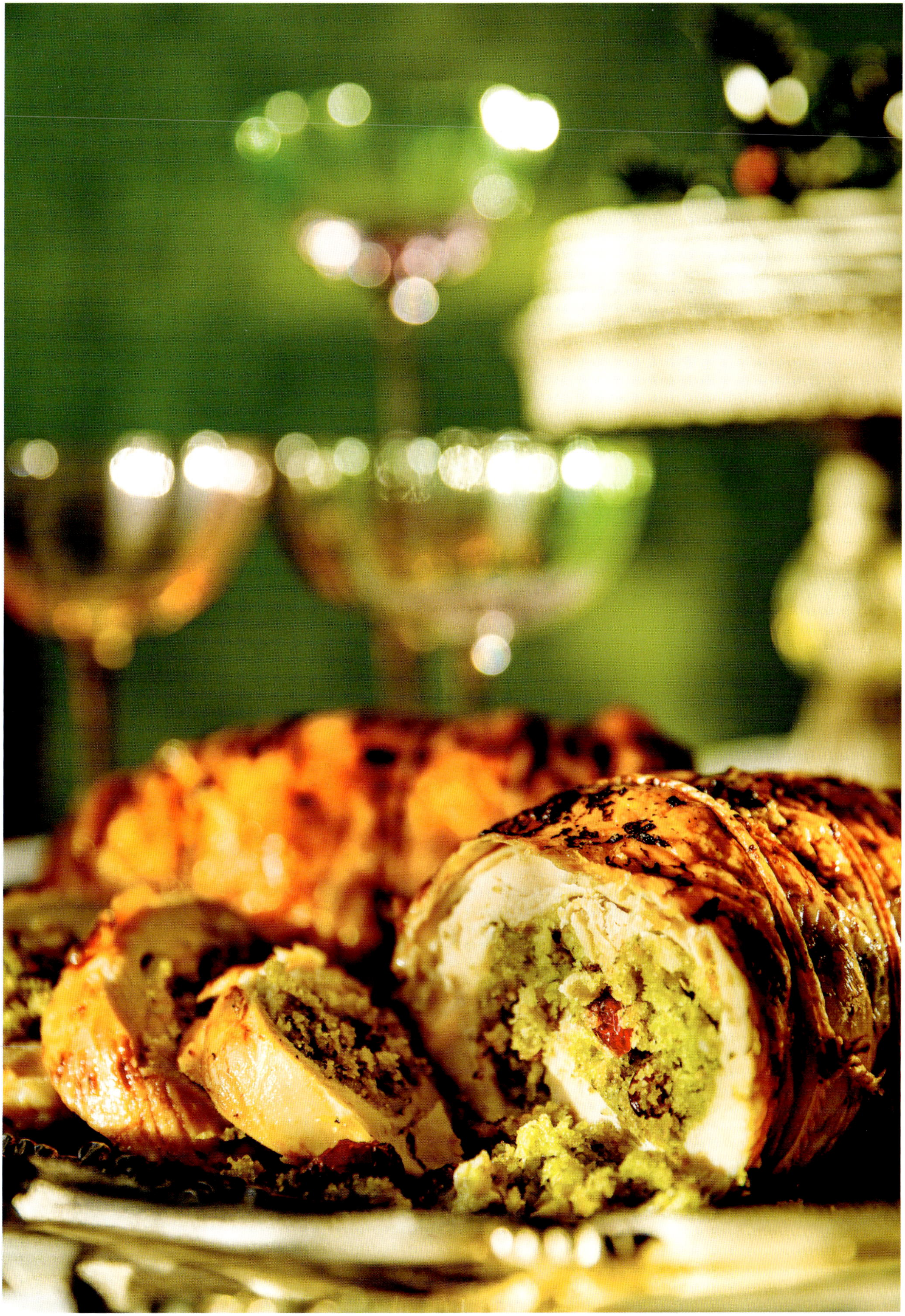

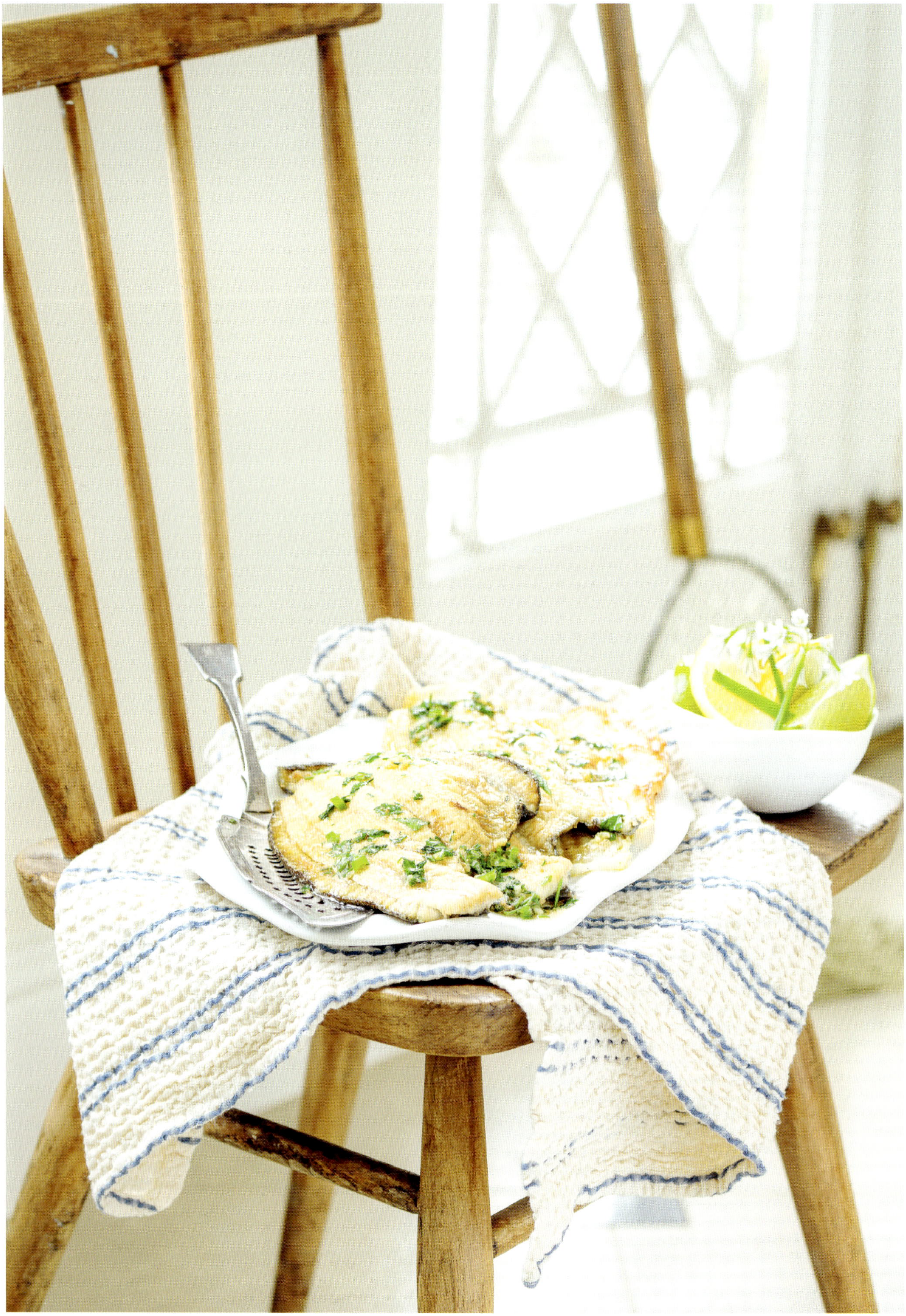

Large Plaice with Garlic Butter Sauce

Nowadays I see this dish on the menus of some of our best restaurants – plaice comes in at a decent price and is every bit as good as some of the pricier flat fish. Pan-frying is the easiest and quickest way to cook plaice, which has a sweet but umami flavour and soft white flesh. This technique seals in all the flavour as well as creating a delicious crispy outer layer.

—

Serves 4
4 x 225–250g plaice fillets
50g plain flour
olive oil, for cooking
100g butter, diced and chilled
2 garlic cloves, crushed
juice of 1 lemon, plus wedges to garnish
1 tbsp chopped fresh parsley
1 tsp snipped fresh chives
sea salt and freshly ground black pepper

Preheat the oven to 100°C (210°F/Gas Mark ½). Heat a large non-stick frying pan over a medium-high heat. Rinse the plaice fillets and pat them dry with kitchen paper. Season the flour on a large flat plate, then use it to dust both sides of the fish. It is best to work one fillet at a time.

Heat a drizzle of oil and a knob of the butter in the pan; once it sizzles, add the plaice, skin-side up. Cook for 2–3 minutes, shaking the pan occasionally, then turn over using a fish slice and cook for another 2–3 minutes. The plaice should be opaque and flake easily with a fork when ready. Put on a warm serving plate and pop in the oven while you cook the remainder in the same way, quickly wiping out the pan with a bit of kitchen paper after each one.

When all the plaice are cooked, wipe out the pan one last time and add a knob of the butter. Tip in the garlic and allow it to sizzle for about 20 seconds, then add the lemon juice and allow it to bubble down. Remove from the heat and add the rest of the butter, swirling around the pan to make a sauce. Season with pepper and add the herbs, tossing to combine. To serve, spoon a couple of tablespoons of the sauce on to each plaice and garnish with lemon wedges.

SERVE WITH ...
Steamed Asparagus with Hollandaise (p.156) makes a perfect pairing, with the nicest boiled Irish potatoes you can find. The **House Salad with Amelda's Dressing** (p.132) will help clean the palate afterwards. If you want something to nibble on first, **Crispy Squid with Smoked Paprika Mayonnaise** (p.8) would be utterly delicious.

AND FOR DESSERT ...
You've worked hard: an **Affogato** (p.168) will mean that everyone goes home very happy – and they might even feel energetic enough to help you tidy up the kitchen before they head off ...

Stuffed Beef Rolls with Tomato Ragu

This recipe is inspired by my love of the witty, gritty TV series The Sopranos. *It's a meal that Tony and his family seemed to have on Sundays, and we would see people coming in and out of the kitchen, checking and stirring, making sure it was just right for everyone to enjoy.*

—

Serves 4

4 small, thin Irish Angus minute sirloin steaks
4 thin slices prosciutto di Parma
6 tbsp olive oil
150ml red wine
1 onion, finely diced
1 celery stick, diced
2 tbsp tomato purée
400ml chicken stock (fresh or made with a stock cube)
2 x 400g tins chopped tomatoes
handful fresh basil leaves
sea salt and freshly ground black pepper
freshly cooked pasta and fresh green salad, to serve

Dry the steaks with kitchen paper and place on a chopping board, cover with parchment paper and gently flatten them with a meat tenderiser or rolling pin to a 3mm thickness. Cover with the prosciutto slices, then roll each steak up tightly like a sausage, securing with a cocktail stick or kitchen string.

Heat the oil in a casserole dish or skillet pan over a high heat. Lower the heat, add the beef rolls and sear on all sides. Increase the heat again, pour in the wine and simmer until reduced by half. Transfer the rolls to a plate and set aside.

Stir the onion and celery into the pan, cook until the remainder of the wine has evaporated, then stir in the tomato purée, mixing well. Add the beef rolls back in, then pour in the chicken stock and the chopped tomatoes. Season with salt and pepper, and tear in the basil. Lower the heat and partially cover with a lid. Cook over a very low heat for 2 hours, stirring occasionally, until the meat is tender when pierced with a fork. Season to taste.

Serve the tomato sauce with some cooked pasta, then serve the meat rolls as a main course with the salad.

SERVE WITH ...

In Southern Italy, the tomato sauce is used to flavour pasta such as tagliatelle or penne for the *primo* (pasta course), while the meat is eaten as a *secondo* (main course) with a simple green salad – all polished off with a nice bottle of red wine.

AND FOR DESSERT ...

Vanilla Panna Cotta (p.182) – literally 'cooked cream' – needs time to set, so make it the night before, or up to 3 days in advance. I love it with whatever fruit is in season, and a drizzle of raw honey can be a lovely final flourish.

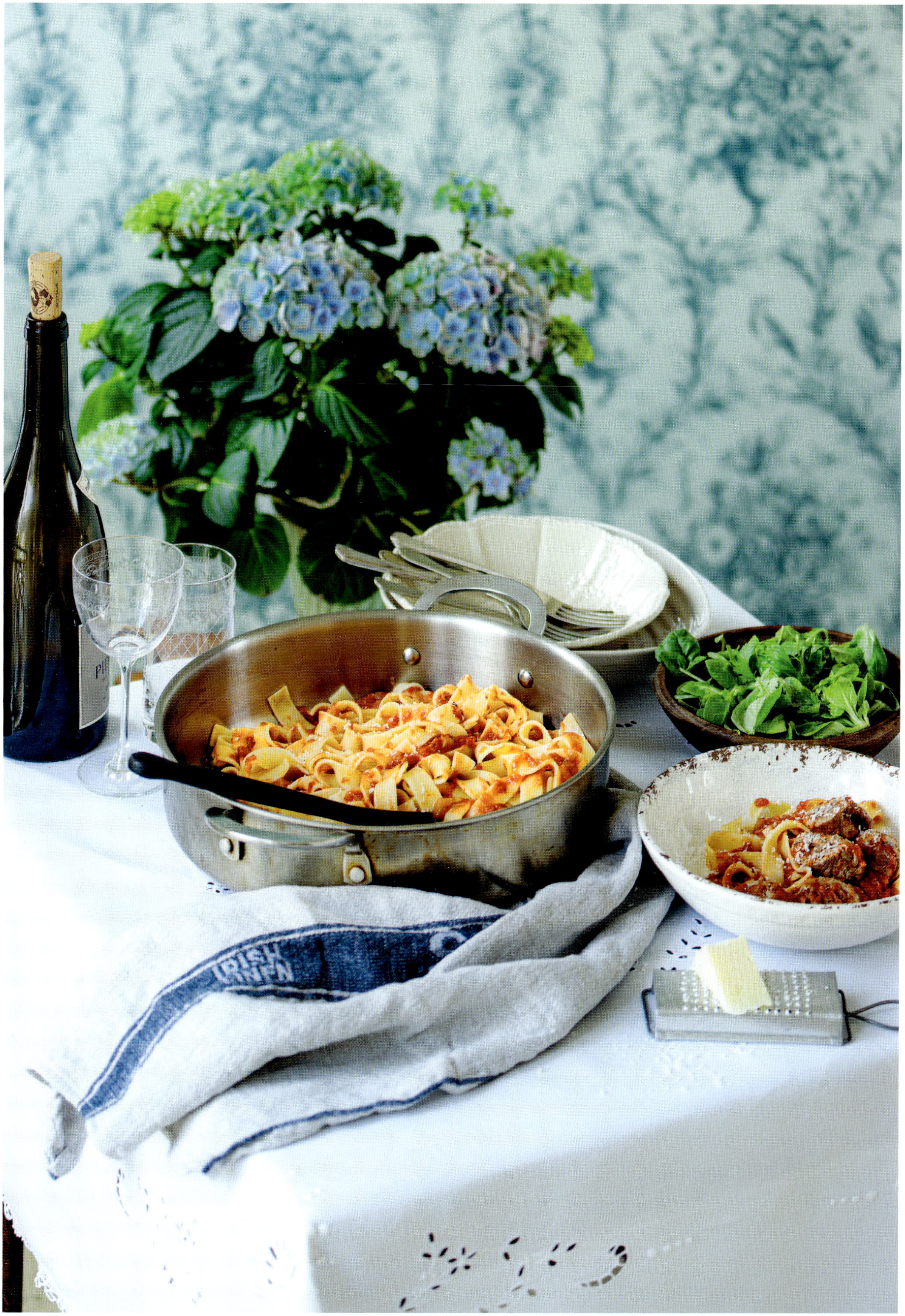
IRISH LINEN

Hake with Red Pepper Sauce

A superb fish to cook and eat, hake can be replaced in this recipe with cod, salmon or sea bass. Whatever you choose, cook the fish at the very last minute, so you appreciate all its freshness. The flavour of the star anise really elevates the sauce into something quite special.

—

Serves 4

4 tbsp olive oil
3 banana shallots, thinly sliced
2 red peppers, cored and thinly sliced
2 star anise
2 tbsp white-wine vinegar
3 tbsp dry vermouth
6 fresh basil leaves, plus extra small sprigs, to garnish
4 x 175g boneless hake fillets, skin on but scaled (from the thick end of the fillet)
plain flour, for dusting
large knob butter
sea salt and freshly ground black pepper

To make the sauce, heat a skillet pan with a lid, add half of the olive oil, then tip in the shallots. Sauté for a few minutes, add the peppers and star anise, and sauté for about 5 minutes until the peppers are soft. Pour in the vinegar and vermouth, and allow it to bubble down until it has completely evaporated, then add 200ml of water and tear in the basil. Simmer over a medium heat until the liquid has reduced by half. Season to taste, remove the star anise and tip into a small pan; then, using a hand blender, blitz to a smooth sauce. Set aside.

Wipe out the skillet pan and add the rest of the olive oil. Dry the hake fillets on kitchen paper, then season to taste and lightly dust the skin with the flour. Add the butter to the pan and, once it begins to sizzle, add the fish, skin side down. Cook for 6–7 minutes or until the skin is crisp and coloured. You may need to press it down gently with a fish slice to stop it curling up. Then turn it over and remove from the heat – the residual heat in the pan will continue to cook the fish.

Warm the red pepper sauce, spoon on to warm plates and top with the hake fillets, skin side up. Garnish with basil sprigs.

SERVE WITH ...
On a summer afternoon, I love this with **Green Couscous** (p.118); I'll have all my prep done, and cook the hake at the last minute on the barbecue. Otherwise, have it as a casual supper with **Green Beans with Goat's Cheese** (p.134) or **Grilled Courgettes with Green Chimichurri Sauce** (p.144).

AND FOR DESSERT ...
Serve **Aperol Spritz Sorbet** (p.173) in delicate, old-fashioned Champagne glasses – you might even decide to start the meal with one if the sun shines ...

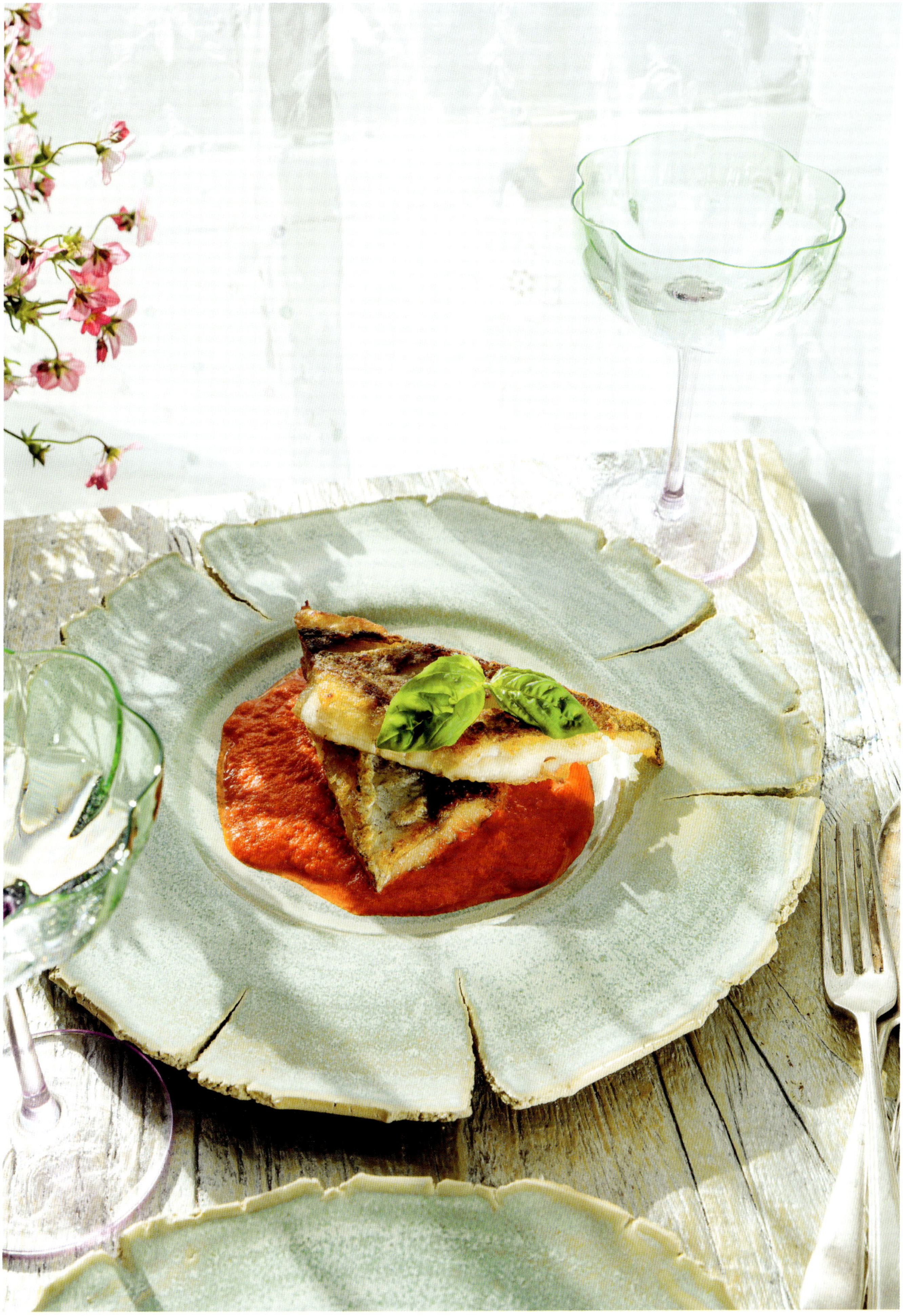

Spiced Roast Cauliflower

This is a vegetarian centrepiece that will wow family and friends. I've used a fabulous Calabrian chilli paste that is so packed full of flavour, it does all the work for you. I was lucky enough to be involved in its launch for Dunnes' Simply Better range. Dukkah is a Middle Eastern blend of nuts and spices; after making it, you'll find yourself adding it to everything.

—

Serves 4

1 large cauliflower, leaves removed and stalk trimmed
50g cashew nuts
50g hazelnuts
2 tbsp black and white sesame seeds
2 tbsp sunflower seeds
1 tsp fennel seeds
½ tsp ground cumin
½ tsp ground coriander
½ tsp cayenne pepper
3 tbsp Calabrian chilli paste (from a jar)
extra virgin olive oil, for drizzling
250g authentic Greek strained yogurt (10% fat)
100g pomegranate seeds
sea salt

Put 3cm of salted water in a lidded pan large enough to fit the whole cauliflower, and bring to the boil over a medium heat. Carefully lower the cauliflower into the pan, then cover and cook for 3 minutes. Turn off the heat and leave for another 10 minutes to steam dry. Lift out the cauliflower and dry well with kitchen paper.

Preheat the oven to 170°C (325°F/Gas Mark 3). Meanwhile, make the dukkah. Roughly chop the cashews and hazelnuts, put in a small baking tin and roast for 5 minutes, then stir in the sesame, sunflower and fennel seeds. Roast for another 2–3 minutes, being careful that the seeds do not burn. Remove from the oven and sprinkle over the cumin, coriander, cayenne and 1 teaspoon of salt. Stir well and set aside until needed. This can be kept in a clean jar for up to 2 weeks.

Increase the oven temperature to 200°C (400°F/Gas Mark 6). Rub the cauliflower all over with the Calabrian chilli paste, making sure you cover the bottom too. Put in a baking tin lined with parchment. Drizzle over a little oil and roast for 20 minutes, then remove from the oven, give it another drizzle of oil, then a good baste and roast for another 25–30 minutes until the cauliflower is golden and crisp in places.

Transfer the cauliflower to a plate. Spoon over about 6 tablespoons of the yogurt and scatter with some of the dukkah and the pomegranate seeds. Carve into wedges or steaks to serve. Have an extra bowl of the yogurt and dukkah on the table so everyone can help themselves.

SERVE WITH ...
This is spectacular enough to serve at Christmas or any other celebration. Surprisingly good at room temperature, it goes perfectly with **Chargrilled Aubergine with Tahini Dressing** (p.120), perhaps alongside little bowls of **Pickled Mixed Vegetables** (p.53) and **Pickled Red Onions** (p.140).

AND FOR DESSERT ...
Peanut Butter Fudge with Goji Berries & Pistachios (p.212) and a round of espressos would round off this meal perfectly.

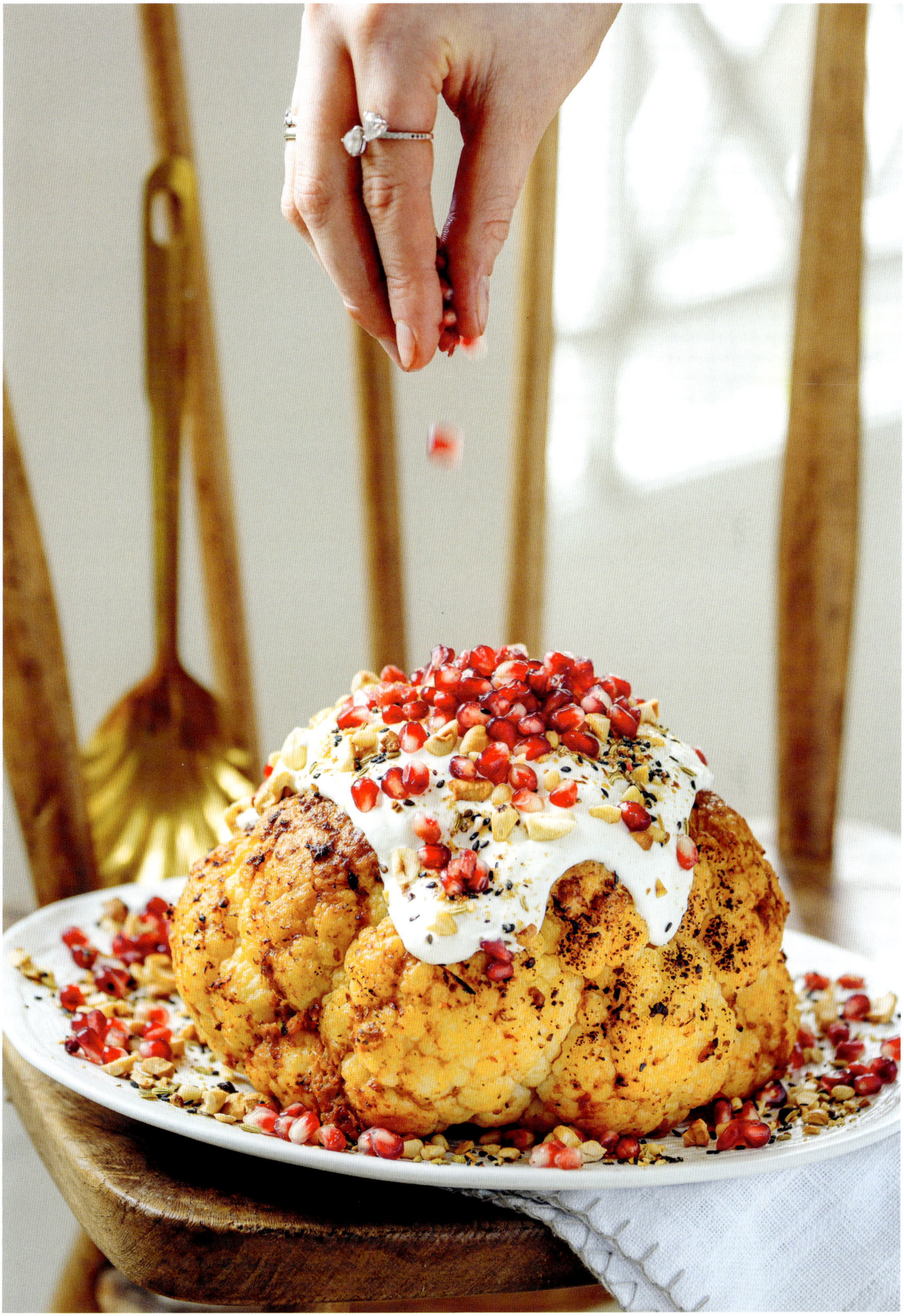

Beef & Medjool Date Tagine

I've been making variations of this tagine for years now and it is wonderful with lamb. If you're looking for a fragrant spiced dish that can be embellished at the last minute, so that it sparkles as it hits the table, look no further. The flavour only improves with time, so this is ideal if you want to get ahead, since it can be left in the fridge for up to 48 hours or frozen.

—

Serves 6–8

2 tbsp hot paprika
1 tbsp each ground coriander and turmeric
2 tsp each ground cinnamon and cumin
1.5kg Irish Angus casserole beef pieces
4 garlic cloves, chopped
2.5cm piece root ginger, peeled and chopped
3 onions, roughly chopped
4 tbsp olive oil
400g tin chopped tomatoes
500ml beef stock (fresh or from a cube)
2 tbsp raw Irish honey
225g Medjool dates, halved and stoned
sea salt and freshly ground black pepper
fresh coriander leaves, toasted almonds, pomegranate seeds and authentic Greek yogurt (optional) to garnish

In a large bowl, mix the paprika, coriander, turmeric, cinnamon, cumin and 2 teaspoons of pepper, then tip half into a small bowl and set aside. Add the beef to the large bowl and coat in the spices. Cover with cling film and chill overnight or for up to 2 days.

Preheat the oven to 170°C (325°F/Gas Mark 3). Place the garlic, ginger and onions into a food processor, and pulse until finely minced. Heat a large heavy-based casserole, add half of the oil and brown the marinated beef in batches. Pour the remaining oil into the pan, add the onion mixture and cook for a few minutes until softened but not coloured. Stir in the reserved spice mixture and cook for another minute or so until well combined.

Blitz the tomatoes in the food processor until smooth. Pour them into the pan with the stock, then add the browned beef with the honey, stirring to combine. Bring to the boil, cover and transfer to the oven. Cook for 2 hours, stirring in the dates halfway through, until the beef is completely tender and the sauce has thickened and reduced. Season to taste.

Garnish the tagine with a dollop of yogurt and scatter over the coriander and almonds. Finish with the pomegranate seeds to serve.

SERVE WITH …

Imagine a pot of this tagine next to a mound of glistening **Green Couscous** (p.118), twinkling lights and the aroma of fragrant spices in the air. The scene is set, and there's no work to do except sit down and enjoy the conversation.

AND FOR DESSERT …

Have a jug of **Apple Mojito** (p.185) ready to pour into tall glasses half-filled with mint sprigs and ice cubes, or stay in a Middle Eastern state of mind with **Moroccan Orange Salad with Pomegranate** (p.170).

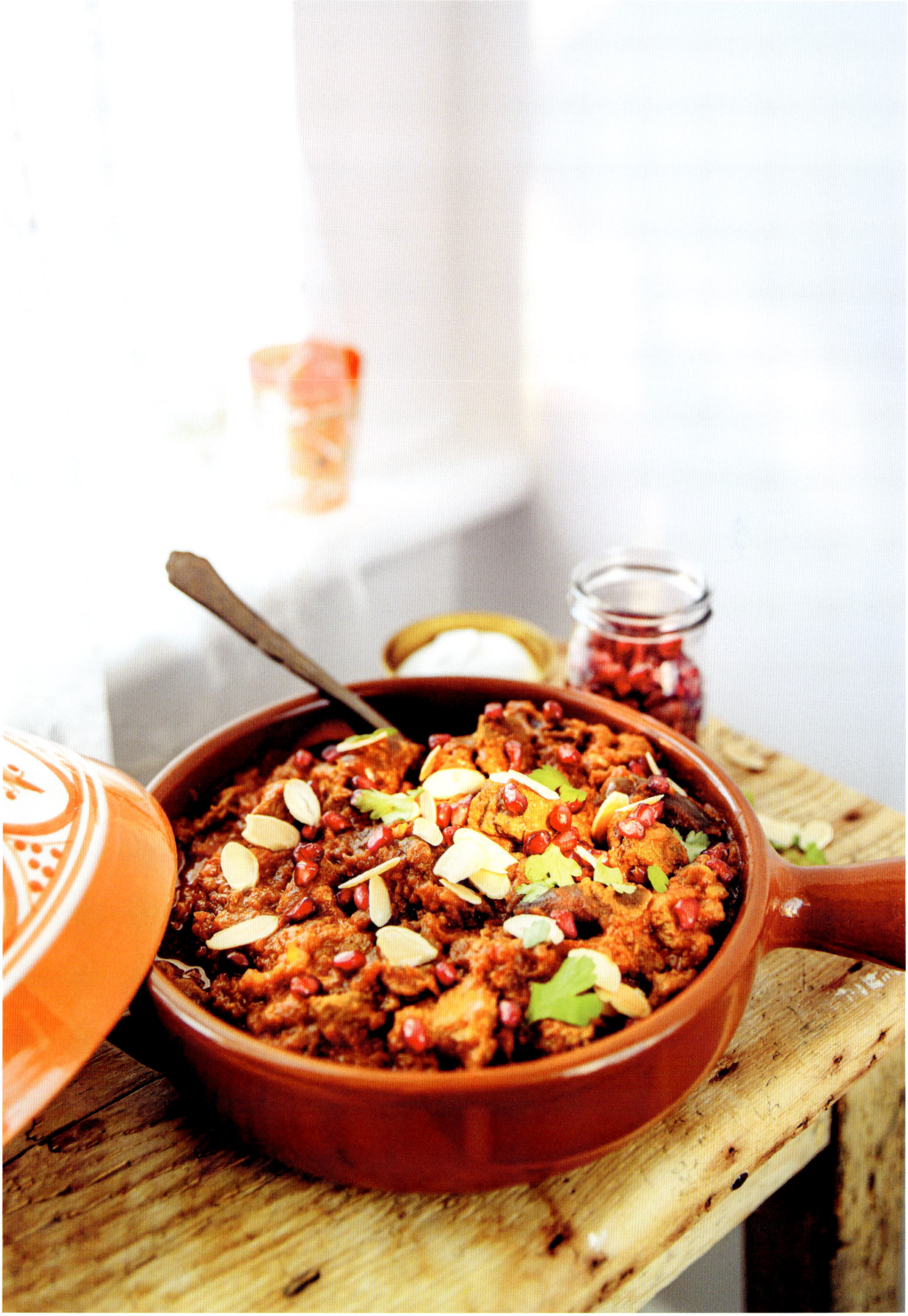

Side Plates

Focaccia with Rosemary & Sea Salt

This is a no-knead bread – in other words, a case of minimal effort producing maximum flavour. Simply give the dough an extended rising time, and you can enjoy this gorgeous focaccia without a hitch. This also works well as a bread for sandwiches. Using a serrated knife, split the bread horizontally. I love it with a smear of pesto, prosciutto di Parma and fresh buffalo mozzarella torn into pieces.

—

Makes 1 large loaf
7g packet dried yeast
2 tsp raw Irish honey
625g plain flour
1 tbsp sea salt flakes, extra for the topping
6 tbsp extra virgin olive oil, plus a little extra
25g butter, at room temperature
handful fresh rosemary sprigs

Whisk the yeast, honey and 600ml of lukewarm water in a large bowl. Leave for 5 minutes to go creamy and foam, then add the flour and salt, and mix with a spatula until a soft dough forms.

Pour 4 tablespoons of the oil into another large bowl and tip in the dough, turning to coat in the oil. Cover with cling film and chill until doubled in size. This process, called cold fermenting, will take 8–24 hours. The slower the yeast growth, the better the flavour.

Generously butter a 33cm x 23cm baking tin, then pour 1 tablespoon of the oil into the centre of the tin. Keeping the dough in the bowl and using a fork in each hand, gather up the edges of the dough furthest from you, then lift up and fold over into the centre of the bowl. Give the bowl a quarter turn and repeat this process. Do this twice more – you want to deflate the dough while forming it into a rough ball. Gently tip the dough into the prepared baking tin, drizzling over any oil left in the bowl, then using your hands turn the dough over so it's completely covered in oil. Leave the dough in a warm place until it has doubled in size (2–4 hours).

Preheat the oven to 220°C (425°F/Gas Mark 7). Check that the dough is ready by poking it with your fingers: it should spring back slowly, leaving a small indentation. If necessary, jiggle the dough to spread it out to the edges of the tin. Using your fingers, dimple the focaccia, creating deep impressions in the dough. Toss the rosemary sprigs into the rest of the oil and scatter on top with a little extra oil and salt flakes. Bake for 25–30 minutes until crisp and golden brown. Leave for 10–15 minutes before slicing into it.

SERVE WITH ...
A basket of homemade bread on the table is a nice way of telling your guests that you've gone to a bit of trouble. This goes with most dishes – I suggest some **Italian Stuffed Conchiglioni** (p.67). Delicious warm, straight from the oven, this focaccia also reheats beautifully the next day.

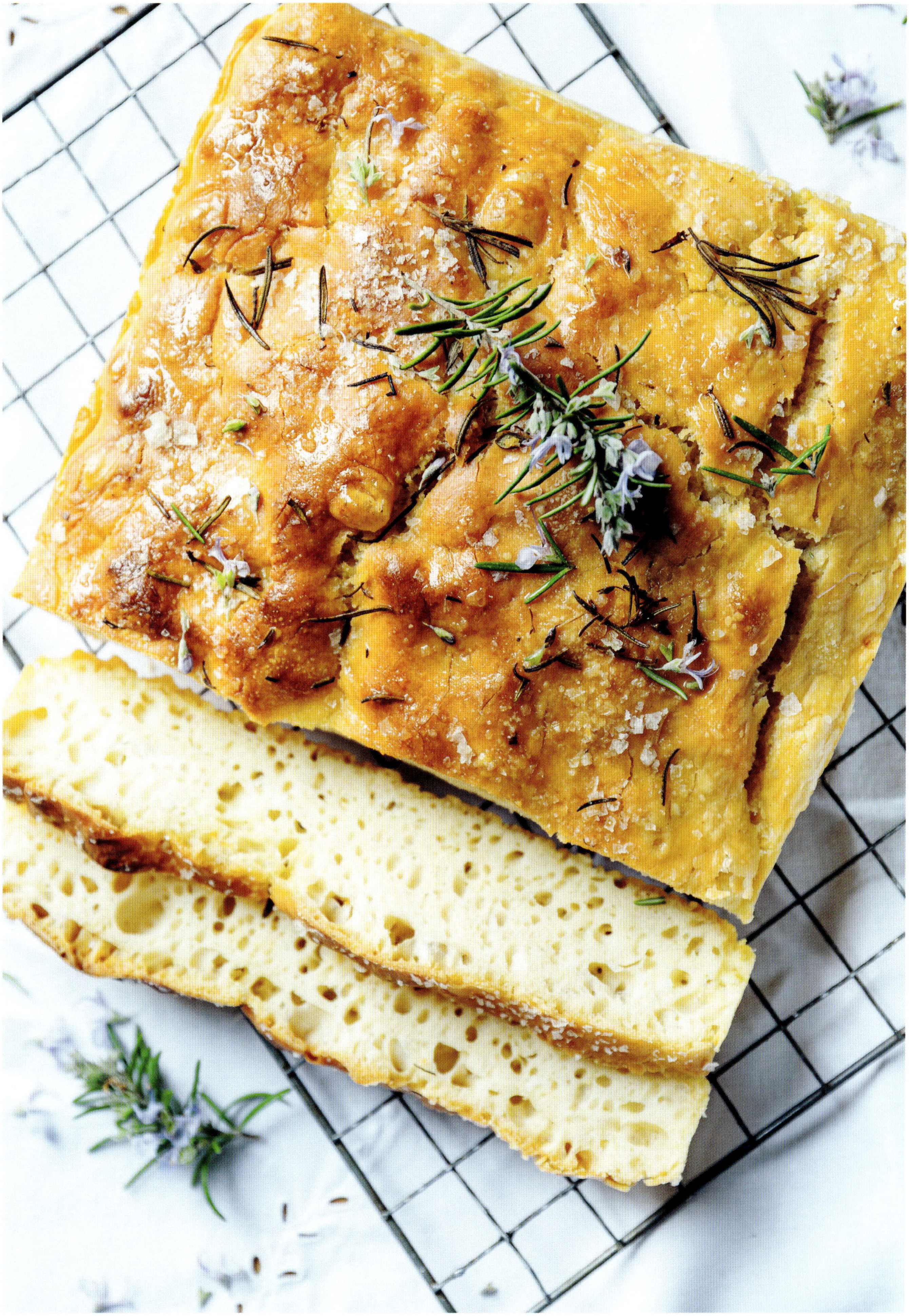

Homemade Flatbreads

These homemade flatbreads are hugely rewarding, and the smell of them cooking on the griddle once everyone has gathered is a lovely contrast with the busyness of everyday life. They are best eaten straight away, while still warm: just brush them with butter, and they're ready for tearing and dipping.

—

Makes 8

300g self-raising flour, plus extra for dusting
½ tsp baking powder
1 tsp sea salt
150g natural yogurt
100g butter
1 tbsp toppings (choose from cumin seeds, minced garlic, chopped fresh coriander or finely chopped chillies)

Sieve the flour, baking powder and salt into a large bowl. Make a well in the centre and add the yogurt with 2 tablespoons of water. Mix lightly to form a dough and tip on to a lightly floured surface. Knead for a few minutes until smooth and pliable, then cut the dough into 8 pieces.

Melt the butter in a small pan and allow the sediment to settle at the bottom. Roll out the dough into rough ovals on the floured work surface and brush with a little of the butter, then scatter over a little of the topping of your choice and fold each piece of dough over on itself, then roll out again into a rough oval shape.

Heat a heavy-based frying pan over a high heat. Cook the flatbreads in the hot frying pan for 1–2 minutes on each side until cooked through, lightly golden and slightly charred in spots. Brush with a little more melted butter and pile up on to a wooden board to serve.

SERVE WITH …

I like to make these to accompany a meze meal. Meze in Greece or Mezze in Turkey and many parts of the Middle East means 'to taste' and is the name for several small dishes or small plates served before a meal with something nice to drink. When putting the dishes together, go for a variety of flavours and textures. **Spiced Cauliflower Bites** (p.21), **Tunisian Carrot Salad** (p.42) and **Pickled Mixed Vegetables** (p.53) would be a lovely combination, perfect with fragrant mains like **Beef & Medjool Date Tagine** (p.108) or **Butter Chicken** (p.85), looking spectacular piled high on a serving dish.

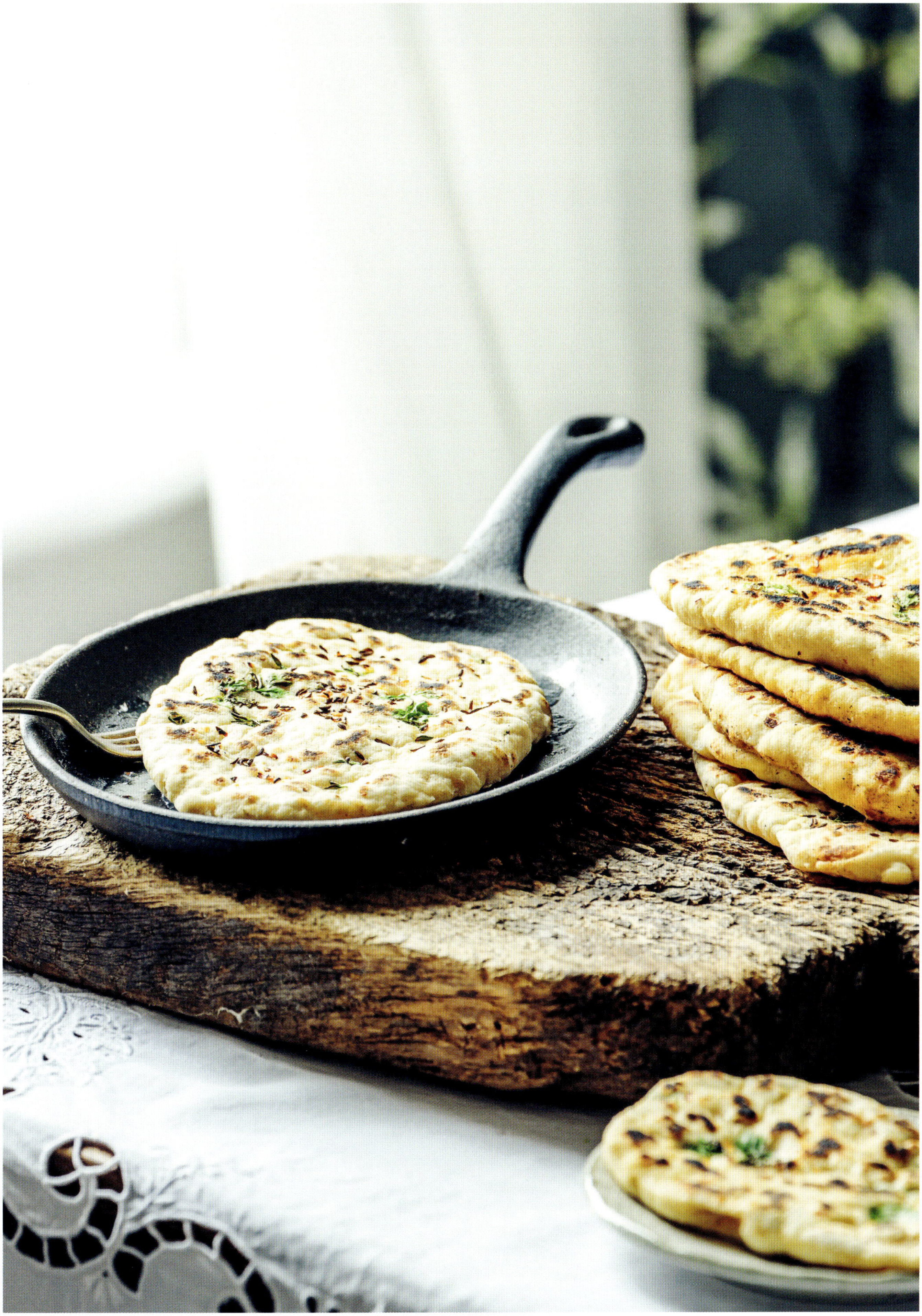

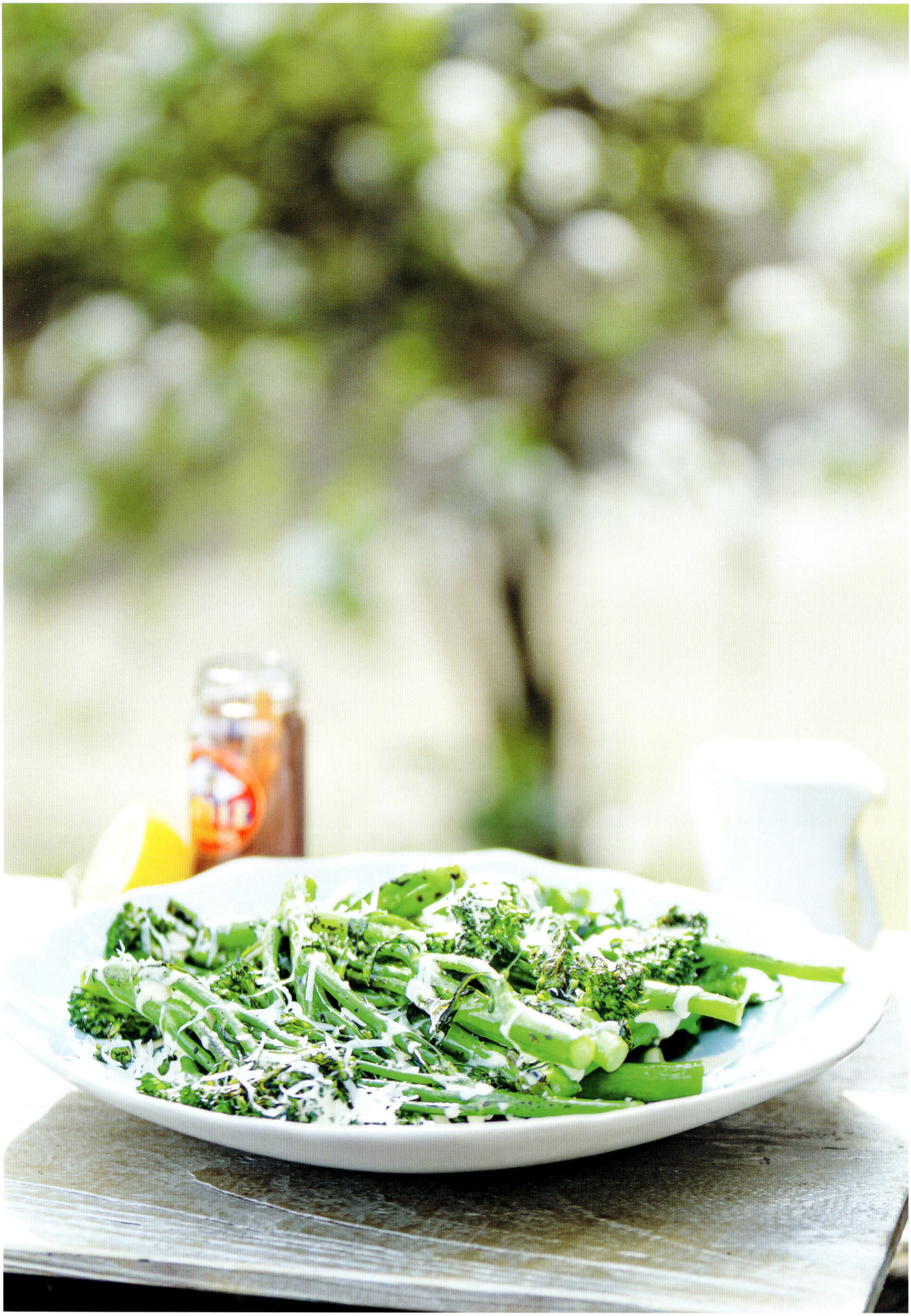

Chargrilled Tenderstem Broccoli with Caesar Dressing

Once you've tried this, you will never want to eat broccoli any other way. It's tricky to make this mayonnaise-style dressing in a food processor because the quantity is too small to emulsify in a large bowl. Instead, use a handheld blender, so long as you have the beaker that comes with it or a narrow jug that is only slightly wider than the head of your blender.

—

Serves 4

1 egg yolk
juice of ½ lemon
½ tsp Dijon mustard
3 anchovies, chopped
1 small garlic clove, crushed
130ml olive oil
1 tbsp freshly grated Parmesan, plus extra shavings to garnish
dash of Worcestershire sauce
400g tenderstem broccoli spears
sea salt and freshly ground black pepper

To make the Caesar dressing, put the egg yolk, lemon juice, mustard, anchovies and garlic into a tall beaker or narrow jug. Add 1 tablespoon of water and 100ml of the olive oil. Leave to settle for 30 seconds, then place your handheld blender at the bottom of the beaker, on top of the yolk, and switch on. Blend, keeping the blender pressed against the base, until you see white mayonnaise beginning to creep out from underneath, at which point you can very slowly begin to draw the blender up the beaker, still blending as you go until all the oil is incorporated. Stir in the grated Parmesan and Worcestershire sauce, and season to taste.

Preheat the griddle pan over a medium-high heat. Toss the broccoli in the rest of the olive oil and season with salt. Griddle the broccoli in batches, sprinkling each batch with a little water to create some steam. Cook for 6–8 minutes, turning with tongs every so often, until tender and slightly charred in places. Arrange the broccoli on a platter and drizzle over the dressing. Scatter over the Parmesan shavings to serve.

SERVE WITH …
This colourful side is just what you need with **Crispy Spatchcock Chicken with Lemon & Herbs** (p.60) or **Crispy Porchetta with Fennel & Herbs** (p.80). It's a great dish for sharing and passing around for all to help themselves as part of a more relaxed meal sitting in the garden, and the broccoli could easily be done on the barbecue to create those crispy bits (which are my favourite part).

Green Couscous

This is my favourite way to serve couscous: soaked in aromatic herb oil, and with a lovely chilli kick. It's great at room temperature, so you can leave it for a few hours after preparing it. Just be sure to fold in the rocket at the last minute, or the leaves will bruise, and scatter with the caramelised onions and toasted pistachios just before serving.

—

Serves 4

120ml extra virgin olive oil
2 large onions, thinly sliced
½ tsp ground cumin
300g couscous
100g shelled pistachios
50g fresh soft herbs (such as flat-leaf parsley, coriander and mint)
1 bunch scallions, trimmed and thinly sliced
1 long green chilli, seeded and finely chopped
100g rocket
sea salt and freshly ground black pepper

Heat 2 tablespoons of the oil in a large non-stick frying pan over a medium heat. Add the onions and cook for 25–30 minutes until it's caramelised and lightly golden. Remove from the heat, add the cumin and season generously with salt. Tip into a bowl and set aside until needed.

Put the couscous in a large bowl and pour over 300ml of boiling water. Cover with cling film and set aside for 10 minutes. Wipe out the frying pan and put back on a medium heat, then toast the pistachios. Tip on to a chopping board to cool down and roughly chop.

Pick all the leaves off the herbs and put into a mini blender. Season with salt and pepper and add the rest of the oil. Blitz to a smooth paste, then stir in the scallions and chilli. Uncover the couscous and gently fluff up with a fork. Fold in the herb mixture and then gently fold in the rocket. Tip on to a platter and scatter over the caramelised onions and the pistachios to serve.

SERVE WITH …

If I'm having my **Beef and Medjool Date Tagine** (p.108), I'll always serve couscous. This also makes great outdoor food alongside **Fragrant Butterflied Lamb** (p.69); for a riot of colour, add a tomato salad. Serving this with **Spiced Roast Cauliflower** (p.106) and **Aubergines Stuffed with Onions, Tomatoes, Chilli & Parsley** (p.76) makes for a rewarding plant-based meal.

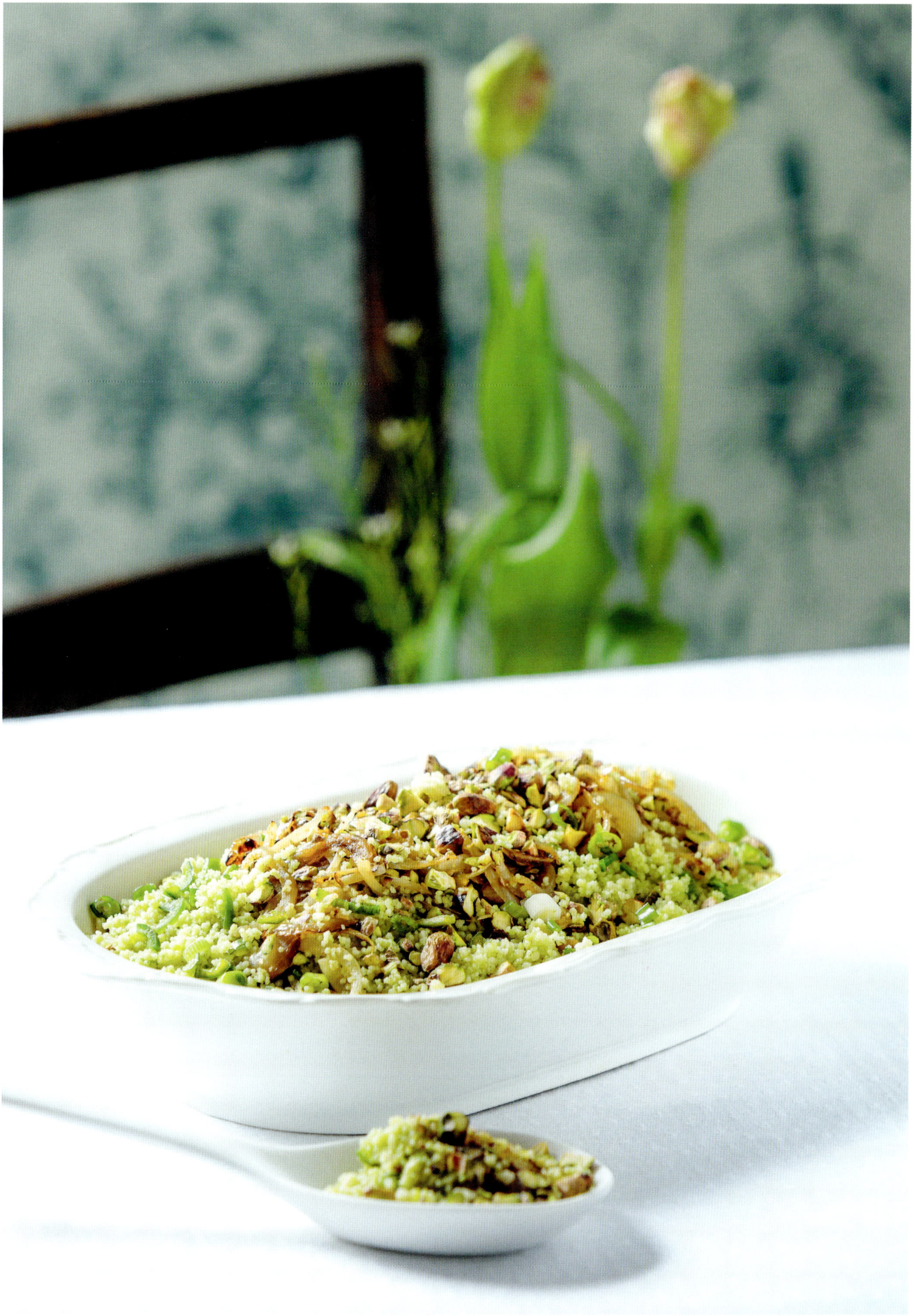

Chargrilled Aubergine with Tahini Dressing

Nicely charred aubergines are a thing of beauty. Their smoky flesh, drizzled with a creamy garlic tahini sauce and scattered with fragrant herbs, is perfect for a summer spread.

—

Serves 4–6
2 large aubergines (or 4 small ones)
Maldon sea salt
about 100ml olive oil
pinch of paprika
handful fresh coriander and mint leaves

For the dressing
4 tbsp light tahini paste
juice of ½ lemon
1 garlic clove, crushed
1 tsp raw Irish honey
sea salt

Cut the aubergines lengthways into 1cm-thick slices and sprinkle with salt. Layer in a colander and set aside in the sink for 40 minutes.

To make the dressing, put the tahini in a bowl and add in the lemon juice. Add the garlic, honey and a good pinch of salt, then whisk to combine. Slowly whisk in 3 tablespoons of water until you have achieved a pourable texture. Leave at room temperature until needed.

Preheat the oven to 110°C (225°F/Gas Mark ¼) and heat a griddle pan over a medium-high heat. Pat the aubergine slices dry with kitchen paper. In batches, brush the aubergine slices with oil and cook for 4–5 minutes on each side until cooked through and lightly charred. Transfer to a baking sheet and keep warm in the oven while you cook the remainder.

Arrange the aubergine slices on a platter, drizzle over the tahini dressing, then add a light sprinkling of paprika and scatter over the coriander and mint leaves to serve.

SERVE WITH …
Like many recipes in this chapter, this will – served generously – stand happily alone for a light lunch, perhaps alongside some **Homemade Flatbreads** (p.114). It is also a fantastic side dish if you are feeding an army, because the aubergines can be prepared in advance and left at room temperature.

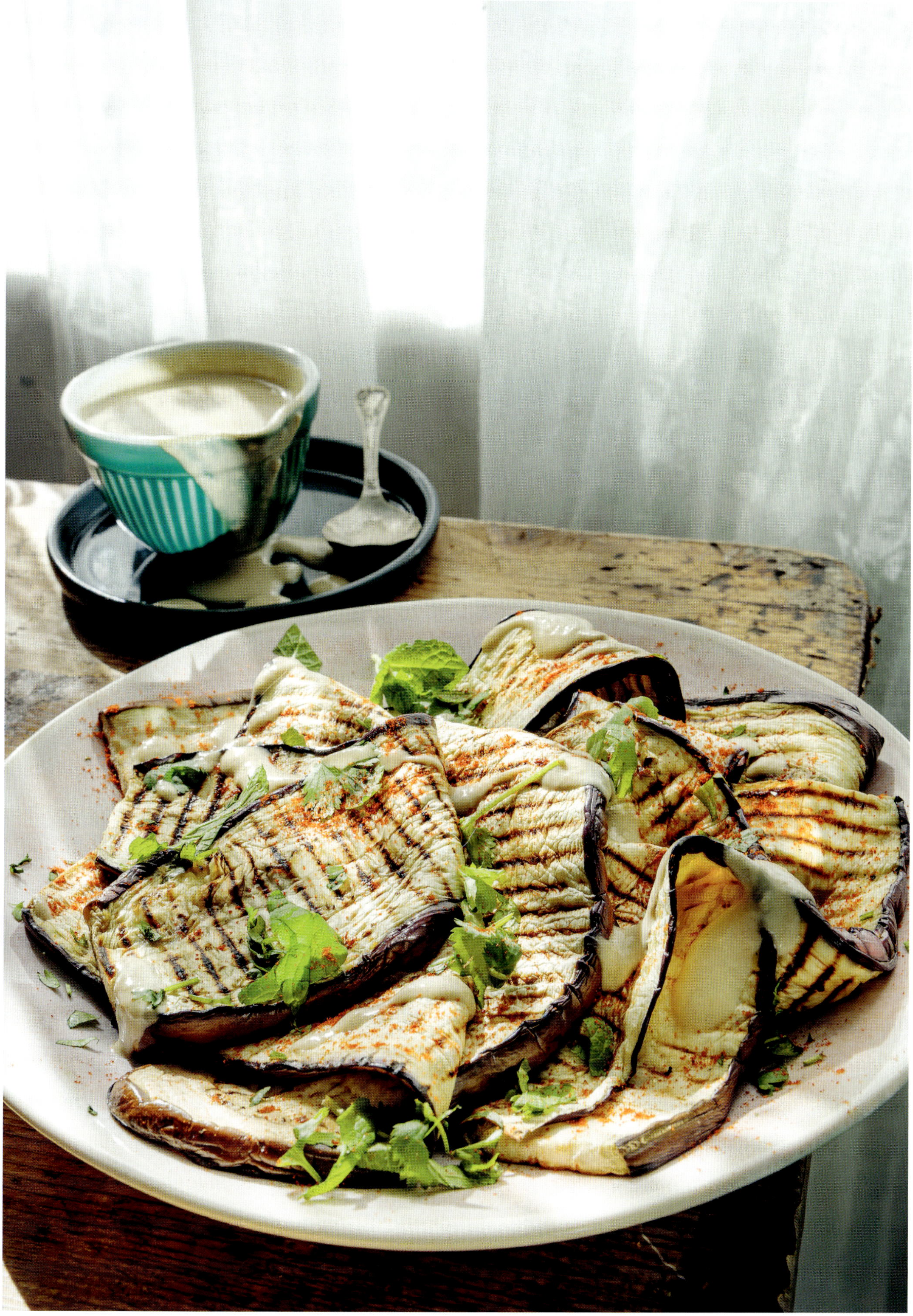

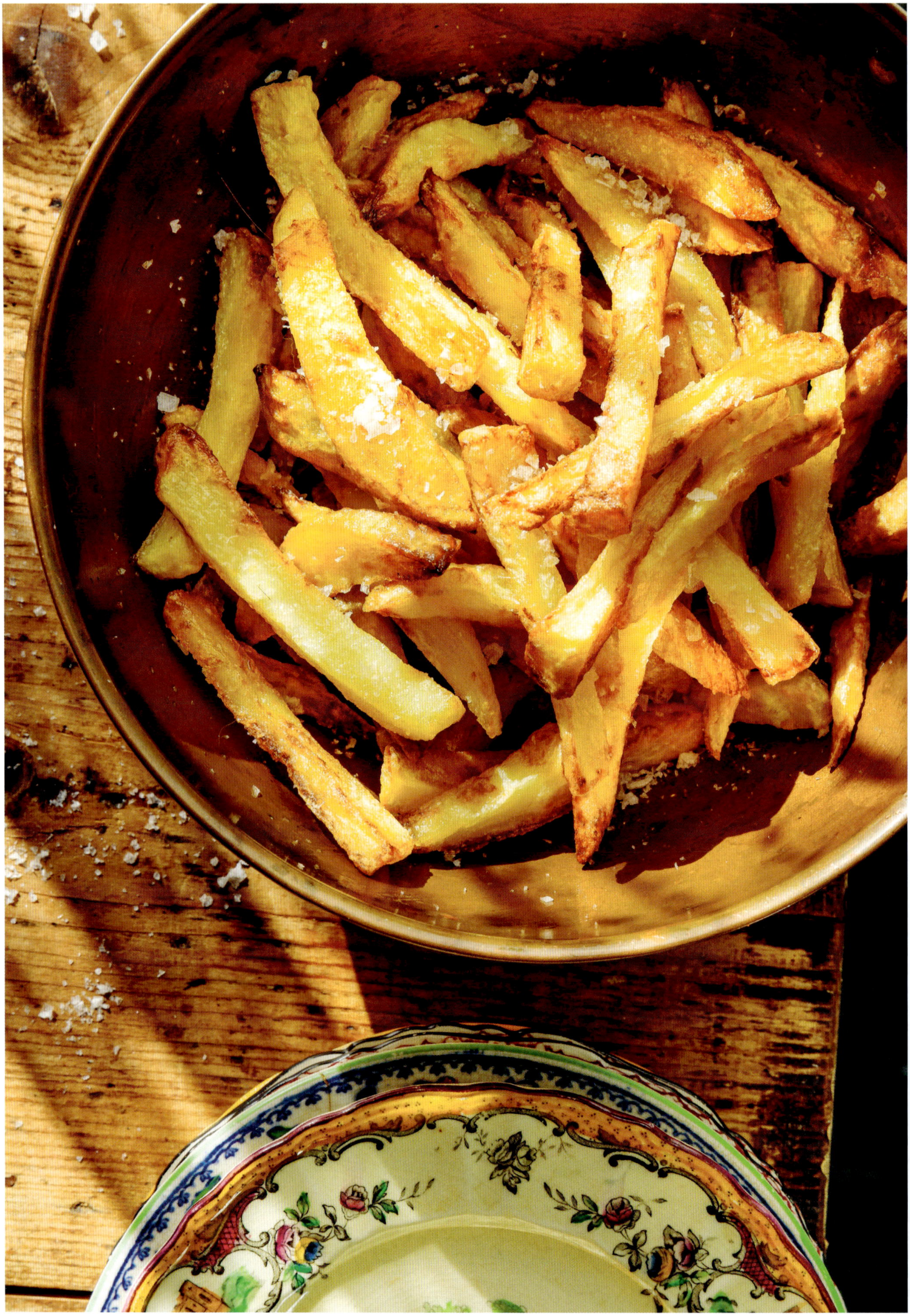

Frites

This recipe teaches you how to make authentic traditional frites. There are no fancy skills involved, but there is a trick: the potatoes are fried twice. The first fry cooks them through and makes them tender. The second fry – which can be done hours later, just before serving – turns them lightly golden and deliciously crisp.

—

Serves 4–6

1kg potatoes (Rooster or Maris Piper)
sunflower or vegetable oil, for deep-frying
sea salt

Peel the potatoes and cut into 1cm batons. Put into a large bowl of cold water and leave to soak for at least 2 hours to remove the starch – this will help them to go nice and crispy when you're frying them.

Preheat a deep-fat fryer to 140°C (275°F), or use a large deep-sided pan no more than a third full of oil. Drain the potatoes, rinse in cold running water and pat dry with kitchen paper.

Fry the potato batons in batches for 6 minutes until lightly golden and cooked through. They should be straw coloured. Drain well on kitchen paper.

Increase the temperature of the oil to 180°C (350°F), and cook the frites again for 2–3 minutes per batch until lightly golden and really crisp. Drain on kitchen paper and pile into a bowl, then season with salt to serve.

SERVE WITH ...

Nobody can resist this perfect, delicious side dish. Make a Friday night supper special by serving it with **Mussels in Spiced Cream** (p.12), or go all in with a showstopping **Chateaubriand with Béarnaise Sauce** (p.96). The **Aromatic Poached Salmon with Avocado & Cucumber Salad** (p.83) is another perfect partner. It's easy enough to put together at the weekend for friends or family, and tastes so good that it will be remembered for a long time.

Smashed Roast Potatoes

This is a great way to roast potatoes, because you can parboil and crush them well ahead of time. Douse them in the flavoured olive oil and leave them to cook longer than you'd think they need – they come out exquisitely crisp and golden.

—

Serves 4–6
500g baby new potatoes (such as Charlotte)
4 tbsp extra virgin olive oil
25g butter
1 garlic bulb, separated into cloves and lightly bashed in their skins
4 fresh thyme sprig, leaves stripped from stems
sea salt flakes

Preheat the oven to 200°C (400°F/Gas Mark 6). Put the potatoes in a large pan of cold salted water. Bring to the boil and cook for 15 minutes until tender. Drain and leave to steam dry for a few minutes.

Arrange the potatoes in a large shallow baking tin, leaving enough space between each one so they have room to spread once smashed. Using the back of a large spoon or a potato masher, push down on each of the potatoes to make them crack open, then season with salt.

Heat the oil, butter, garlic and thyme in a small pan, and drizzle the mixture over the potatoes. Roast for 1 hour, turning once about half way through, until the potatoes are crisp and golden. Remove from the oven and pile on to a platter. Garnish with a little salt to serve.

SERVE WITH …
In our house we'd happily eat these with anything, but they work particularly well with the **Turkey Roulade with Maple Glaze** (p.98) as a Christmas lunch, alongside some **Honey-Glazed Spiced Carrots with Pistachio & Dill** (p.160). Just remember to make twice as many potatoes as you think anyone will eat!

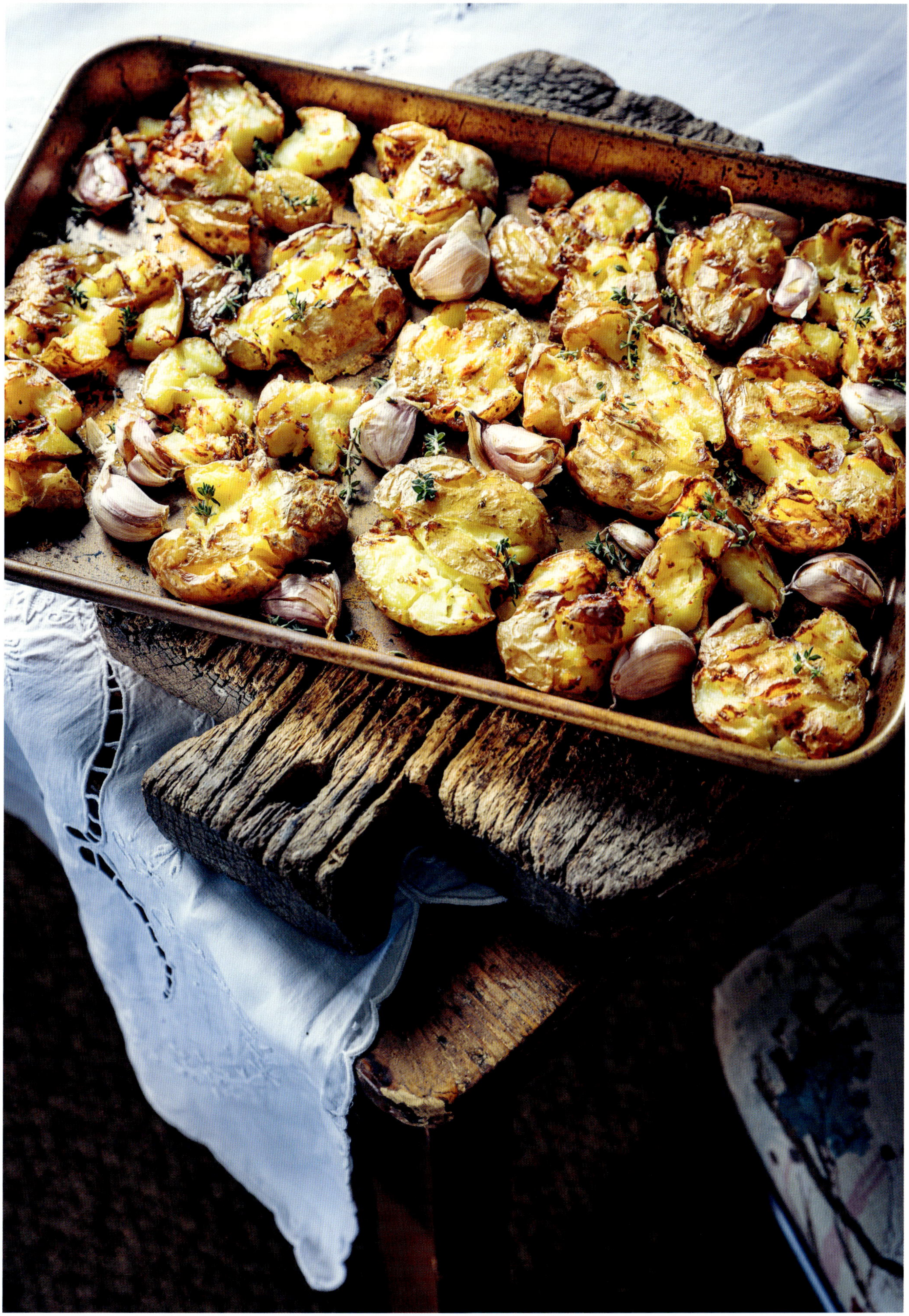

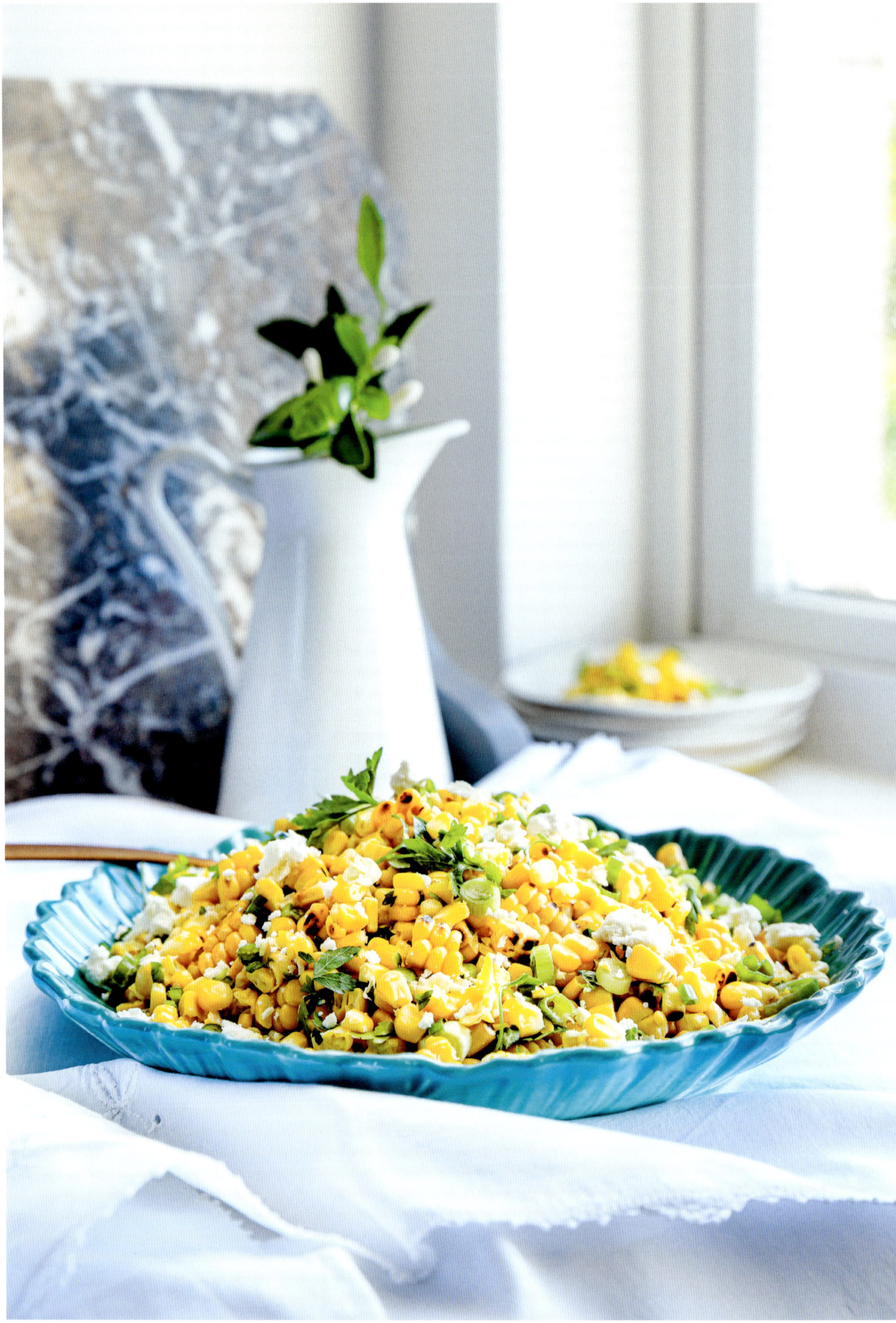

Grilled Corn Salad

Corn is at its most tantalisingly sweet and smoky from the barbecue, though you can chargrill it indoors with great results. I've garnished this dish with some feta cheese, which is a good substitute for cotija, a Mexican cheese made from cow's milk that is also white in colour and firm in texture, with a salty, milky flavour.

—

Serves 4

4 fresh corn on the cob, husks removed
1 tbsp extra virgin olive oil, plus extra for brushing
1 tbsp mayonnaise
1 garlic clove, crushed
finely grated rind and juice of 1 lime
3 scallions, trimmed and thinly sliced
20g fresh coriander or flat leaf parsley, leaves stripped and roughly chopped
¼ tsp smoked paprika
1 mild green chilli, seeded and diced
50g feta cheese (barrel aged if possible)
sea salt and freshly ground black pepper

Preheat a griddle pan to a medium-high heat. Brush the corn with olive oil and char for 2 minutes on each side (or better again, use the barbecue). Leave to cool a little.

Put the mayonnaise in a large bowl with the olive oil, garlic, and lime rind and juice. Quickly slice the kernels off the corn while they are still warm, and fold into the dressing. Leave until cool, then stir in the scallions with most of the coriander or parsley, the smoked paprika and chilli, and season to taste. Crumble over the feta with the rest of the coriander to serve.

SERVE WITH...
This is glorious on a sunny day with any barbecued food, or serve alongside **Tacos with Chicken Tinga** (p.74). Put together a spread by adding **Summer Slaw** (p.163), plenty of sliced **Sticky Damson Ham with Star Anise** (p.58) and a bowl of steaming jacket potatoes with a knob of butter.

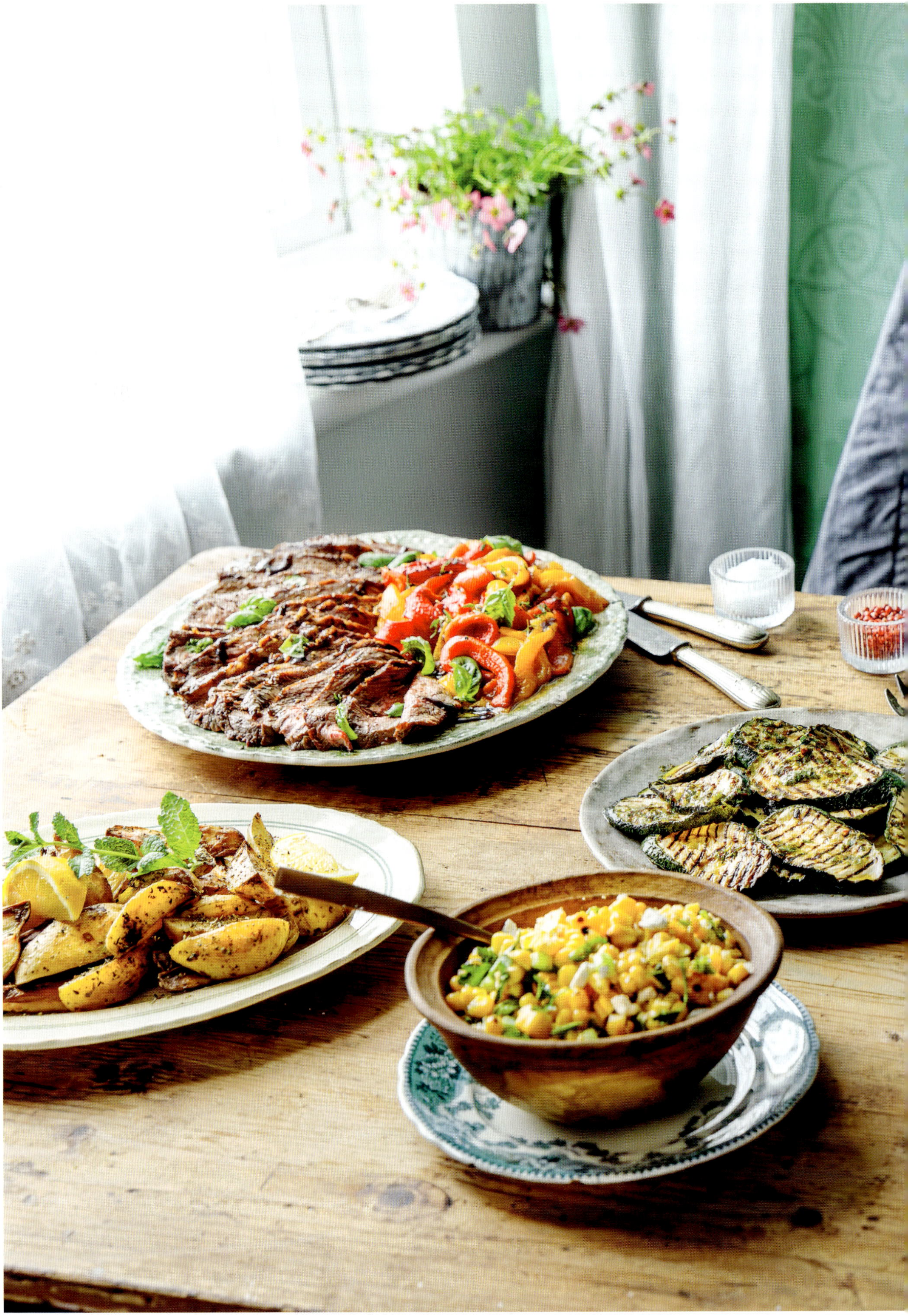

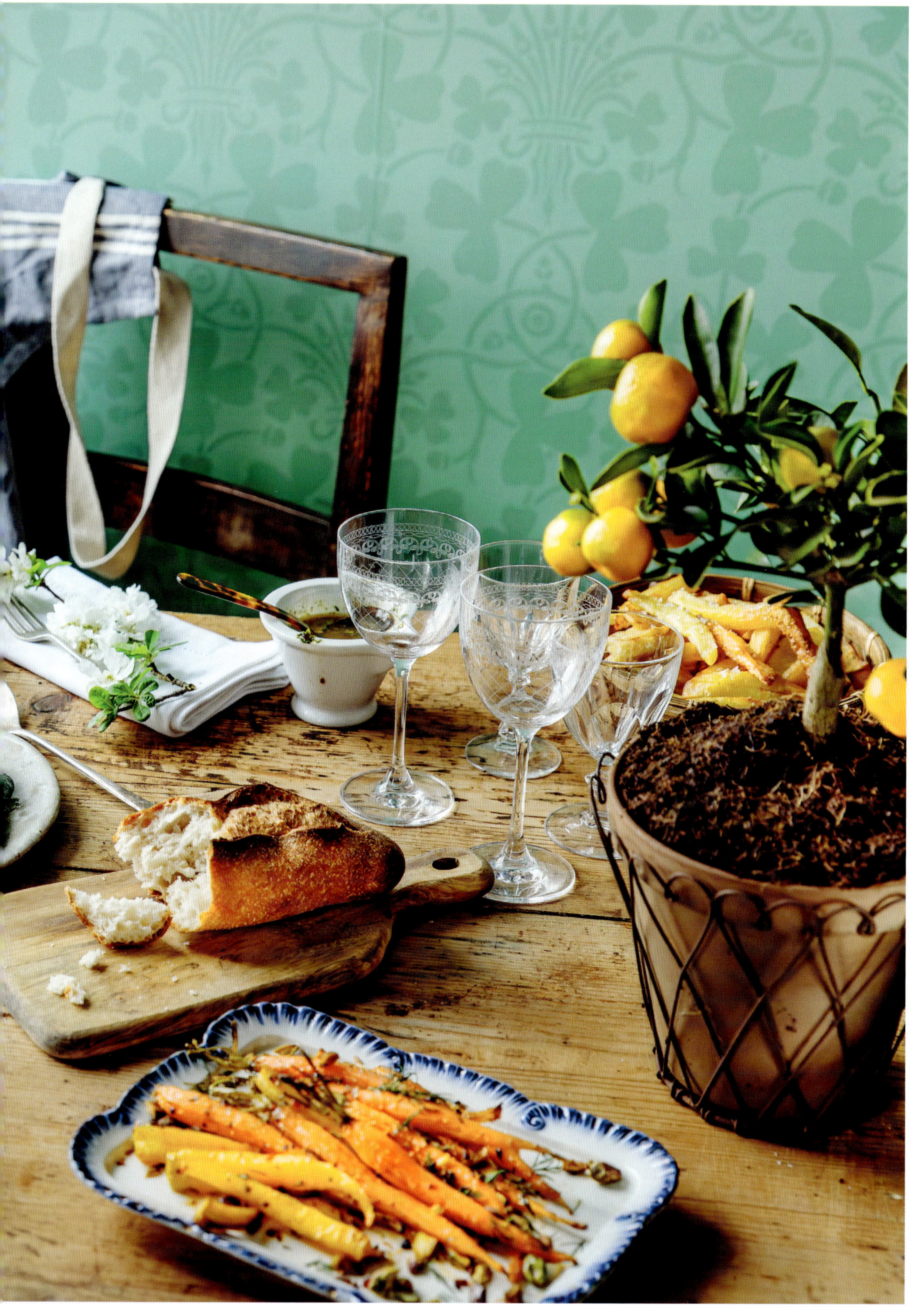

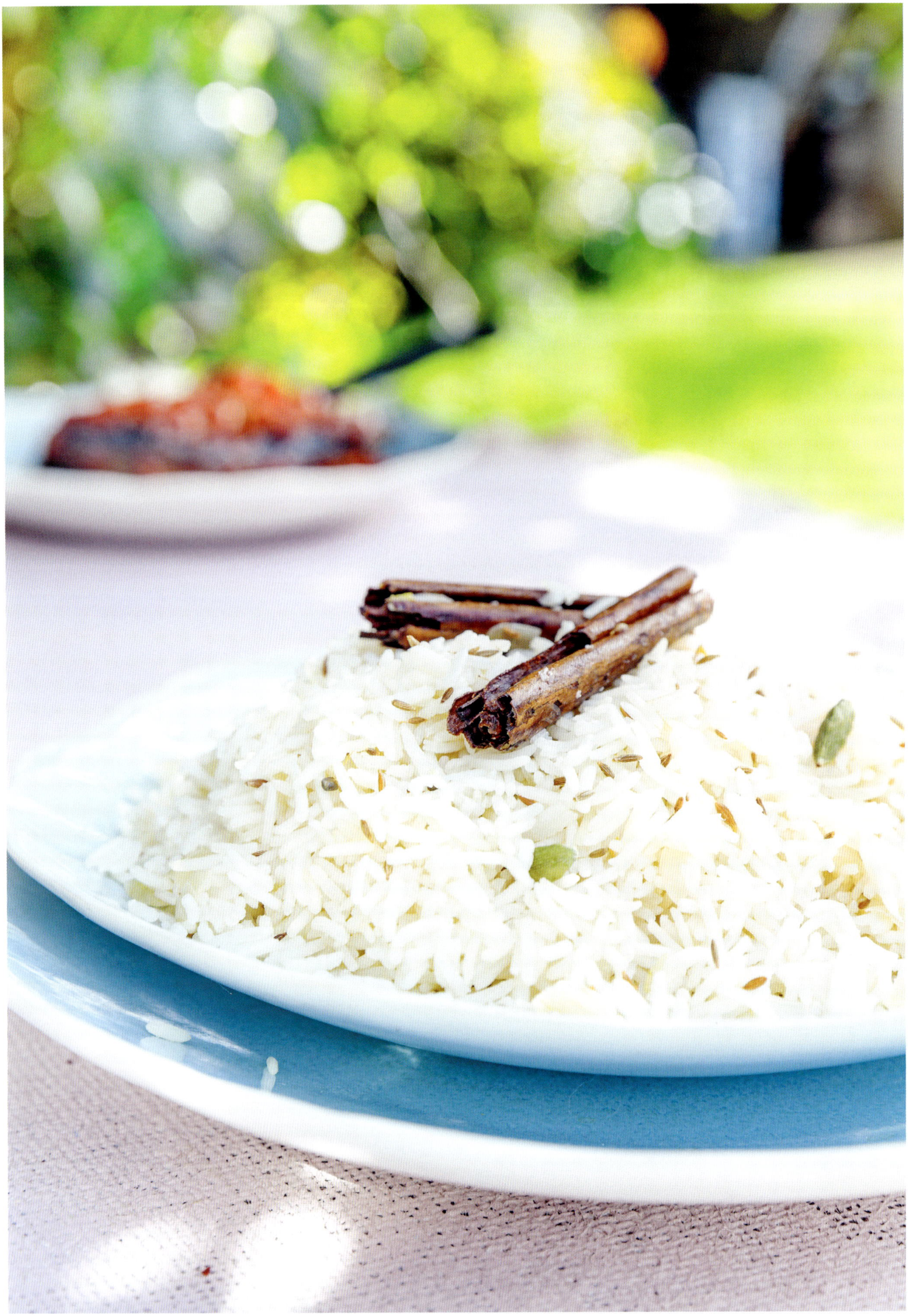

Pilau Rice

The secret to perfectly fluffy pilau rice is to leave it to steam in its own heat, without removing the lid. Here I've added a nice bit of butter for a richer flavour, along with whole cardamom, cloves, cumin, bay leaves and cinnamon, all of which will fill your kitchen with a heady fragrance.

—

Serves 4–6
300g white basmati rice
25g butter
1 large onion, finely chopped
good pinch of sea salt
1 cinnamon stick, broken in half
1 tsp cumin seeds
4 whole cloves
6 green cardamom pods, bashed
2 bay leaves

Put the rice into a large bowl and cover with cold water, then set aside to soak for 30 minutes. Tip into a sieve and rinse under cold running water, then drain well. Repeat the rinsing process until the water is only slightly cloudy, then leave in the sink to drain completely.

Heat a heavy-based pan over a medium heat. Add the butter and, as soon as it stops sizzling, add the onion and salt. Sauté for about 10 minutes until softened and golden. Stir in the spices and add the bay leaves, then sauté for another 1–2 minutes.

Add the drained rice and stir through the onion mixture until coated, then add 500ml of water. Stir again, then cover the pan and increase the heat. Once it is boiling, remove the lid and stir the rice a final time. Cover again and reduce the heat to low. Simmer for 2 minutes, then turn off the heat and leave to stand for 10 minutes without disturbing. Uncover, then stir a final time and cover again for 5 more minutes. Fluff up the pilau rice with a fork and tip into a warm dish to serve.

SERVE WITH ...
With its mild aromatic flavour, this restaurant-style pilau rice is the perfect accompaniment to a curry feast featuring my mouth-watering **Butter Chicken** (p.85). It would also be delicious with **Aromatic Poached Salmon with Avocado & Cucumber Salad** (p.83).

House Salad with Amelda's Dressing

This 'anytime salad' is fresh, vibrant and packed full of the very best of home-grown produce. It's named after my wife Amelda, who always makes the dressing in our house. The tangy dressing with a hint of sweetness will bring these simple vegetables to life. I like to use my hands to toss a salad to ensure I don't damage or bruise the delicate butterhead lettuce leaves.

—

Serves 4

For the dressing
1 tbsp apple cider vinegar
1 small garlic clove, crushed
1 tbsp Dijon mustard
pinch of sugar
4 tbsp extra virgin olive oil
1 tbsp snipped fresh chives
1 tbsp chopped mint, plus extra leaves to serve

For the salad
2 butterhead lettuces
¼ cucumber, halved and cut into wafer-thin slices
100g cherry tomatoes on the vine, halved
4 radishes, thinly sliced
1 tbsp rinsed capers
sea salt and freshly ground black pepper

First, make the dressing: put the vinegar in a screw-topped jar with the garlic, mustard and sugar, and season generously. Shake to dissolve, then add the oil, chives and mint, and shake again to form an emulsion.

Remove the outer leaves from the lettuce, then roughly tear them up. Drizzle the salad dressing along the walls of your bowl, then add the lettuce leaves, season with salt and pepper, and lightly toss until the dressing is evenly distributed. Add in the cucumber, cherry tomatoes, radishes and capers, then lightly toss again. Tear over some mint leaves to serve.

SERVE WITH ...
This salad goes with almost every meal; it's quick to put together and adds lovely colour to the table. It works particularly well with rich dishes, such as the exquisite **One-Pot Fish Pie** (p.62) or the **Slow-Cooked Onion & Goat's Cheese Tart** (p.86). Alternatively, use it to refresh your palate following a plate of **Beef Ragu Lasagne** (p.64) or **Macaroni Cheese with 'Nduja Crumbs** (p.95).

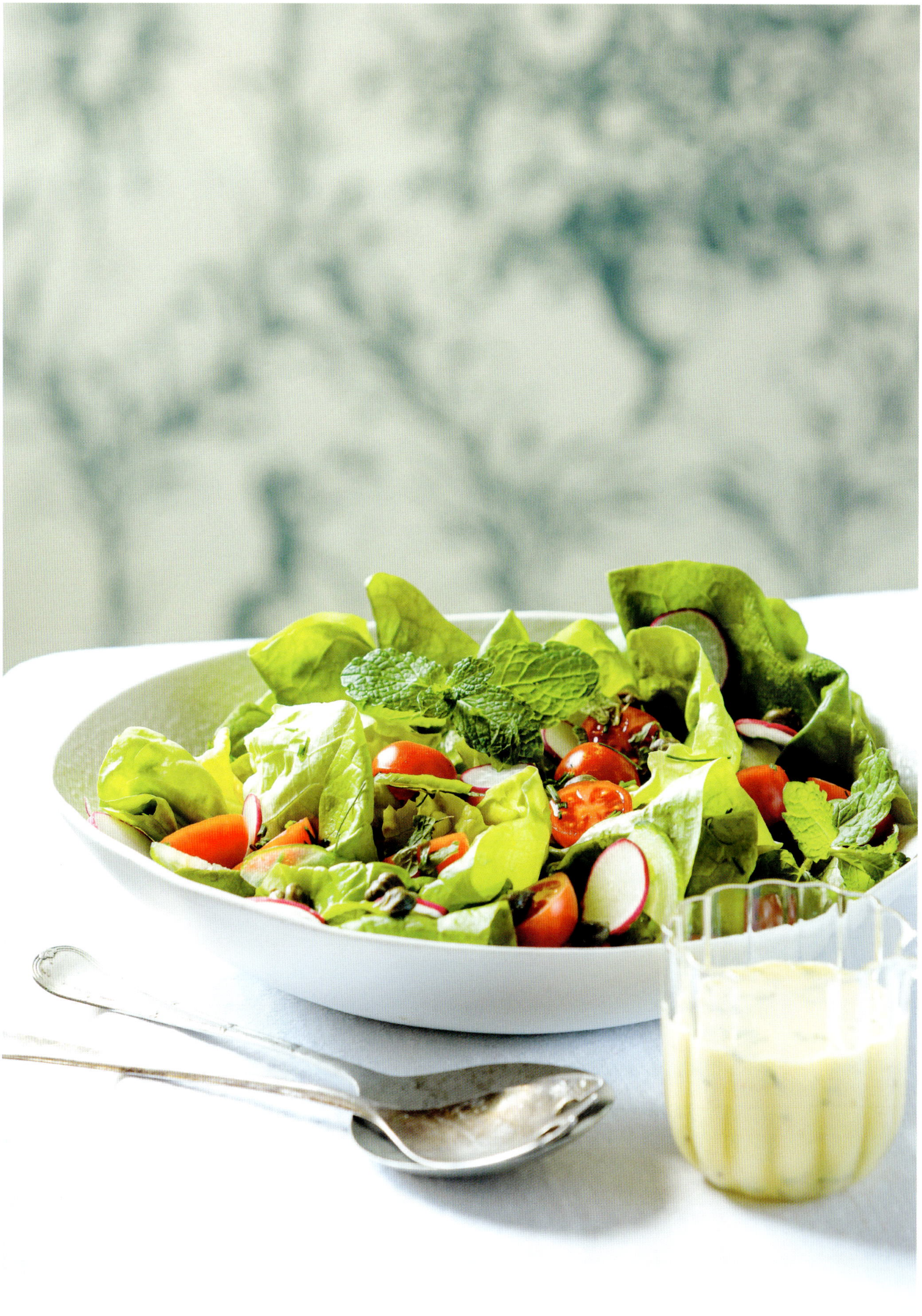

Green Beans with Goat's Cheese

This is a simple side dish – made stellar by the addition of some creamy goat's cheese, buttery shallots and crunchy walnuts, which add a wonderful contrast to the green beans.

—

Serves 4-6
400g fine green beans, trimmed
50g walnut halves
1 tbsp olive oil
2 shallots, thinly sliced
knob of butter
50g goat's cheese
sea salt and freshly ground black pepper

Cook the green beans in a large pan of boiling salted water for 2 minutes until bright green; then, using a slotted spoon, plunge them into a bowl of ice-cold water to prevent further cooking. Drain in a colander, then dry on kitchen paper and set aside.

Heat a large non-stick frying pan over a medium heat and toast the walnuts for 2–3 minutes, then tip on to the chopping board and leave to cool before roughly chopping.

Add the oil to the pan and sauté the shallots for 4–5 minutes until softened but not coloured. Add the butter and, once it stops sizzling, tip in the green beans and season with salt and plenty of pepper. Toss until evenly combined and cook for another 4–5 minutes until the beans are completely tender.

Tip the beans on to a platter. Crumble over the goat's cheese, scatter over the walnuts and add another good grinding of black pepper to serve.

SERVE WITH ...
Green beans start to appear in farmers' markets at the beginning of the summer. This side dish goes really well with **Iberico Pork with Red Gooseberry Relish** (p.92), but it will also give a nice twist to a succulent **Turkey Roulade with Maple Glaze** (p.98).

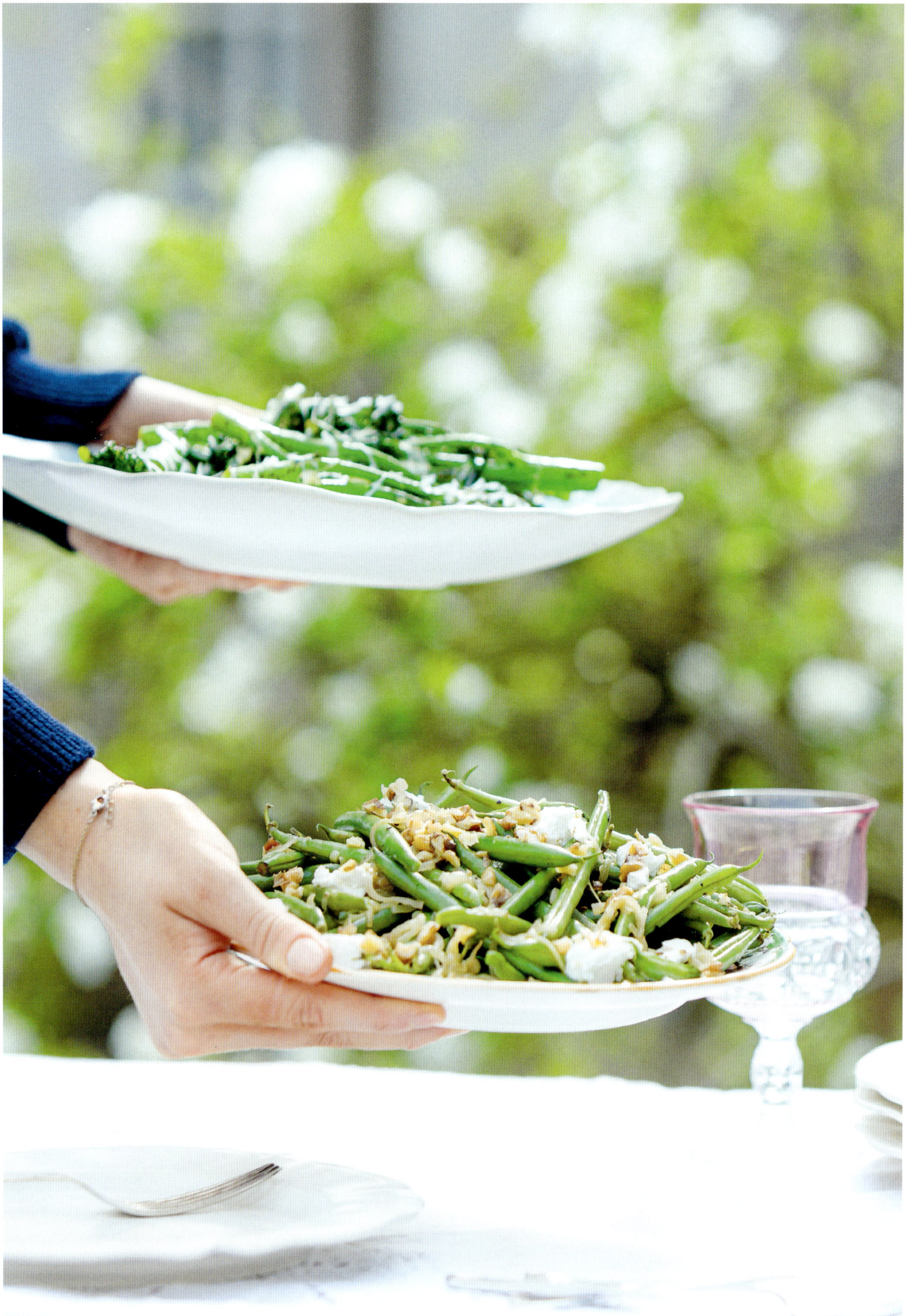

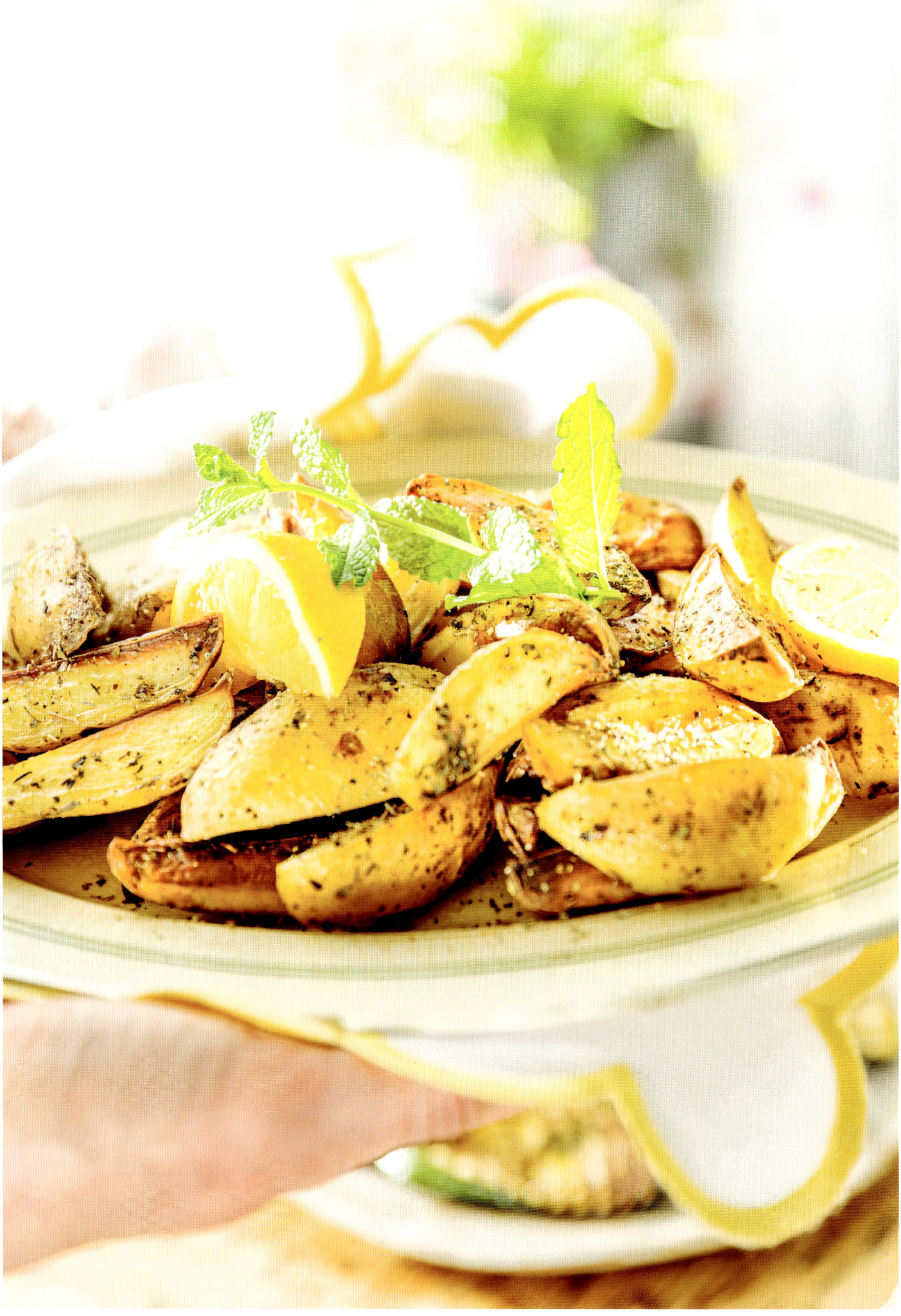

Lemon Roast Potato Wedges

You can expect these clever potato wedges to turn deliciously crispy with hardly any attention in the kitchen. What you're after is a fine golden colour with intense lemon and garlic flavours.

—

Serves 4–6

1kg waxy potatoes (Cyprus new season or similar yellow-fleshed varieties)
4 tbsp olive oil
1½ tsp dried oregano
500ml fresh chicken stock (from a carton)
juice of 1 lemon, plus extra lemon wedges, to garnish
1 garlic bulb, split into cloves, peeled and bashed
1 fresh mint sprig, to garnish
sea salt and freshly ground black pepper

Preheat the oven to 200°C (400°F/Gas Mark 6). Cut the potatoes into even-sized wedges and put in a large roasting tray so that they all fit in one layer. Drizzle over the oil and toss to coat, then season generously with salt and pepper. Sprinkle over the oregano and mix with your hands to ensure the wedges are evenly coated.

Pour in the chicken stock and lemon juice, then tuck in the garlic cloves. Bake for 80 minutes until the potatoes have soaked up all the liquid and are lightly caramelised. Transfer to a platter and garnish with lemon wedges and a mint sprig to serve.

SERVE WITH …

For a summer feast, serve alongside **Chicken Shawarma** (p.88) and **Pickled Red Onions** (p.140). You can also put these potatoes on the table for everyone to tuck into, with **Hake with Red Pepper Sauce** (p.104) or **Large Plaice with Garlic Butter Sauce** (p.101), plus a steamed green vegetable.

Braised Petits Pois with Bacon

A celebration of spring, this classic French dish takes only minutes to make, but it is unbelievably good. Traditionally, this uses tender new-season peas cooked with butter lettuce, but I like making it with frozen peas and wedges of Gem lettuce, which give some structure and crunch to the finished dish.

—

Serves 4–6
1 tbsp olive oil
100g smoked streaky bacon lardons
4 tbsp white wine
1 bunch scallions, trimmed and thinly sliced
400g frozen petits pois
150ml fresh chicken stock (from a carton)
2 little Gem lettuces, cut into quarters
40g butter, chilled and diced
4 tbsp chopped fresh flat-leaf parsley
sea salt and freshly ground black pepper

Heat a sauté pan over a medium heat. Add the oil with the bacon lardons and sauté until they are golden and have released their fat. Pour in the wine and add the scallions, then allow the mixture to bubble for 2 minutes. Add the petits pois and chicken stock, then bring back to the boil and cook for 3 minutes.

Carefully place the lettuce quarters on top of the petits pois mixture, with the stalks facing upwards. Cover with a lid and cook for 2 minutes, then turn off the heat. Remove the lettuce and put on a plate. Add the butter into the petits pois mixture and give everything a good stir, then simmer gently until the butter has formed a smooth emulsion sauce. Season to taste and stir in the parsley.

Tip most of the petits pois mixture into a warm dish and arrange the lettuce on top, then finish with the rest of the petits pois mixture to serve.

SERVE WITH …
This goes rather well with the **One-Pot Fish Pie** (p.62) or the **Cottage Pie** (p.71). Of course, it is also perfect with any roast dinner – and the buttery sauce means you can get away with not making any gravy.

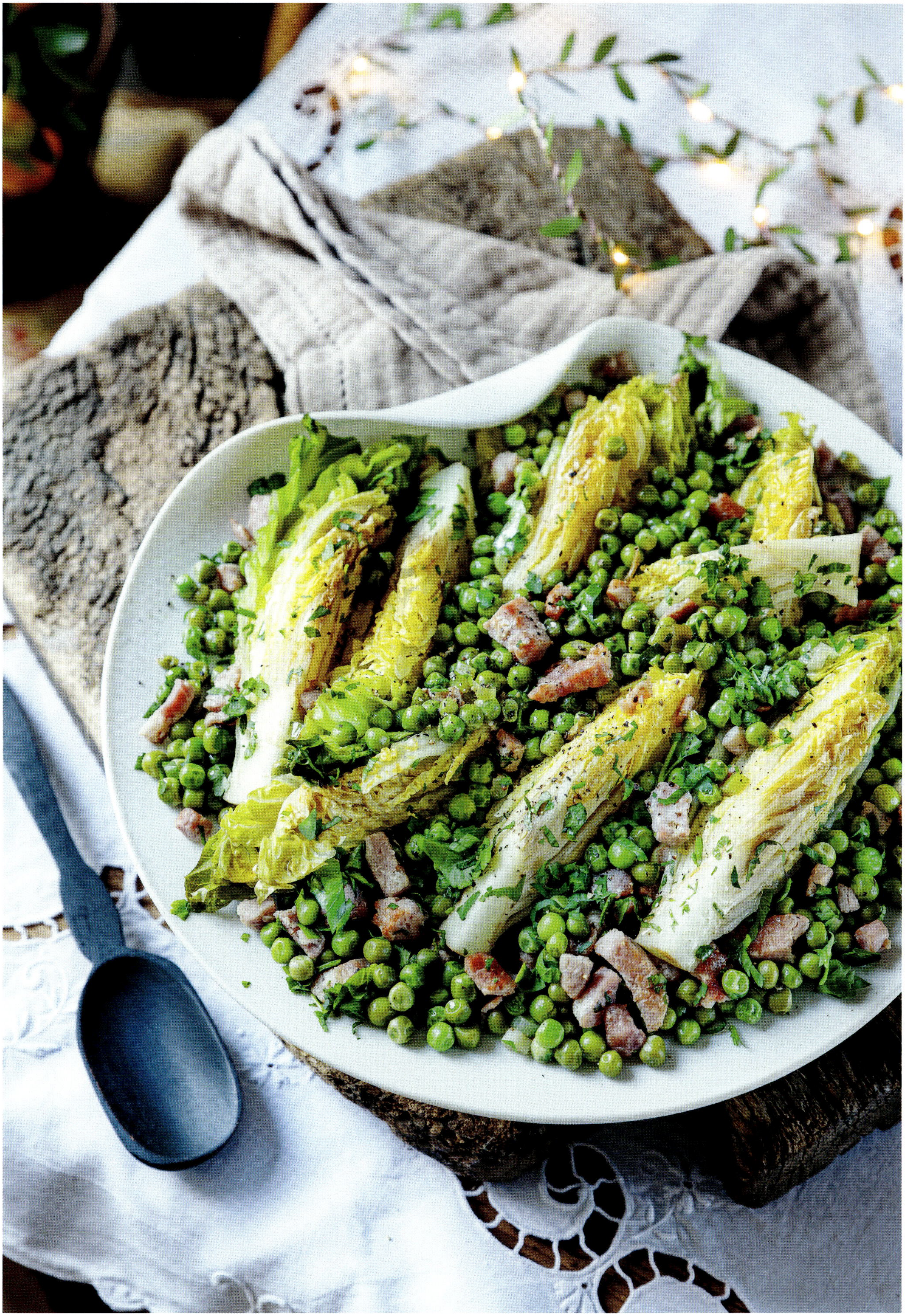

Pickled Red Onions

This recipe might be simple, but it has layers. Pickling transforms raw red onions from pungent and crunchy to irresistibly tangy. These pickles are the perfect condiment for almost anything, and I find myself using them a lot.

—

Makes 600ml jar

400ml apple cider vinegar
4 tbsp caster sugar
4 tsp sea salt flakes
1 tsp mixed peppercorns
1 star anise
2 fresh thyme sprigs
4 small red onions, halved and sliced into rings

Pour the vinegar into a pan and add the sugar, salt, spices and thyme. Bring to a simmer, stirring for 1 minute until the sugar and salt have dissolved. Remove from the heat.

Put the sliced onions in a sieve and pour over a whole kettle of boiling water. Drain well and tip on to kitchen paper to remove any excess water. When cool enough to handle, pack into a clean 600ml jar and pour over the warm flavoured vinegar. Leave to cool completely and pickle for at least 2 hours. This will keep for up to 3 months unopened; once opened, keep in the fridge and use within 2 weeks.

SERVE WITH …
These colourful, spiced, sweet-and-sour pickled onions add piquancy and a sharp finish to dishes such as **Tacos with Chicken Tinga** (p.74) and **Chicken Shawarma** (p.88).

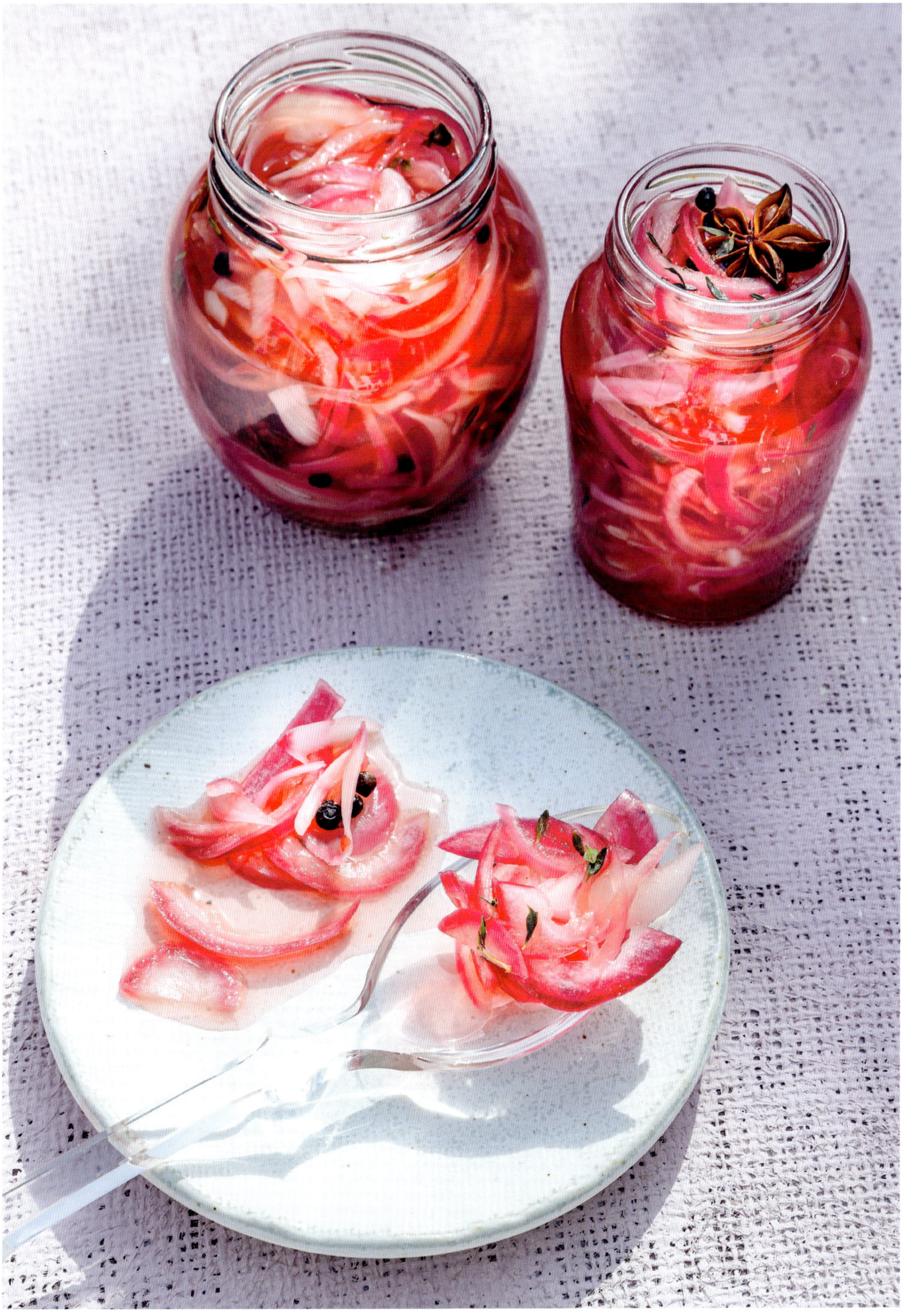

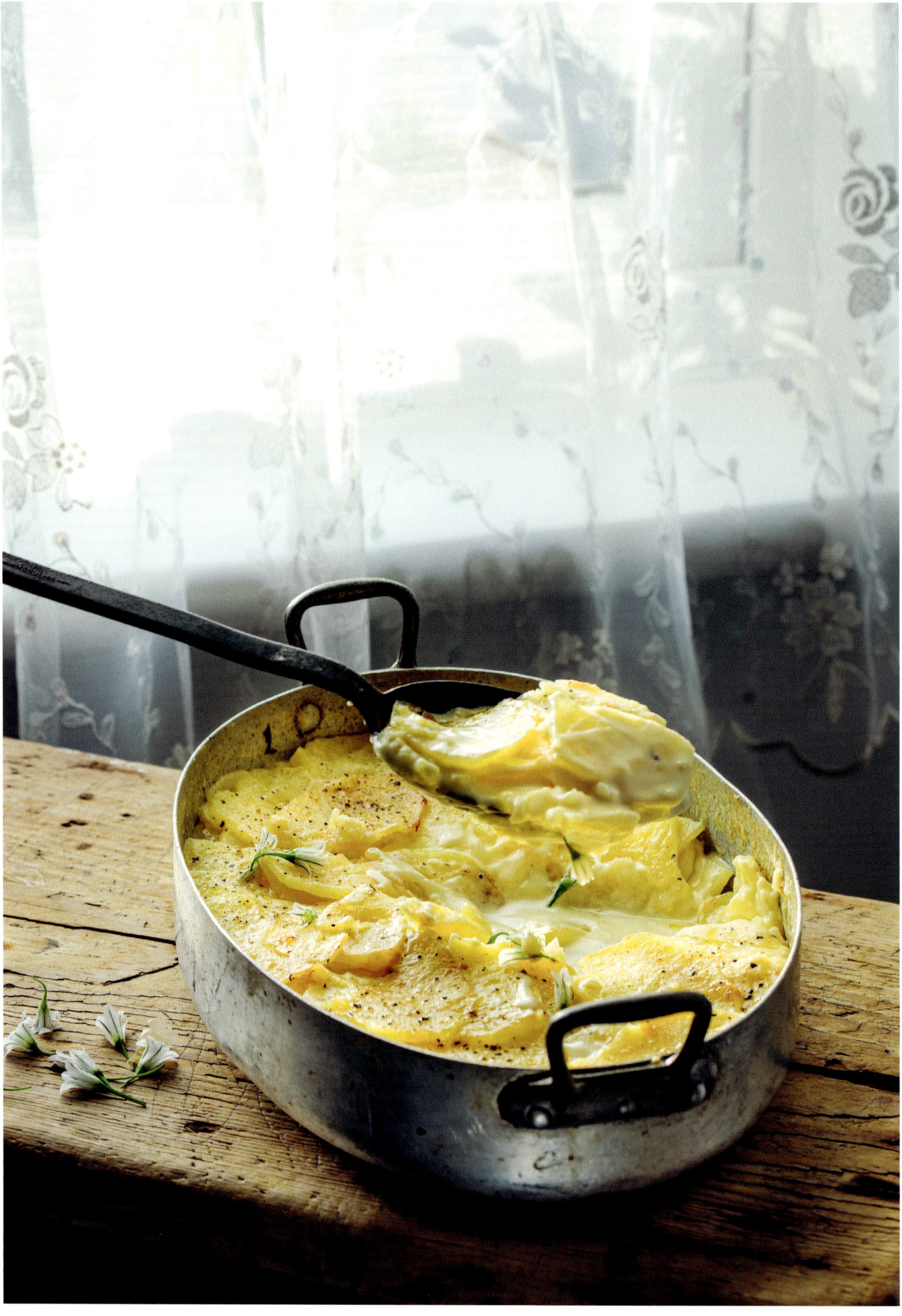

Potato Gratin

There is something immensely satisfying about potato gratin, with its golden crust and soft, creamy inside. Rich and filling, it brings out greediness in even the most reticent eater. Normally I serve it in the dish in which it cooks, but if you are entertaining, it might be helpful to have it already portioned out when you take it to the table.

—

Serves 4–6
1kg floury potatoes (such as Rooster or Maris Piper)
900ml cream
120ml milk
good pinch of freshly grated nutmeg
4 garlic cloves, finely grated (on a microplane)
butter, for greasing
wild garlic, to serve (optional)
sea salt and freshly ground white pepper

Peel the potatoes and cut into 3mm slices with a mandolin. Spread them on a tray and sprinkle with plenty of salt. Rub the slices together, then heap them up in a pile and leave for 10 minutes. The salt will extract the excessive water and soften the potatoes.

Put the cream and milk in a pan large enough to take all the potatoes later. Season lightly with salt, add plenty of pepper and the nutmeg, then stir in the garlic. Place over a high heat and bring to the boil, then reduce the heat to low and simmer to reduce the liquid by about a quarter, stirring occasionally to ensure it doesn't stick to the bottom.

Preheat the oven to 120°C (250°F/Gas Mark ½). Press the potatoes gently in a tea towel with your hands to squeeze out all the excess water. Add to the reduced cream mixture and bring back to the boil. Remove from the heat and, using a large spoon, spread the mixture out evenly in a buttered ovenproof dish. The gratin should be at least 6cm thick. Cover tightly with tin foil and bake for 90 minutes, or until the potatoes are completely tender when pierced with a sharp knife but not at all coloured.

The gratin can now be cooled down and chilled for at least 6 hours, although overnight is best to firm up. At this point it can be cut into portions and arranged on a non-stick baking sheet, or kept whole. When ready to serve, preheat the oven to 170°C (32°F/Gas Mark 3) and cook the gratin pieces for about 20 minutes until warmed through; if you are cooking the whole dish, it will take 30–40 minutes until bubbling and golden. Garnish with wild garlic, if desired.

SERVE WITH ...
Serve with the **House Salad with Amelda's Dressing** (p.132) for a light meal; alternatively, this is a great accompaniment to the **Turkey Roulade with Maple Glaze** (p.98) or the **Crispy Spatchcock Chicken with Lemon & Herbs** (p.60).

Grilled Courgettes with Green Chimichurri Sauce

This is a simple yet seductive salad with a vivid colour, a tangy sharpness and a terrific taste. A little bit of this, a little bit of that ... the purpose of a dish like this is that it complements many different types of food, and it adds variety and interest to the plate.

—

Serves 4–6
20g flat-leaf parsley
½ tsp dried oregano
2 garlic cloves, peeled
1 shallot, chopped
½ tsp dried chilli flakes
1 tbsp red-wine vinegar
5 tbsp extra virgin olive oil
4 courgettes, trimmed and cut into 2cm slices on the diagonal
sea salt and freshly ground black pepper

To make the sauce, pick all the leaves off the parsley and put in a NutriBullet or liquidiser, then add the oregano, garlic, shallot, chilli flakes and red-wine vinegar. Add 3 tablespoons of the olive oil and season to taste. Pulse to a roughly chopped sauce consistency. Set aside until needed.

Preheat a griddle pan over a high heat. Put the courgettes in a bowl, drizzle over the rest of the oil and season generously with salt. Toss until evenly coated and cook on the griddle for 3–4 minutes until just tender and lightly charred, turning once. Transfer to a plate while you finish the remainder. Arrange the courgettes, warm or at room temperature, on a platter and drizzle over the green chimichurri sauce to serve.

SERVE WITH ...
This is a real winner with **Roast Picanha & Chargrilled Pepper Salad** (p.72) as part of an al fresco lunch, perhaps washed down with a refreshing jug of **Apple Mojito** (p.185).

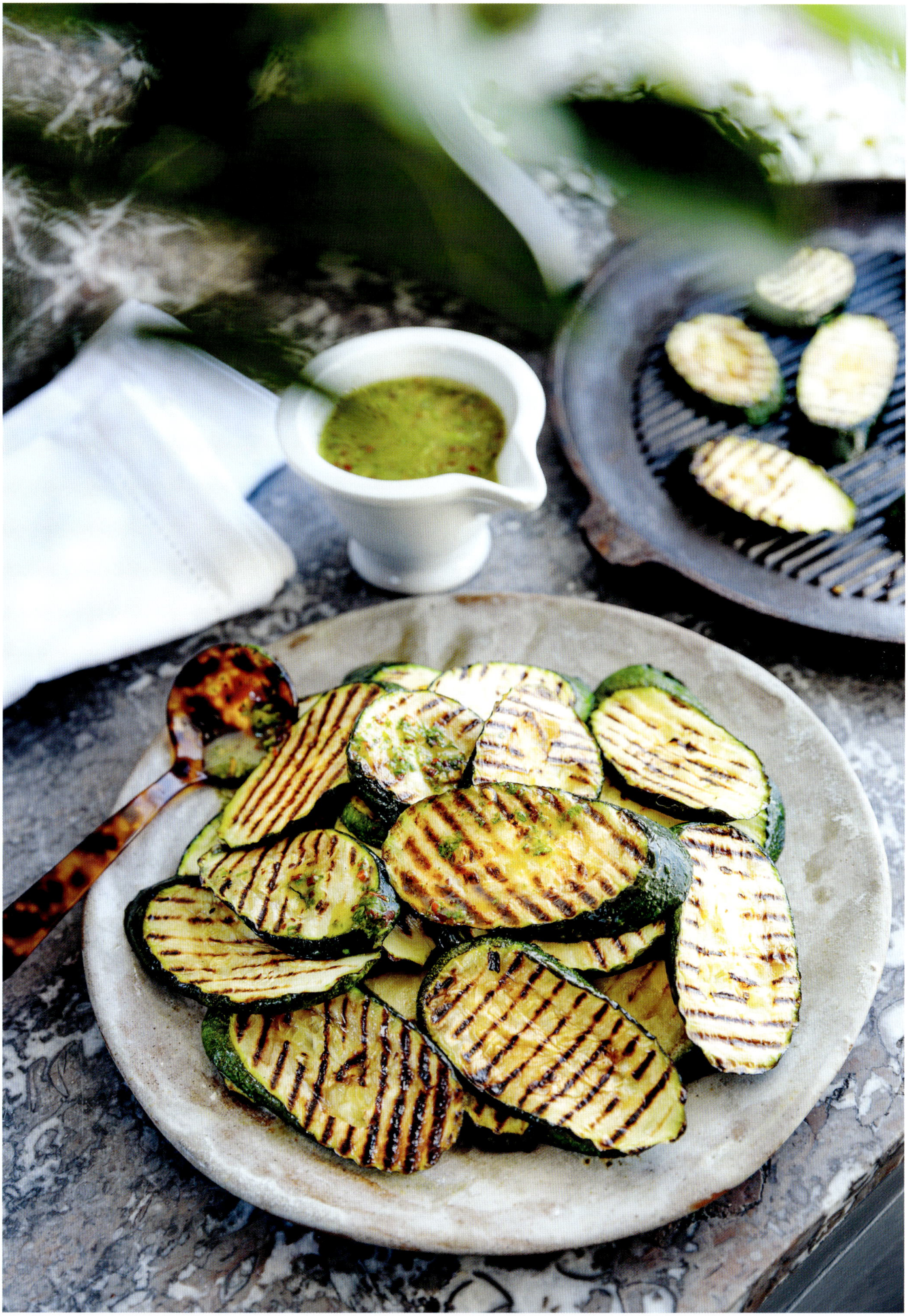

Warm Potato Salad

The secret to a delectable potato salad is simple: use fresh new season potatoes, peel once they're cooked and toss in dressing while they are still warm. I normally use Golden Wonder or Kerr's Pinks as I like the way the potatoes break down a little around the edges, but you might prefer to use a waxy potato like Pink Fir Apple or Charlotte. I like it just as it is without the mayonnaise as it is less rich but of course you could fold in a few tablespoons just before serving if that is what you prefer.

—

Serves 4-6

1kg new season potatoes
2 tbsp white wine vinegar
a pinch of sugar
1 tsp Dijon mustard
6 tbsp extra-virgin olive oil
1 large scallion, trimmed and very finely chopped
2 tbsp snipped fresh chives
2 tbsp chopped fresh flat-leaf parsley
sea salt and freshly ground black pepper
mayonnaise, to serve (optional)

Scrub the potatoes well and put into a large pan. Cover with water and add a good pinch of salt. Bring to the boil, then cover and cook for about 15 minutes until the potatoes are almost tender. Pour off most of the water, replace the lid and cook over a gentle heat so that the potatoes steam until they are tender.

Meanwhile, put the vinegar in a screw-topped jar with the sugar and a good pinch of salt. Shake until dissolved, then add the mustard, oil and plenty of pepper and shake again until emulsified.

Peel the potatoes while they are still warm and cut into dice. Place in a serving bowl and fold in the dressing with the scallion until evenly combined. Finally fold in the chives and parsley and leave at room temperature until ready to serve. Have a separate dish of mayonnaise to hand around separately, if liked.

SERVE WITH ...
I think we all have childhood memories of this type of dish, which was regularly served in our house with a green salad and some cold meats on a warm summer's day. It goes with almost anything and I find everyone loves a good potato salad. Serve alongside the **Slow Cooked Onion & Goat's Cheese Tart** (p.86) or with thin slices of **Sticky Damson Ham with Star Anise** (p.58). It would also make a welcome addition to the **Smoked Salmon Wreath** (p.37) for a light lunch before the days turn cold but are still bright.

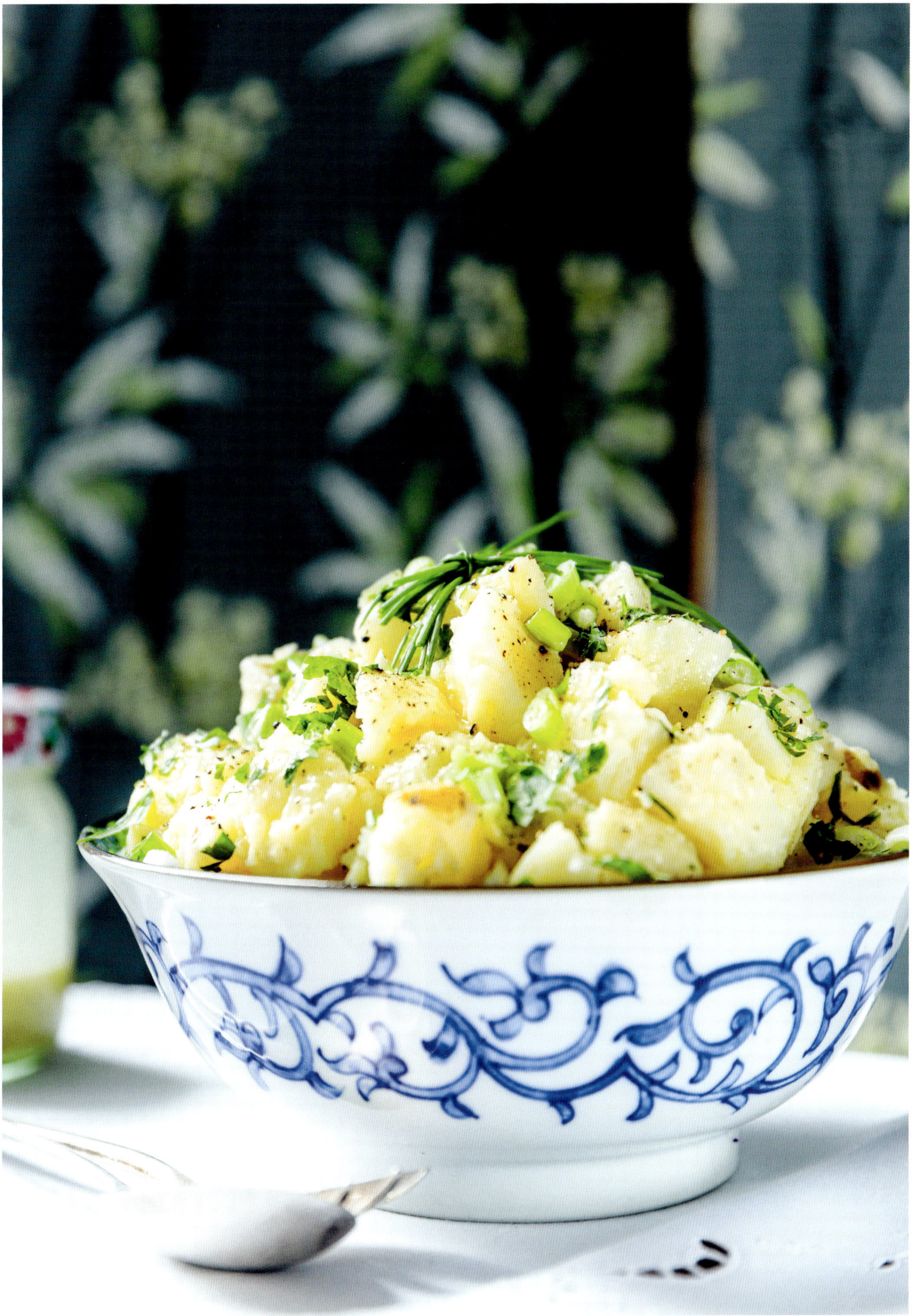

Slow-Roast Tomatoes with Puy Lentils

Slowly roasted with fresh thyme, cherry tomatoes yield intensely sweet-tart flavours – and they get the best chewy texture. They are a great dish if you want to stretch the meal out further.

—

Serves 4–6

400g cherry tomatoes
1 tsp fresh thyme leaves
6 tbsp extra virgin olive oil
1 tsp balsamic vinegar
300g Puy lentils
2 shallots, finely chopped
20g fresh flat-leaf parsley, leaves stripped and roughly chopped
100g rocket
sea salt and freshly ground black pepper

Preheat the oven to 170°C (325°F/Gas Mark 3). Cut the cherry tomatoes in half and arrange in a baking tin lined with parchment paper. Season with salt and pepper, and sprinkle over the thyme leaves. Drizzle over 2 tablespoons of the oil and the balsamic vinegar. Roast for 25–30 minutes until reduced by half and lightly charred. Remove from the oven and leave to cool completely.

Rinse the lentils in a sieve under cold running water, then place in a pan with 600ml of water. Add a pinch of salt and bring to the boil, then reduce the heat and simmer for 15–20 minutes or until just tender.

Meanwhile, heat 1 tablespoon of the olive oil in a frying pan over a medium heat and sauté the shallots for 4–5 minutes until softened but not coloured. Tip into a salad bowl, then stir in the cooked lentils with the remaining 3 tablespoons of olive oil and the slow-roast cherry tomatoes.

When the lentils have cooled to room temperature, gently fold in the parsley and rocket, then season to taste. Pile into a suitable dish to serve at room temperature.

SERVE WITH ...
This dish is an absolute dream for a picnic, with a tub of creamy goat's cheese and some nice crusty bread. For a weekend summer lunch, try it with **Fragrant Butterflied Lamb** (p.69). As you slowly creep into autumn, serve it alongside a **Slow-Cooked Onion & Goat's Cheese Tart** (p.86).

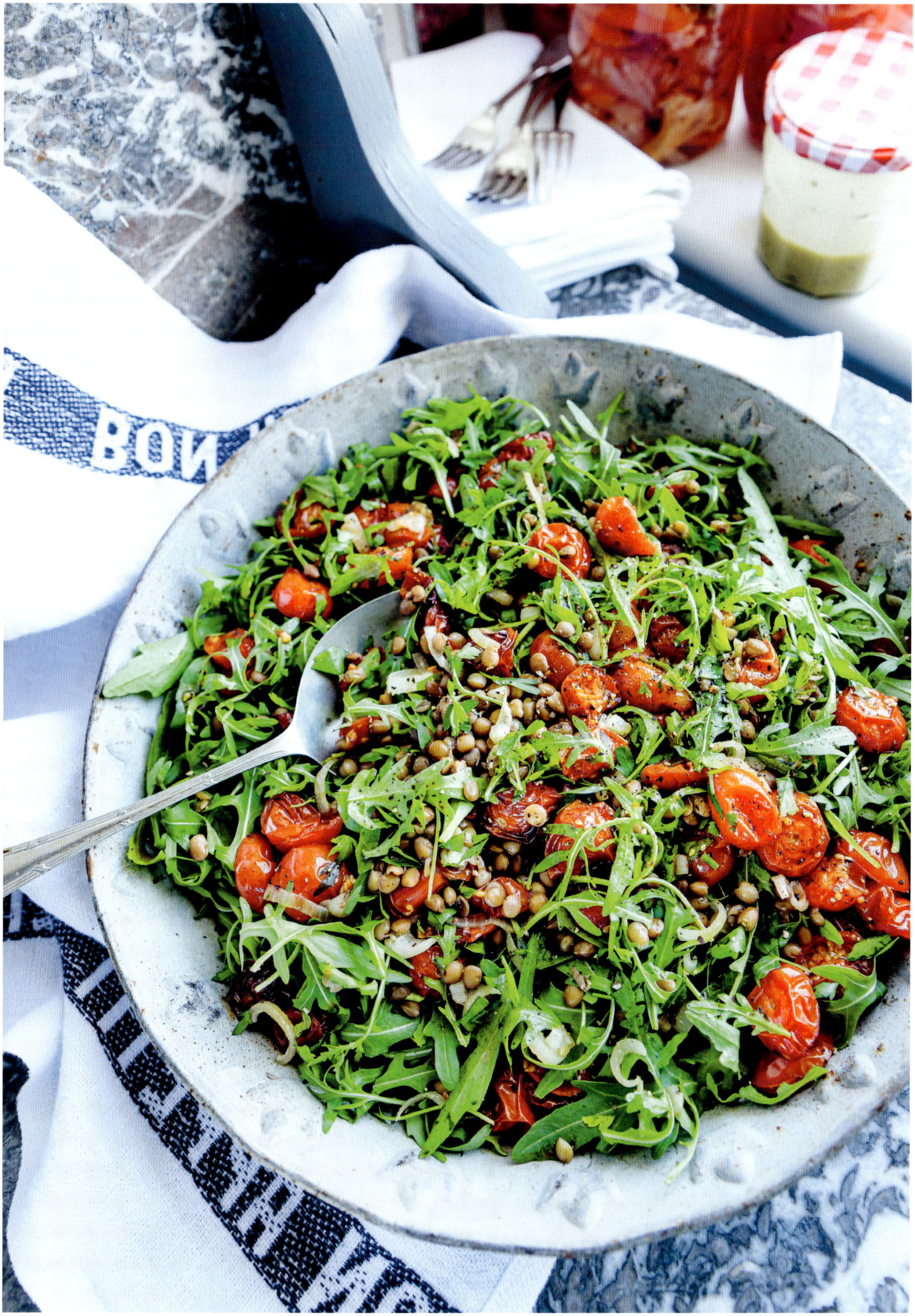

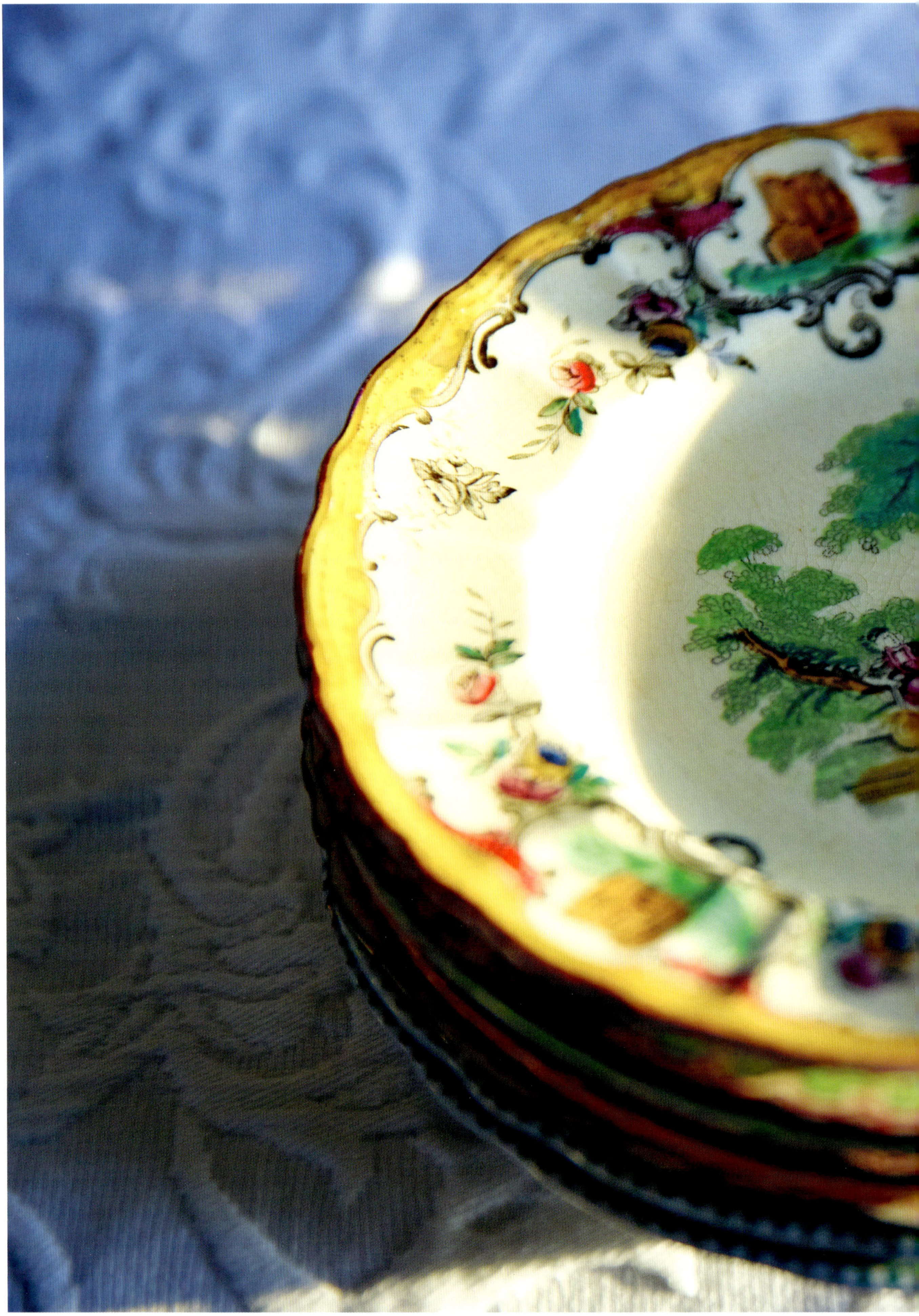

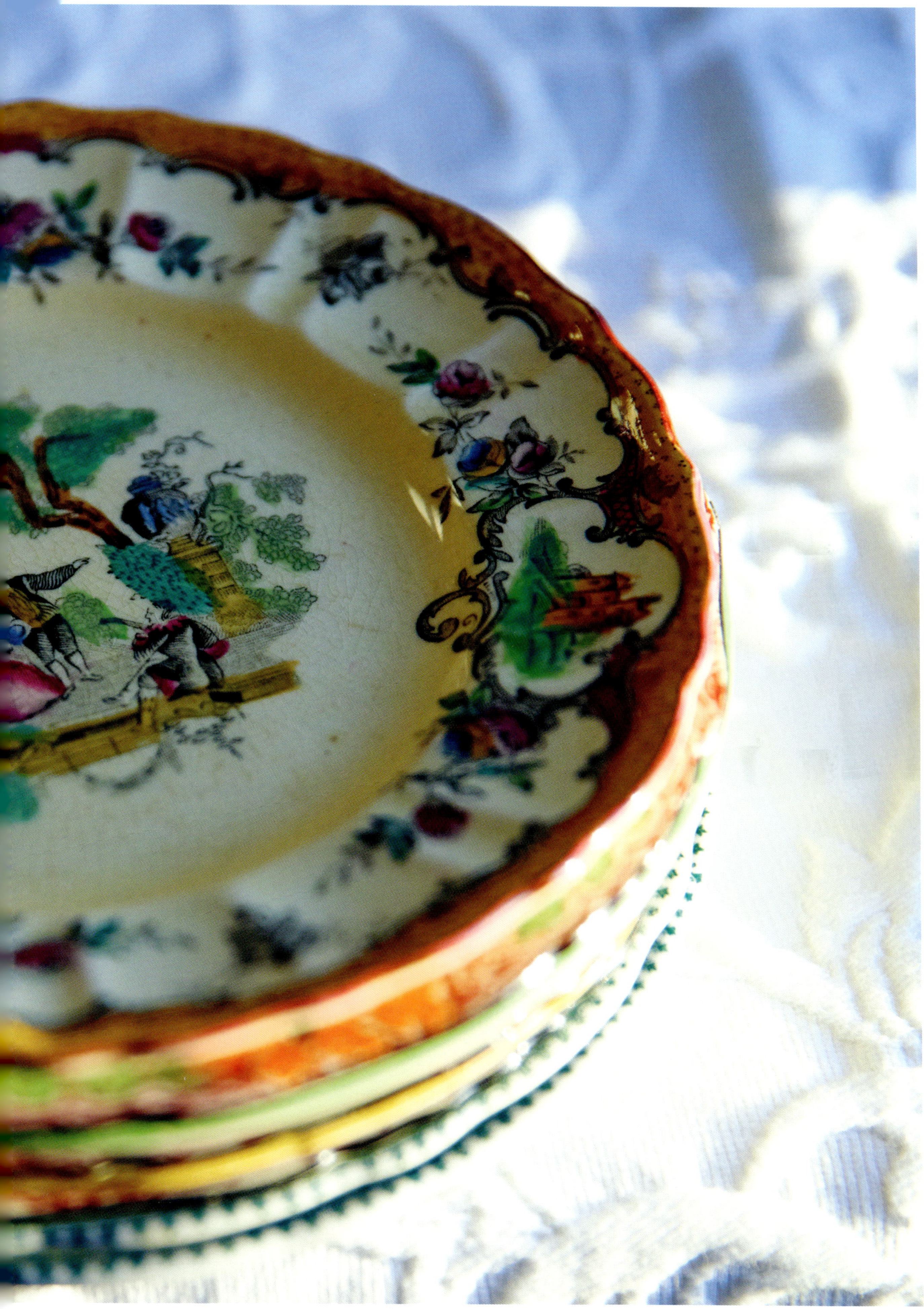

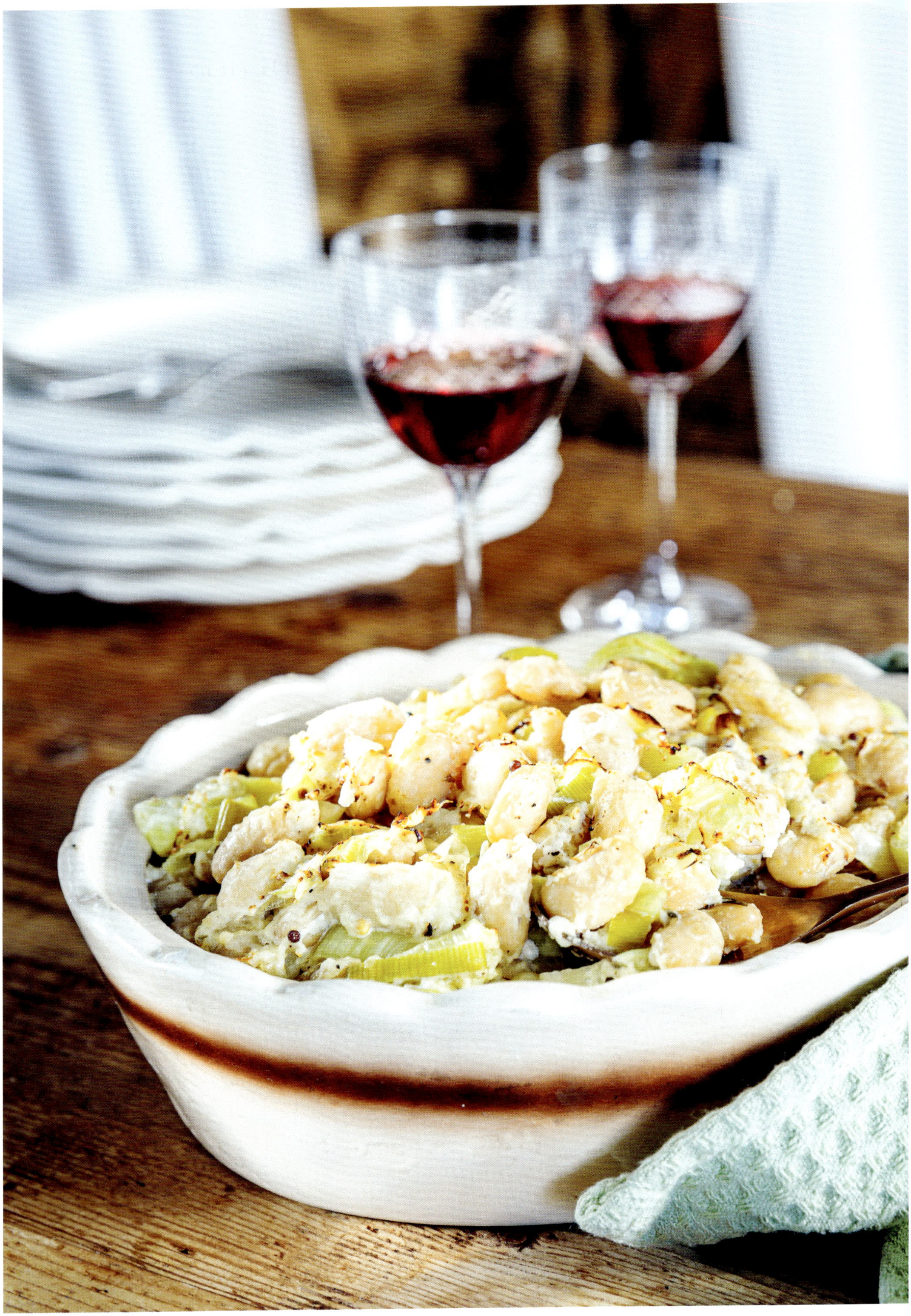

Creamy Butter Beans with Leeks

When we were young, my mum prepared the biggest feasts on Sundays, and everyone would talk around the dinner table for hours. She would also teach me things, like adding herbs from the garden, and my passion for cooking is largely down to her. This is a great side to any Sunday roast; alternatively, serve it for lunch with salads and other grains on the side. I know you'll love it.

—

Serves 4–6
2 tbsp olive oil
knob of butter
400g baby leeks or 2 small leeks, trimmed and sliced
2 garlic cloves, finely chopped
1 tsp fresh thyme leaves
2 x 250g cartons butter beans, drained and rinsed
4 tbsp dry white wine
1 heaped tsp wholegrain mustard with honey
150g crème fraîche
50g freshly grated Pecorino
sea salt and freshly ground black pepper

Preheat the oven to 200°C (400°F/Gas Mark 6). Heat a large ovenproof frying pan or shallow casserole dish over a medium heat. Add the oil and butter and, once the butter stops sizzling, add the leeks, garlic and thyme. Season to taste with salt and plenty of pepper, and sauté for 2–3 minutes until the leeks are softened but still hold their colour. Stir in the butter beans and cook for another minute, then drizzle over the wine and allow to bubble down. This should happen almost instantly.

Remove from the heat and stir in the mustard and crème fraîche with a good handful of the Pecorino. Scatter the rest of the Pecorino on top and place in the oven for 10–15 minutes until bubbling and golden brown. Serve straight away.

SERVE WITH …
Rich in protein and with a wonderfully creamy texture, butter beans are among life's delights. This dish would be exquisite served alongside the **Crispy Porchetta with Fennel & Herbs** (p.80).

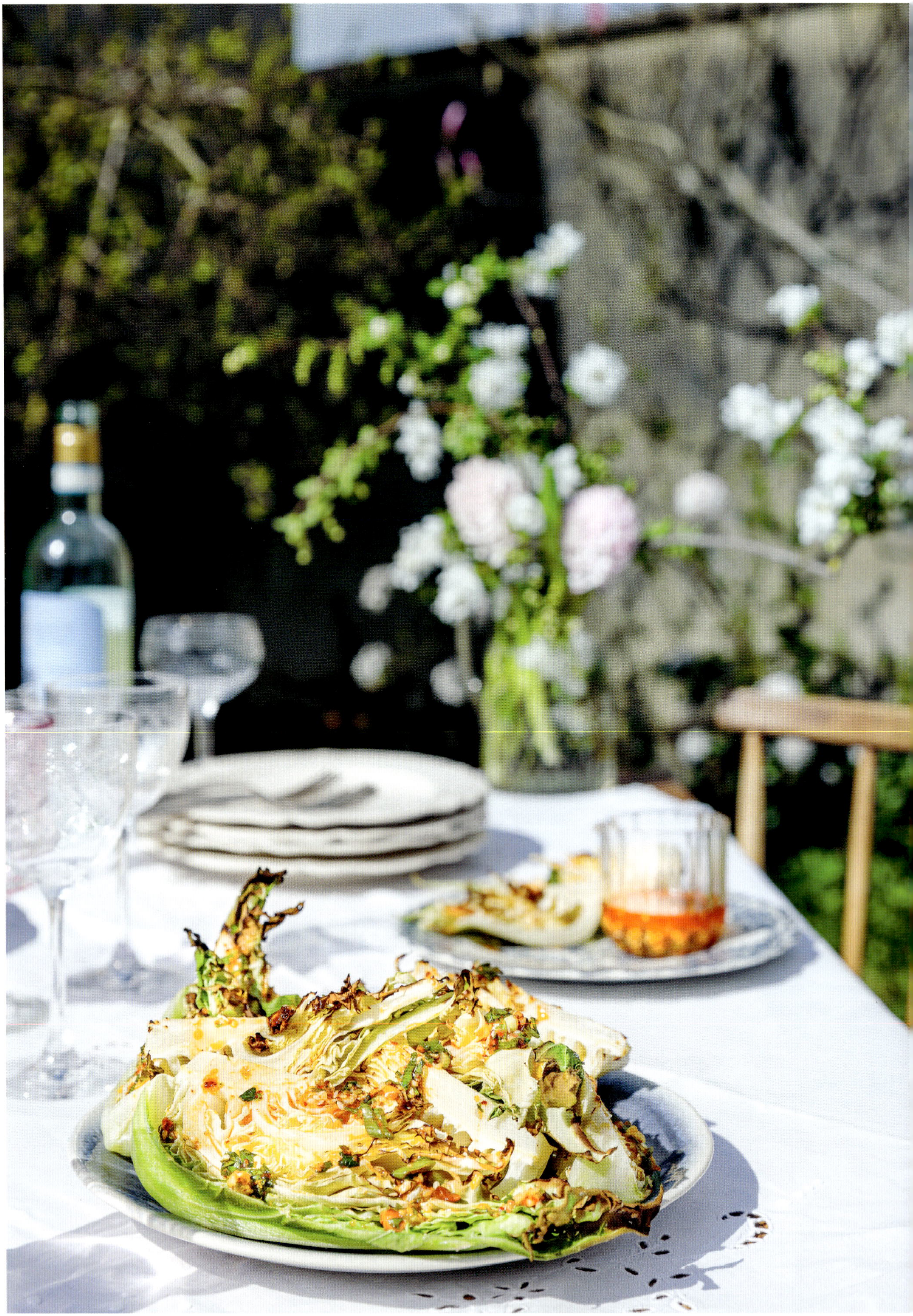

Chargrilled Cabbage with Kimchi Dressing

You can prepare much of this dish in advance: prep the cabbages and make the dressing, then leave them somewhere cool in the kitchen – no need for the fridge. When it comes to cooking, it's better if the cabbage wedges aren't too crowded in the oven, because it is the space between them that allows them to chargrill so gloriously. You might need to use more than one baking sheet.

—

Serves 4–6

3 sweetheart cabbages
3 tbsp olive oil
50ml rice-wine vinegar
2 tbsp sunflower oil
2 tsp sesame oil
½ tsp caster sugar
½ tsp freshly grated root ginger
1 scallion, finely chopped
1 tbsp chopped fresh coriander
1 tsp paprika
50g kimchi
1 tbsp chilli and peanut rayu
sea salt and freshly ground black pepper

Preheat the oven to 180°C (350°F/Gas Mark 4). Trim the cabbages as necessary, then cut in half and cut each half into 3 wedges. Arrange in a single layer on as many baking sheets as necessary and drizzle over the olive oil, then season with salt and pepper. Roast for 25 minutes until lightly charred.

Meanwhile, make the dressing. Put the rest of the ingredients in a screw-topped jar and shake until emulsified. Arrange the chargrilled cabbage wedges on a plate and spoon over the kimchi dressing to serve.

SERVE WITH...
Thinly sliced **Sticky Damson Ham with Star Anise** (p.58) for an ultra-modern twist on bacon and cabbage. Alternatively, making **Iberico Pork with Red Gooseberry Relish** (p.92) would leave you with plenty of oven space to blister the cabbage wedges to your heart's content.

Steamed Asparagus with Hollandaise

For me, hollandaise is the mother of all emulsion sauces, especially when it's made with our amazing Irish butter. Believe me when I say that it will transform your asparagus into a feast. It does not reheat, so you can't make it in advance; however, this version only takes a few minutes to prepare.

—

Serves 4–6
20–25 fresh green asparagus spears
2 egg yolks
100g butter, diced
1–2 tsp lemon juice
sea salt

Holding each asparagus spear between your index finger and your thumb, snap it near the root end, where it begins to get tough. Cook them in a large pan of boiling salted water for 4–6 minutes. The time will depend on the thickness of the spears, but it is easy to check: the root end should pierce easily with a small sharp knife.

To make the hollandaise, put the egg yolks in a heavy-based pan over a low heat; if you want to err on the side of caution, use a heatproof bowl set over a pan of simmering water. Add 2 teaspoons of cold water and whisk thoroughly. Add the butter, a bit at a time, whisking continuously. As one piece melts, add the next. If it starts to become too thick or if it looks like it might scramble, quickly take the pan off the heat and add 1–2 tablespoons of cold water – that should fix it. Add enough lemon juice and salt to taste.

Drain the asparagus and tip on to a platter, then spoon over the hollandaise sauce to serve.

SERVE WITH …
We use asparagus in every possible way during the precious few weeks when it's in season. This is a simple but superb recipe – it will be a complete revelation, meltingly tender, sweet and delicate. This goes perfectly with **Large Plaice with Garlic Butter Sauce** (p.101).

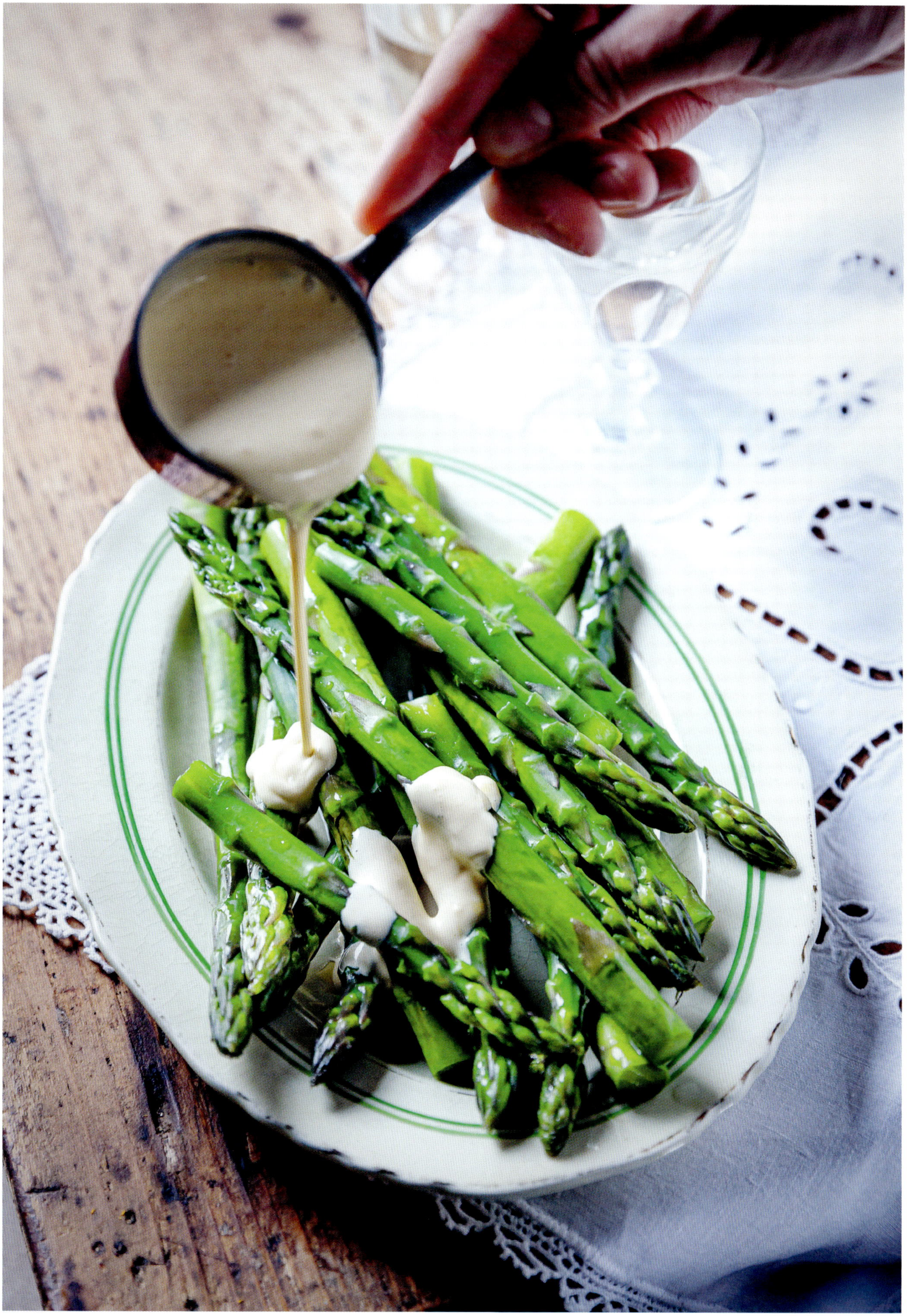

Tomato & Cucumber Salad with Whipped Feta

I like to make this salad with baby plum tomatoes because they tend to be sweeter and more flavoursome; however, a mix of shapes, sizes and colours would also give a stunning appearance to an otherwise simple dish.

—

Serves 4
225g feta cheese (barrel aged if possible)
225g authentic Greek yogurt (10% fat)
1 lemon
200g baby plum tomatoes
200g baby cucumbers
2 tbsp extra virgin olive oil
1 tsp red-wine vinegar
1 tsp dried mint
75g Greek black olives
small handful fresh basil or mint leaves
sea salt and freshly ground black pepper

Drain the feta and put into a food processor with the yogurt and a light grating of the lemon rind. Then cut the lemon in half and squeeze in the juice from one half. Pulse until whipped. Set aside.

Cut the tomatoes in half and chop up the cucumbers. Put both in a bowl, and add the olive oil, red-wine vinegar and mint. Stir to combine, then add a squeeze of lemon juice to taste. Season generously with salt and pepper.

Spread the whipped feta on a board and spoon the tomato and cucumber mixture on top. Scatter over the olives and the basil or mint leaves to serve.

SERVE WITH …
This goes remarkably well with my **Greek Beef & Macaroni Pie** (p.79). Put both on the table, together with a basket of freshly baked **Focaccia with Rosemary & Sea Salt** (p.112).

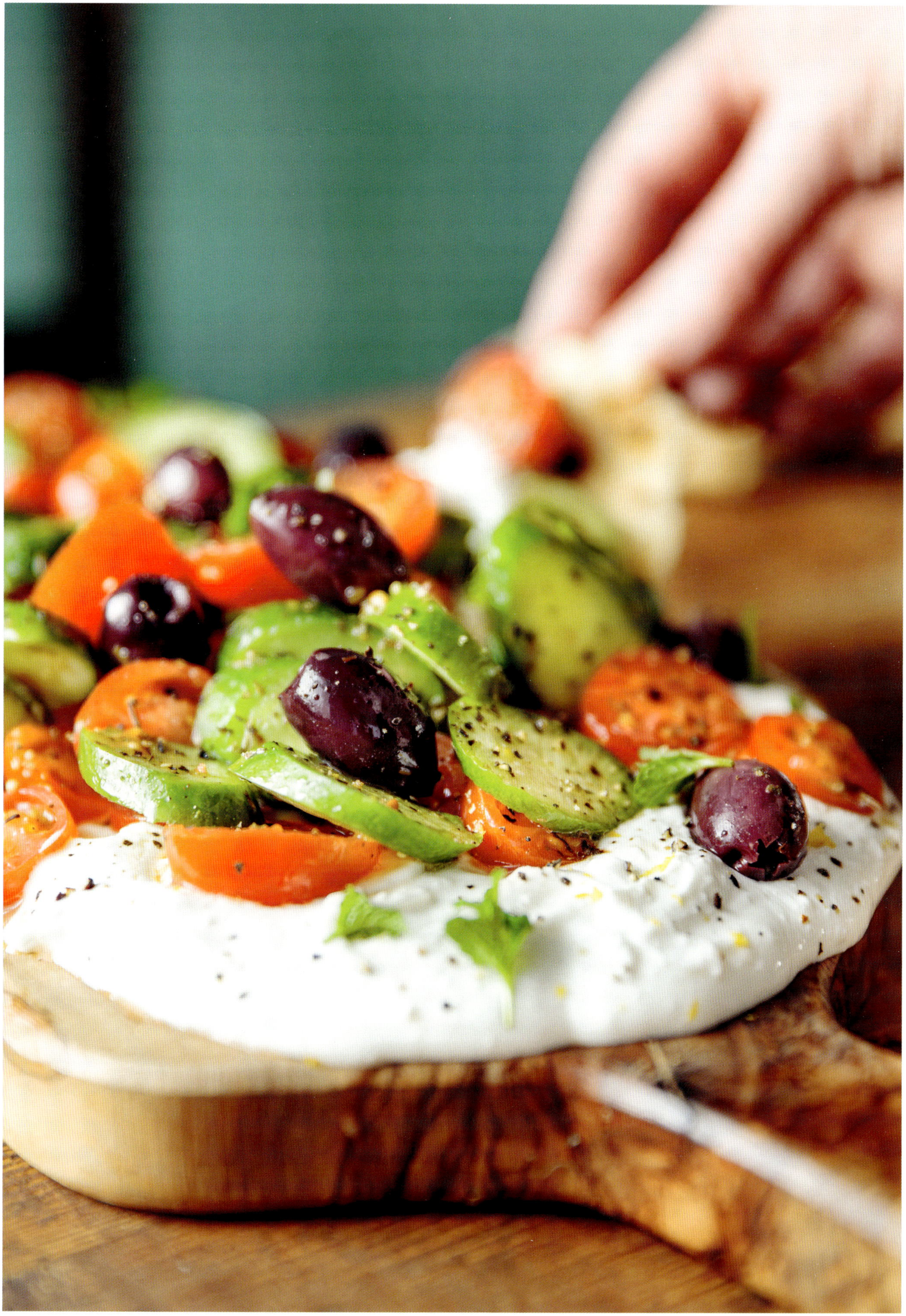

Honey-Glazed Spiced Carrots with Pistachio & Dill

This is such a beautiful dish: baby carrots glistening in spicy caramelised juices ... Just stunning! My preference is to use baby carrots (no peeling or chopping involved, other than trimming their little tops), but you can also slice regular carrots into batons.

—

Serves 4–6

50g shelled pistachio nuts
400g baby rainbow carrots
2 tbsp extra virgin olive oil, plus a little extra for drizzling
2 tbsp raw Irish honey
2 tsp spicy red pepper and herb seasoning
handful fresh dill sprigs
sea salt

Preheat the oven to 180°C (350°F/Gas Mark 4). Put the pistachio nuts in a roasting tin and toast for 5 minutes, then tip on to a chopping board and roughly chop.

Scrub the carrots and trim the tops. Put in a roasting tin with the oil and season with salt. Roast for 30 minutes. Mix the honey with the spicy pepper and herb seasoning. Drizzle over the roasted carrots and cook for another 10 minutes until soft and caramelised.

Arrange the carrots on a serving platter, drizzling over any juices left in the tin and a little extra oil. Scatter over the dill sprigs and pistachio nuts to serve.

SERVE WITH ...

These carrots look wonderfully theatrical on the table and the recipe scales up nicely, so it works well for a large crowd – it's one that I always end up doing over the festive season, when we celebrate with family and friends. This dish goes very well with **Crispy Spatchcock Chicken** (p.60).

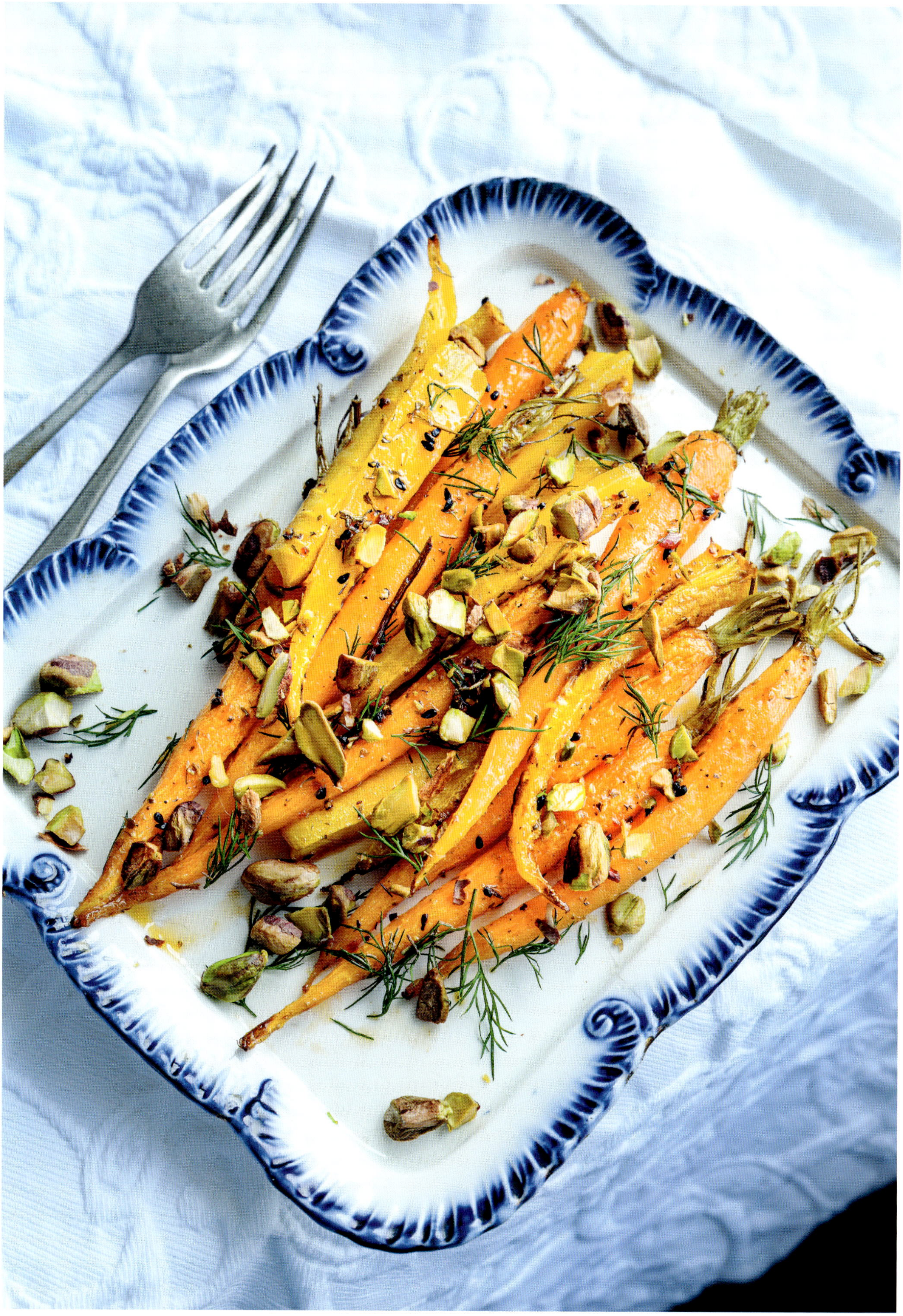

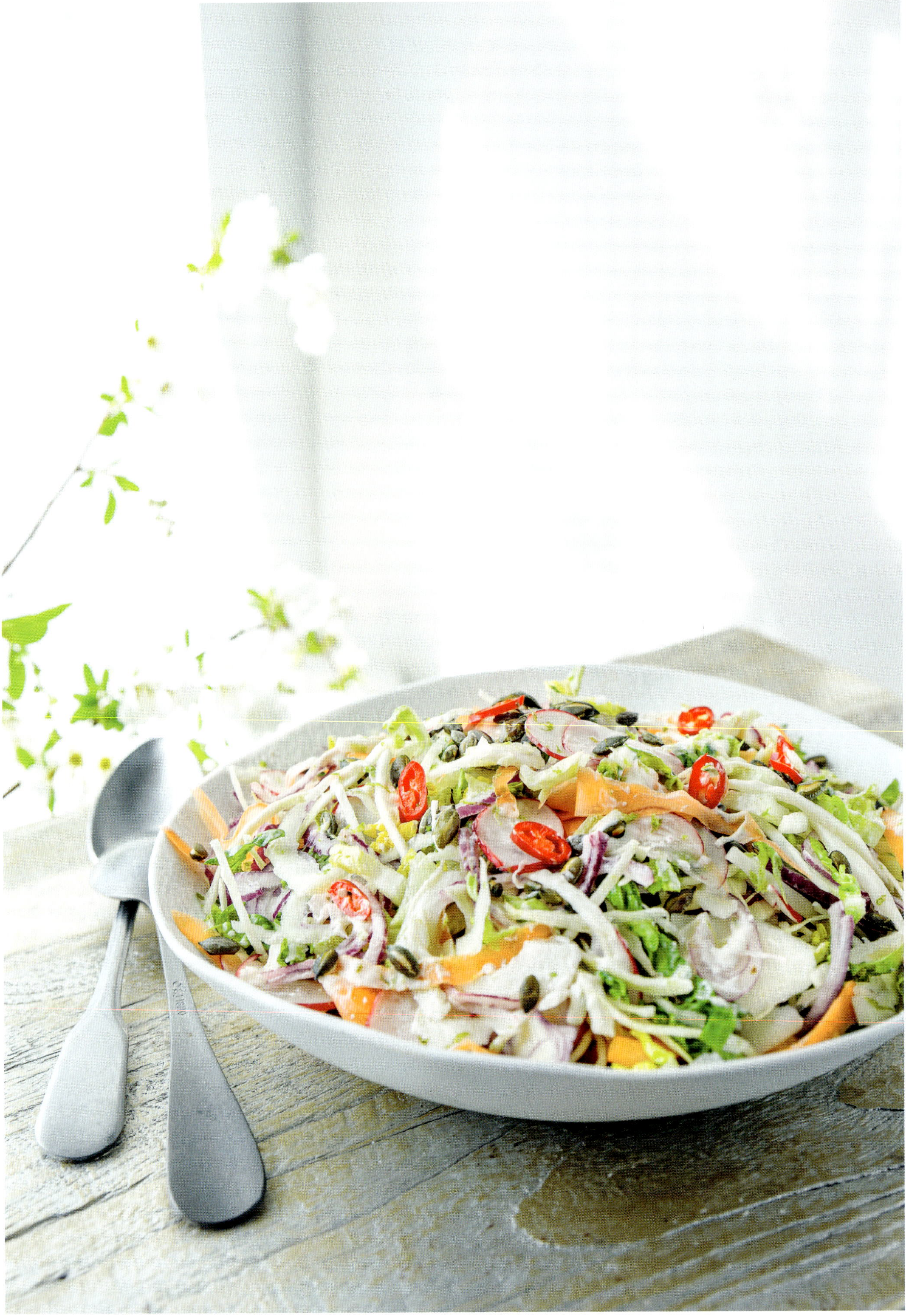

Summer Slaw

Bursting with flavour, this crunchy fresh salad is a million miles away from a traditional coleslaw; however, the principles are the same. I like to use a mandolin to prep all the vegetables. About 10 minutes before you are ready to eat, toss the slaw with the dressing so that it keeps its crunch.

—

Serves 4–6
For the dressing
120g mayonnaise
120g soured cream
2 tbsp extra virgin olive oil
finely grated rind and juice of 1 lime
1 tsp raw Irish honey
1 tsp ground cumin

25g pumpkin seeds
½ small white cabbage
100g radishes
1 red onion
1 mild red chilli
2 large carrots
2 little Gem lettuces, thinly sliced
20g fresh coriander, leaves stripped and roughly torn
sea salt and freshly ground black pepper

To make the dressing, mix the mayonnaise, soured cream, olive oil, and lime rind and juice in a small bowl with the honey and cumin, then season generously.

Toast the pumpkin seeds in a heavy-based frying pan for a few minutes. Tip on to a plate to cool and go crunchy.

Cut the cabbage into two wedges, cut away the tough core, then thinly slice using a mandolin. Trim and thinly slice the radishes, red onion and chilli the same way, then change the setting on the mandolin and cut the carrots into julienne.

Mix the cabbage, carrots and red onion in a bowl; then, using your hands, fold in the radishes and little Gem. Scatter over the chilli and coriander, then drizzle over enough of the dressing to lightly coat everything. If there is any dressing leftover, serve it alongside. Scatter the toasted pumpkin seeds on top to serve.

SERVE WITH …
Use this as a topping for **Tacos with Chicken Tinga** (p.74) or over big steaming plates of slow-cooked barbecued meats or fish. To be honest, this slaw is delicious with anything, and you'll find yourself going back for more.

Apple & Fennel Salad

This is a truly beautiful salad with bright green hues. Use the best and freshest ingredients you can lay your hands on, and think of it as a wonderful pick-me-up before a more indulgent meal.

—

Serves 4–6
100g walnut halves
juice of 1 lemon
1 tsp raw Irish honey
4 tbsp extra virgin olive oil
1 fennel bulb or 200g baby fennel
3 Granny Smith apples
3 celery stalks
handful fresh dill sprigs (optional)
sea salt and freshly ground white pepper

Toast the walnut halves in a heavy-based frying pan over a medium heat, tossing regularly. Tip on to a chopping board and coarsely chop.

Put the lemon juice, honey and olive oil in a screw-topped jar, and season generously with salt and pepper. Shake until well emulsified.

Using a mandolin or a sharp knife, thinly slice the fennel. Cut the apples into quarters, then remove the cores and thinly slice. Peel the celery along its ridges, then trim and thinly slice.

Add the fennel, apple and celery to a large bowl. Give the dressing another good shake and drizzle on top. Toss until coated, then transfer to a serving bowl or platter. Scatter over the walnuts and the dill sprigs, if liked, to serve.

SERVE WITH …
This makes a lovely side dish to **Crispy Spatchcock Chicken with Lemon & Herbs** (p.60), or you could serve it as a starter to **Hake with Red Pepper Sauce** (p.104).

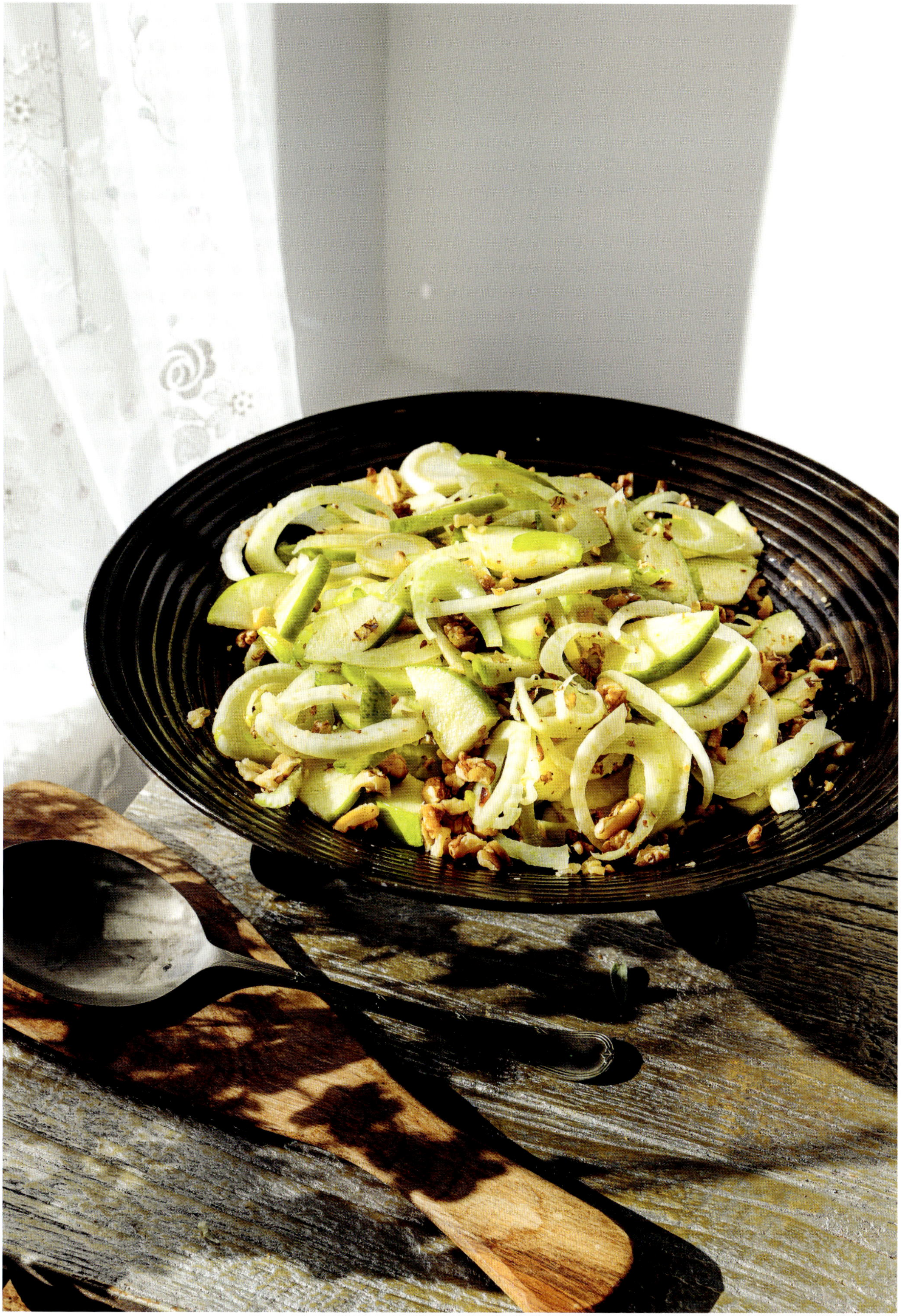

Sweet Things

Affogato

If you are after a light and sophisticated after-dinner treat, whip up an affogato. Affogato means 'drowned' in Italian, and that is essentially what is happening here ... The sweetness of the ice cream tempers the bitterness of the espresso coffee, and the contrasting temperatures balance each other out. The cold glasses keep the ice cream solid, leaving you to scoop the perfect mix of cold and hot with each mouthful.

—

Serves 4
500ml carton vanilla ice cream or gelato
4 tbsp nut liqueur (Frangelico or Amaretto)
4 shots hot espresso coffee
50g block plain chocolate (optional)

Scoop the ice cream or gelato into balls and put on a suitable tray lined with parchment paper. Put back in the freezer for at least 4 hours or overnight to firm up.

Put the ice cream balls into small cold glasses and pour the liqueur around the edges. Pour a hot shot of espresso coffee over each one, and stir the ice cream into the hot coffee so that it melts a little. Using a microplane, finely grate a little chocolate on each one, if liked.

SERVE AFTER ...
This Italian coffee dessert will delight anyone with a sweet tooth. A perfect after-dinner indulgence, it's particularly good for a spontaneous last-minute summer supper party because it takes no more than five minutes to make. Plus, it can be a great little pick-me-up after an all-day affair. Traditionally, Italian meals happen on Sundays, when large extended families spend hours cooking together before sitting down to a multicourse meal. What makes this style of eating so special is that it is designed to slow everyone down to enjoy the moment and savour the food, which ultimately improves digestion. This dessert lends itself especially well to that style of occasion.

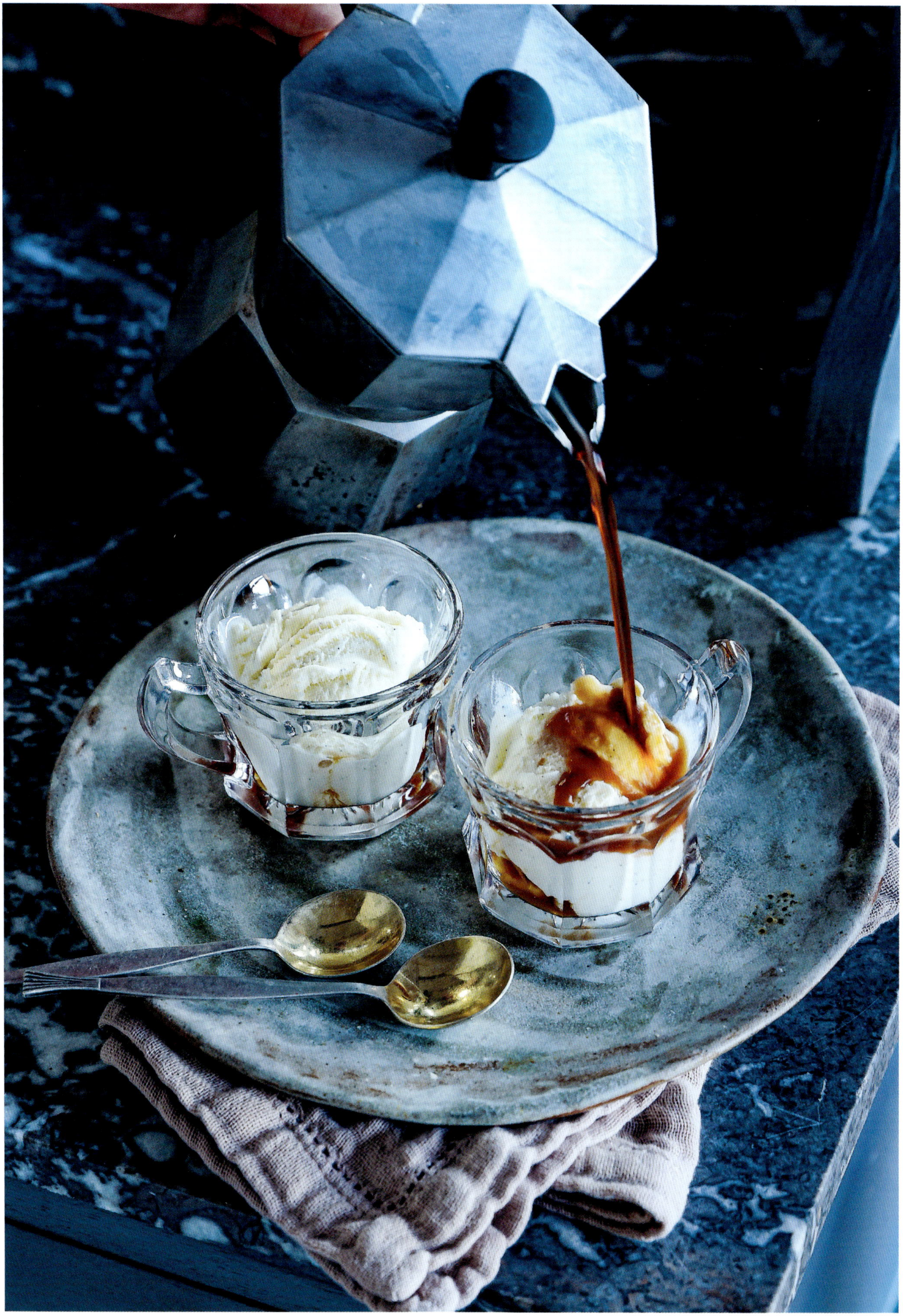

Moroccan Orange Salad with Pomegranate

Use the nicest, sweetest oranges you can find for this dessert. The first harvest of oranges comes into our supermarkets at the beginning of the winter season, or wait till early spring and take it to another level by using blood oranges, which bring a great pop of colour and a flavour booster.

—

Serves 4

6 large oranges
seeds and juice of 1 large pomegranate
2 tbsp extra virgin olive oil
6 tbsp freshly squeezed orange juice
handful fresh mint leaves
salt and freshly ground black pepper

To get lovely slices of orange without any bitter pith, take a slice off the bottom and top of each orange, then carefully cut away the skin and pith following the curve of the fruit until you have removed all the peel and pith. Cut the peeled oranges into slices. Reserve any juice for the dressing.

Arrange the orange slices on a large plate and sprinkle with the pomegranate seeds. Whisk together the olive oil and orange juice along with any pomegranate juice, then season lightly to taste. Drizzle the dressing over the salad, then roughly tear the mint leaves and scatter on top to serve.

SERVE AFTER …

A refreshing dessert on a hot day, and it's perfect after **Fragrant Butterflied Lamb** (p.69) or **Crispy Porchetta with Fennel & Herbs** (p.80) as a palate cleanser. This recipe involves nothing more than assembly, so you can throw it together at the last minute, or make it in the morning and give the oranges time to soak up the dressing. With its riot of colours, it's a very pretty dish requiring minimal effort.

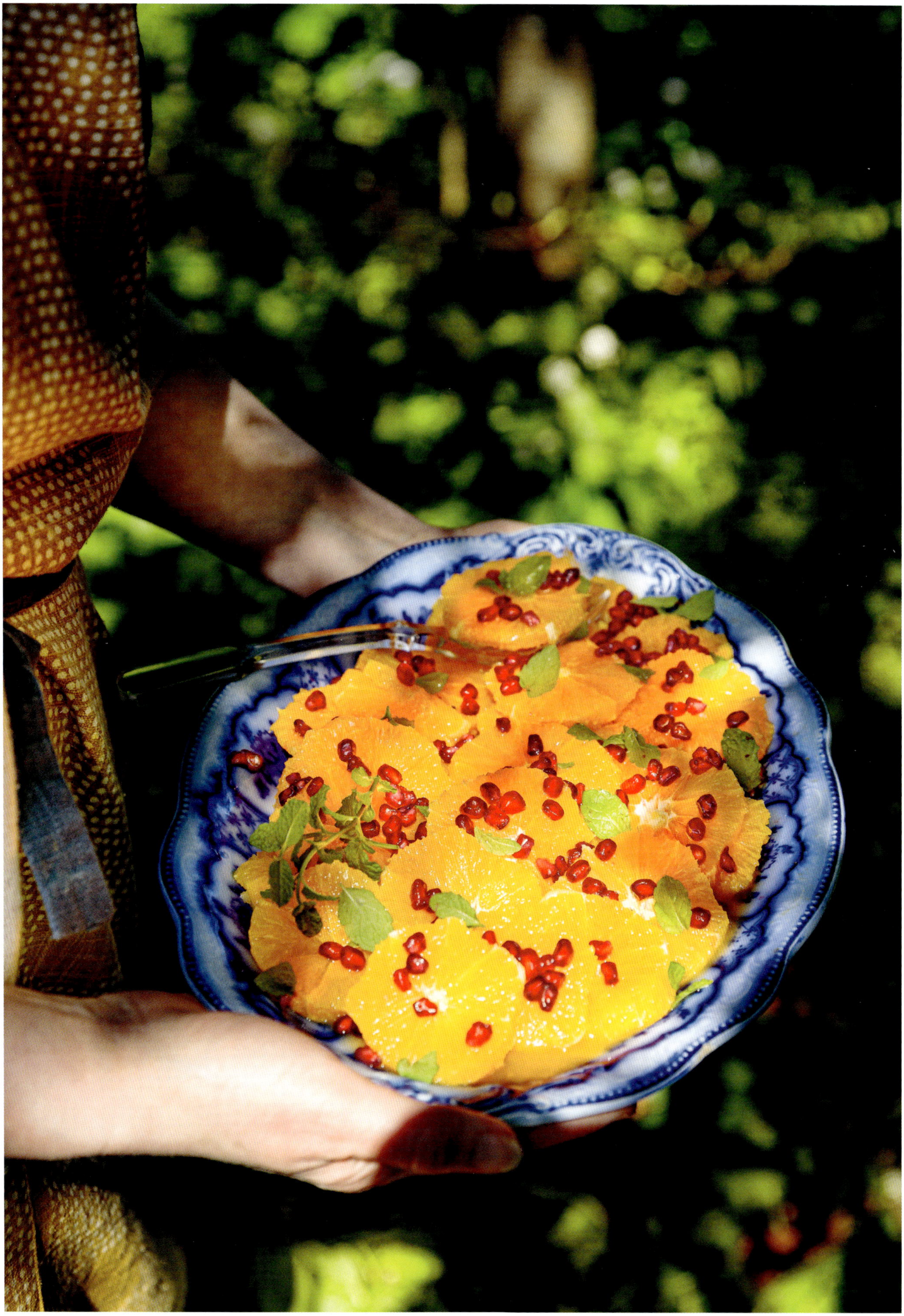

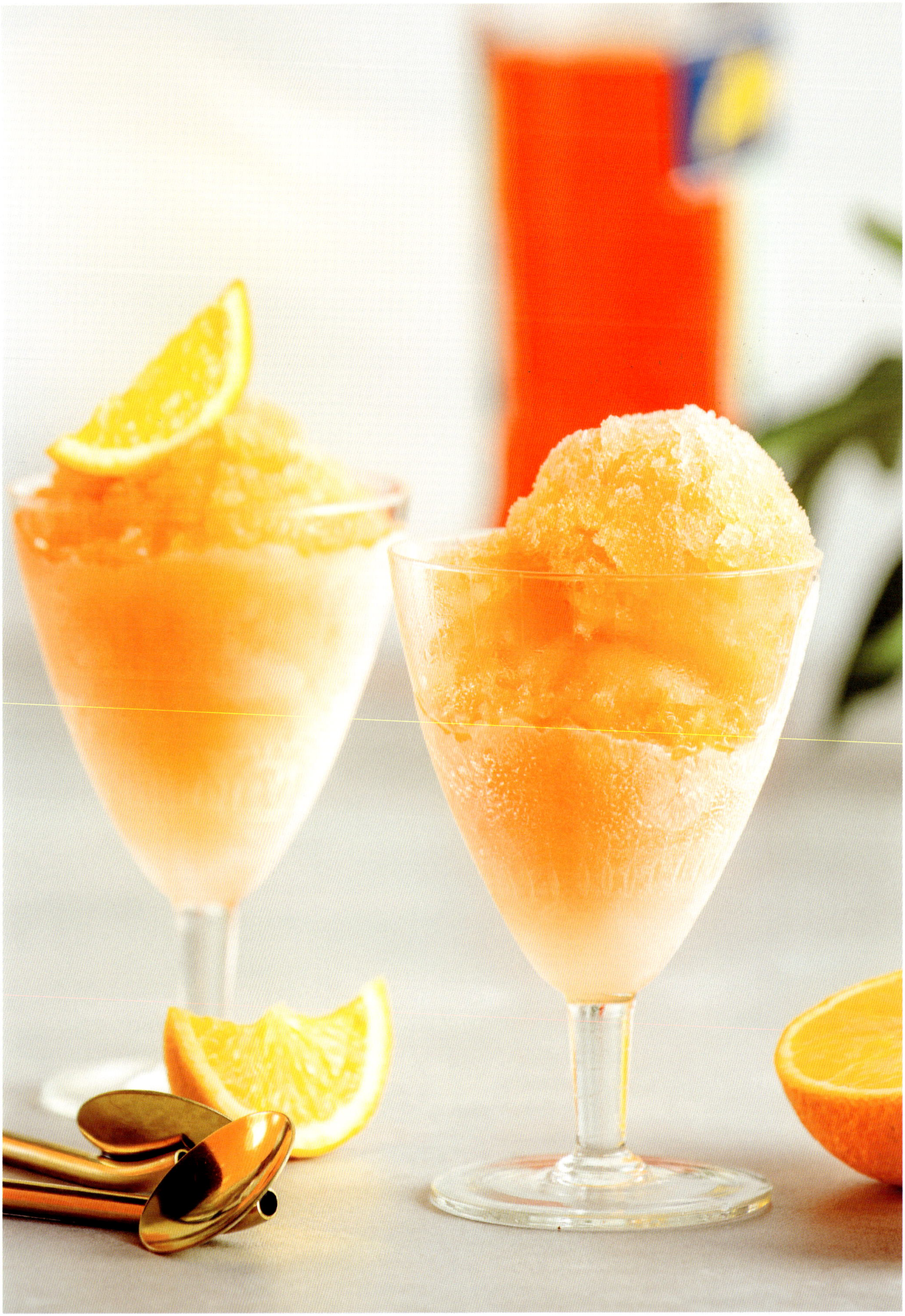

Aperol Spritz Sorbet

Aperol Spritz – also known as Spritz Veneziano – is a refreshing orange cocktail make from Aperol and Prosecco. It's always been a popular drink in Italy, particularly in Venice, and it is fast becoming popular here too. What better way to do it justice, then, than to make it into a beautiful sorbet to enjoy at the end of a meal on a hot summer's day?

—

Serves 4
300g caster sugar
about 6 large oranges (blood or regular, depending on the season), plus extra slices to decorate
100ml Aperol

Put the sugar and 200ml of water in a small heavy-based pan over a low heat. Cook for a few minutes until the sugar has dissolved, stirring occasionally. Increase the heat and bring to the boil, then boil fast for 1–2 minutes. Remove from the heat and leave to cool.

Squeeze the juice from the oranges and strain into a measuring jug – you are looking for 400ml – then stir in the Aperol. Add the cooled-down sugar syrup and stir to combine. Pour into a shallow 2-litre rigid plastic container, then cover with a lid and freeze for 2–3 hours.

Remove the partially frozen sorbet from the freezer and blitz in a food processor until the ice crystals are all broken down. Return to the freezer and leave overnight. About 15 minutes before serving, transfer the sorbet to the fridge to soften slightly. Scoop the sorbet into balls and arrange in flute glasses and decorate with the orange slices to serve.

SERVE AFTER …
Light and vibrantly coloured, this goes well after almost anything, especially Italian dishes like **Stuffed Beef Rolls with Tomato Ragu** (p.102) or **Italian Stuffed Conchiglioni** (p.67). For an added twist, place a scoop of sorbet into a flute glass and top with chilled Prosecco – it's a fantastically simple cocktail to have up your sleeve.

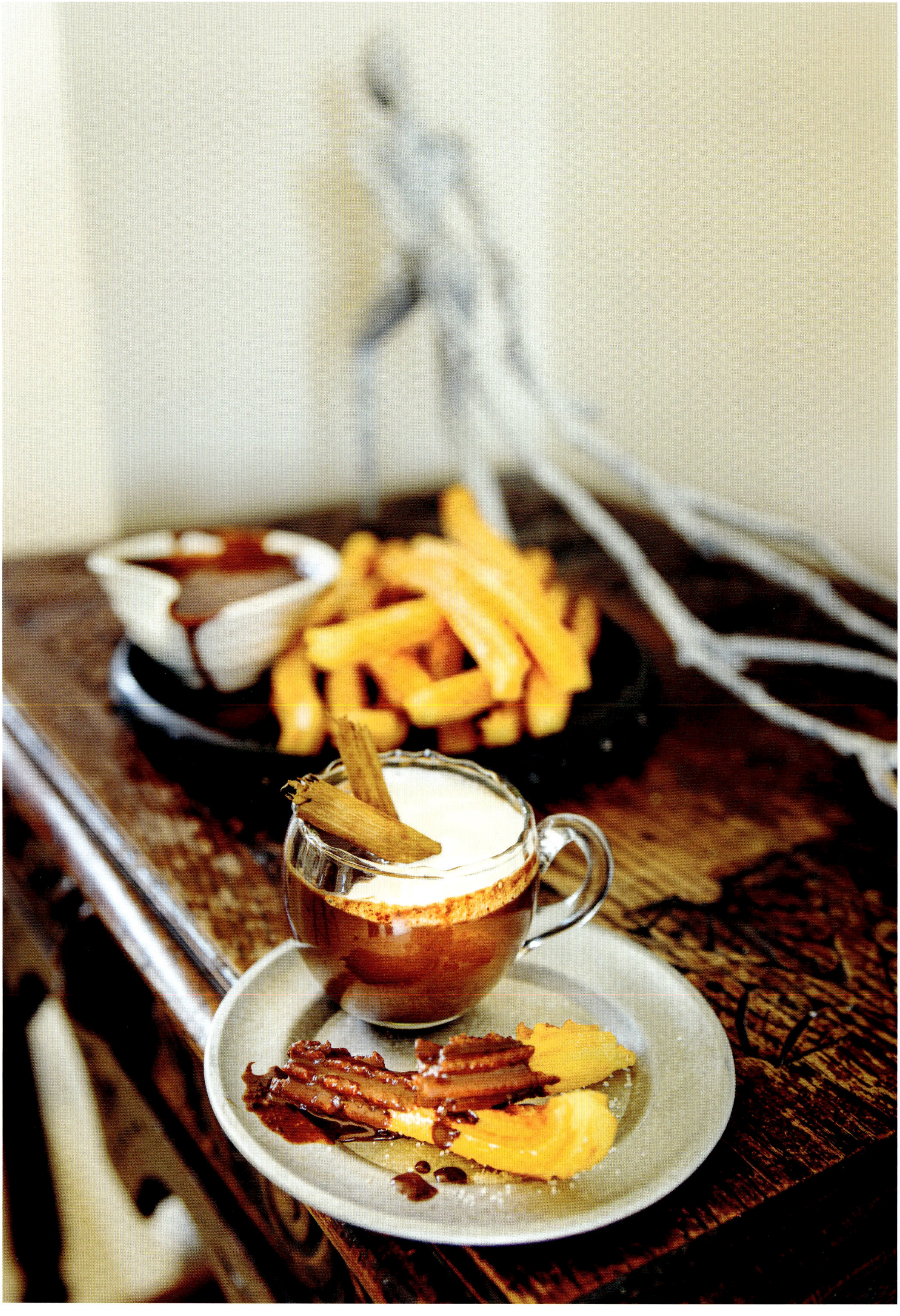

Hot Chocolate with Cinnamon Churros

Originally from Spain, but also popular in France, Portugal, the USA, Latin America and Spanish-speaking Caribbean islands, churros are a fried-dough snack sometimes referred to as a Spanish (or Mexican) doughnut. The snack gets its name from its shape, which resembles the horns of the Churro breed of sheep reared in the Spanish grasslands of Huarocho.

—

Serves 4–6
5 tbsp sunflower oil
1 tbsp ground cinnamon
finely grated rind of 1 lemon
200g plain flour
½ tsp salt
1 egg
vegetable oil, for deep-frying
6 tbsp caster sugar
6 cinnamon sticks, to serve (optional)

For the hot chocolate
225g plain chocolate, broken into squares
900ml milk
175ml cream, plus extra whipped to decorate

To make the churros, place 300ml of water in a pan with the sunflower oil, half of the cinnamon and the lemon rind. Bring to the boil. Meanwhile, sieve the flour and salt into a bowl. Once the water mixture is at a rolling boil, tip in the flour and salt, beating well with a wooden spoon over a low heat until the mixture leaves the sides of the pan. Leave to cool a little, then beat in the egg.

Heat the vegetable oil in a deep-fat fryer to 180°C (350°F). Spoon the churros mixture into a piping bag fitted with a 2.5cm star-shaped nozzle. Carefully pipe 7.5cm lengths directly into the heated oil and cook for 3–4 minutes until golden, turning once. You may have to do this in batches – it is important not to overcrowd the pan.

To make the hot chocolate, melt the chocolate in a bowl set over a pan of simmering water. Next, place the milk and cream in a small heavy-based pan. Using a spatula, add the melted chocolate and stir to combine. Heat gently for a few minutes, stirring continuously, until piping hot but not boiling.

Meanwhile, mix the remaining cinnamon with the sugar on a flat plate. Remove the cooked churros from the oil with a slotted spoon, quickly drain on kitchen paper, then roll in the cinnamon sugar. Pile on to a plate and finish cooking the rest of the churros in the same way. When ready to serve, pour the hot chocolate into mugs or large cappuccino cups. Decorate with the cinnamon sticks, if liked, and place the plate of churros in the centre of the table so that everyone can help themselves.

SERVE AFTER...
For full nostalgic effect, try this after a comforting dish of **Cottage Pie** (p.71) or **One-Pot Fish Pie** (p.62), with a side of **Braised Petits Pois with Bacon** (p.138).

Summer Blush

This is my go-to cocktail for summer lunches, suppers and parties because it is so refreshing and easy to make. I love it because there is no mixing involved, and everything can be poured straight into the glasses.

—

Serves 4-6
4 tbsp elderflower cordial
4 tbsp pomegranate seeds
1 chilled bottle of Prosecco
handful fresh mint leaves

Pour a couple of teaspoons of the elderflower cordial into each flute glass, and add the pomegranate seeds. Top up with the chilled Prosecco and decorate with mint leaves to serve.

SERVE WITH ...
When I have people over, I like to serve a cocktail as they arrive: it is a perfect way to lead into dinner and I find that after one or two, people are going to revert to their wine of choice. In the summer, there's nothing nicer than sitting outside on a nice evening with a glass of this. Watch as it immediately lifts everyone's spirits and sets the party tone. Mind you, this is so good that we have been known to serve it after dinner, too, alongside a fruity dessert such as **Vanilla Panna Cotta with Clarke's Strawberries** (p.182) or **Lemon Posset with Passion Fruit** (p.180).

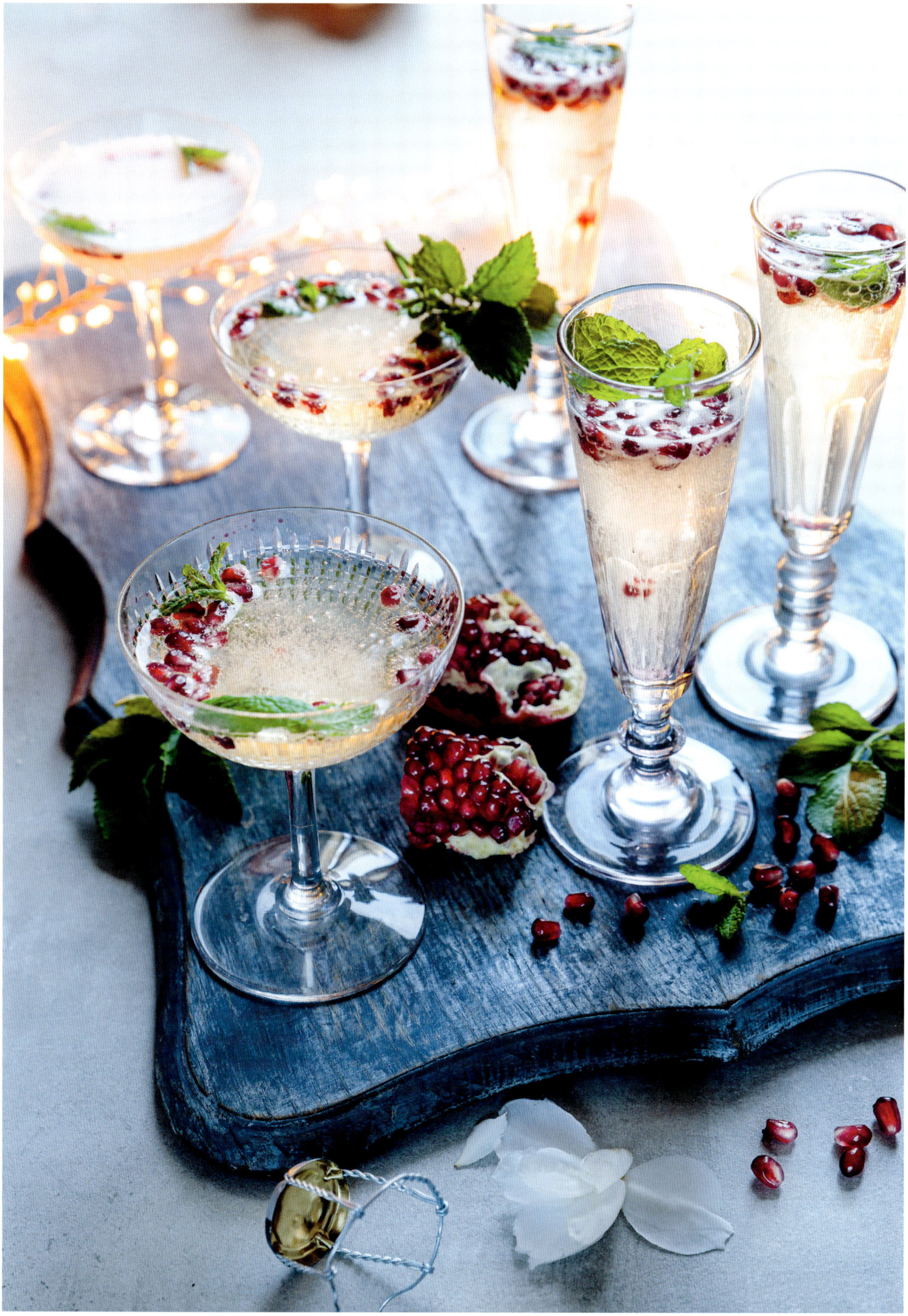

Mango with Lime, Chilli & Star Anise

Alphonso mangoes from Pakistan can be found all through the summer in good greengrocers and Asian supermarkets – and they are worth making a special trip for. I just love serving them in this spicy, fresh syrup, elevated even further with a scoop of praline ice cream. The tequila has a fruity, sweet, almost earthy taste with notes of honey, citrus, vanilla, caramel, oak and black pepper. If you splash out on an aged tequila, it will be smoother and richer – it's the perfect combination for a hot summer's day.

—

Serves 4
4 tbsp agave syrup
finely grated rind and juice of 2 limes
1 mild red chilli, seeded and finely chopped
1 star anise
2 large ripe mangoes
2–4 tbsp tequila, to taste
4 fresh mint leaves, finely shredded
praline ice cream, to serve (optional)

Place the agave syrup into a small pan with the lime rind and juice, chilli and star anise. Bring to a gentle simmer and cook gently for 5 minutes, then turn off the heat. Set aside to cool and allow the flavours to infuse for 20 minutes.

Peel the skin off the mangoes over a bowl to catch any juices, then cut the flesh into bite-sized pieces. Stir in the cooled syrup with the tequila to taste. Put in the fridge to marinate for 1 hour, then spoon the mango with some of the syrup into glasses and decorate with the mint. Add a scoop of ice cream to each glass, if liked, to serve.

SERVE WITH ...
If you're feeling brave or are in a party mood, offer tequila shots with lime wedges and sea salt flakes with this, or consider freezing and then blending in a food processor for an instant frozen cocktail with a fiery kick.

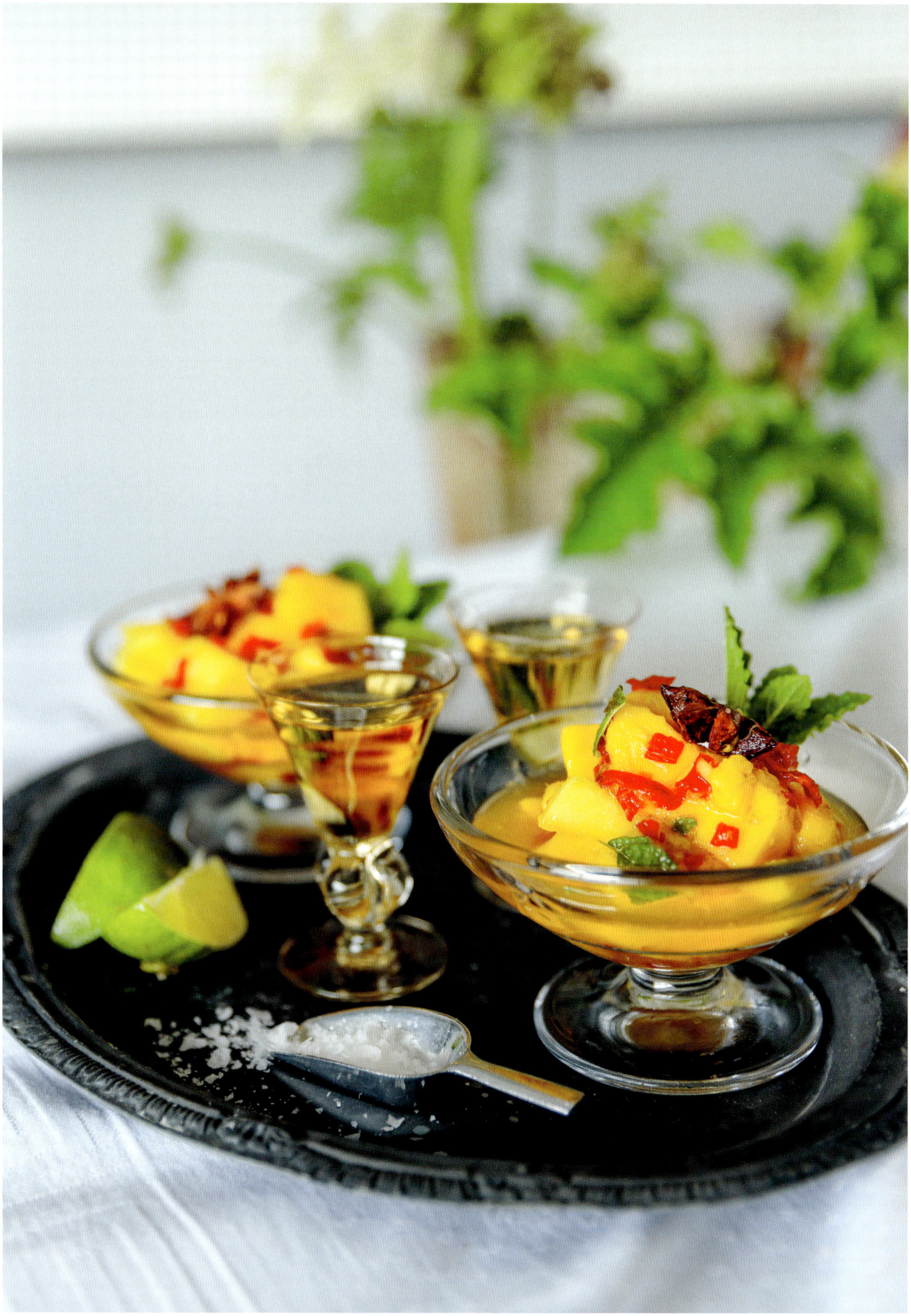

Lemon Posset with Passion Fruit

This is probably the simplest dessert you'll ever make – yet, it can look really elegant, and packs a big citrus punch with a passion-fruit kick. It's divine, and it will become your go-to, quick-but-impressive way to end a meal – it certainly is in our house …

—

Serves 4
1 vanilla pod
600ml cream
90g caster sugar
finely grated rind and juice of 1 lemon
1 large passion fruit
thin shortbread biscuits, to serve

Cut the vanilla pod in half and, using a teaspoon, scrape out the seeds into a heavy-based pan. Pour in the cream, then add the sugar with the lemon juice and rind. Cut the passion fruit in half and scoop in the seeds, reserving some for decorating, then heat gently, stirring until the sugar has melted. Bring to the boil and simmer for 1 minute.

Remove the lemon mixture from the heat and pour into stemmed glasses or pots. Chill for at least 2–3 hours, though overnight is best. Decorate with the rest of the passion fruit seeds and serve set on a plate alongside some thin shortbread biscuits.

SERVE AFTER …
There is something wonderfully comforting about this lemon posset, its velvety cream spiked with zesty lemon and passion fruit. I don't think you can improve upon a simple meal of **Chateaubriand with Béarnaise Sauce** (p.96) and **Smashed Roast Potatoes** (p.124) followed by this dessert.

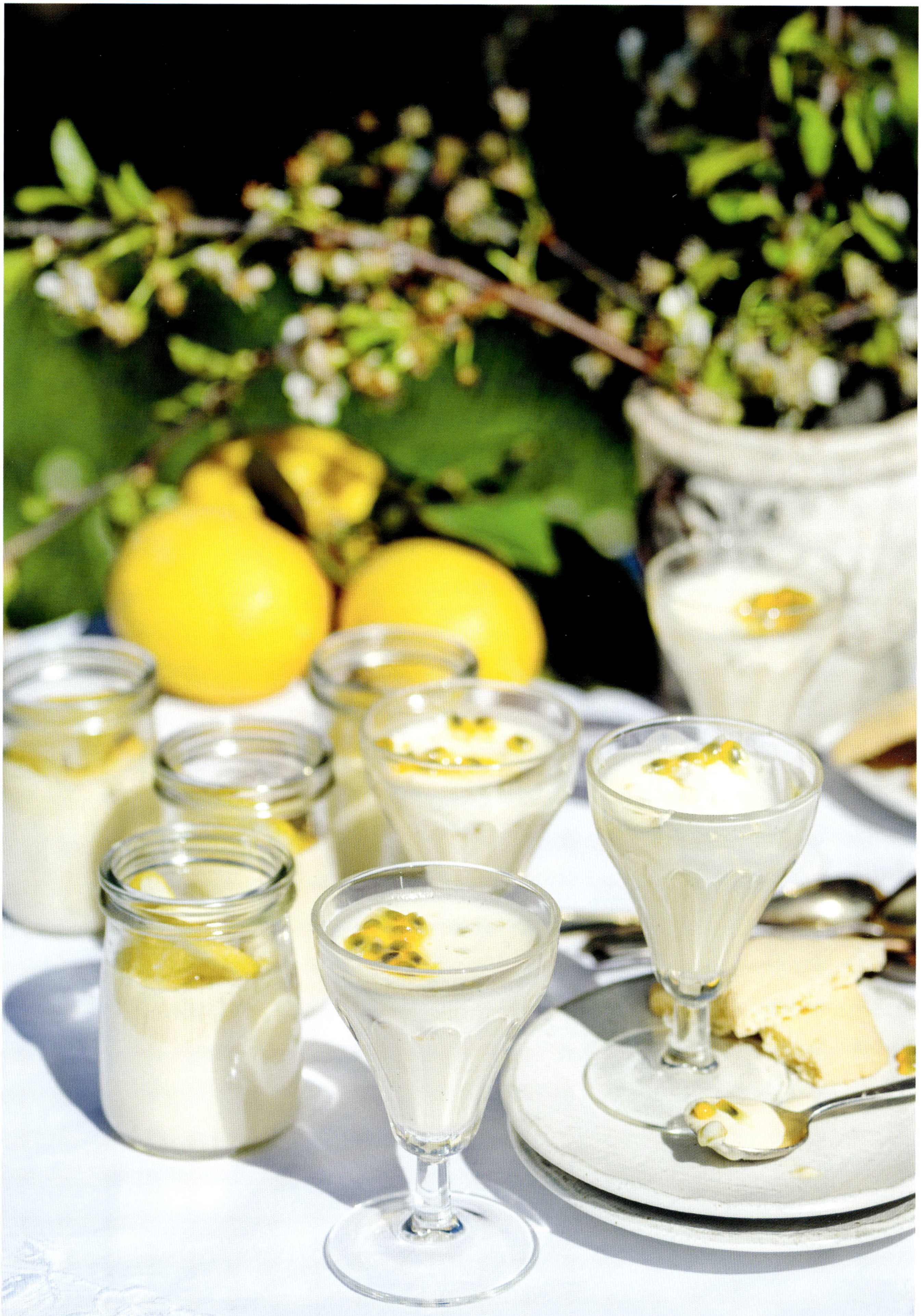

Vanilla Panna Cotta with Clarke's Strawberries

Give this classic Italian dessert a twist with a delicate creamy vanilla flavour and a fresh strawberry topping. It's the perfect dessert for a chilled summer gathering. If you want to make it less rich, simply replace 200ml of the cream with milk.

—

Serves 4
1 vanilla pod
3 sheets gelatine
600ml cream
100g caster sugar
300g large strawberries (preferably Pat Clarke's)
½ lemon
2–3 tsp icing sugar, to taste

To make the panna cotta, split the vanilla pod in half and scrape out the seeds. Put the gelatine sheets into a bowl of cold water and leave them to soak for 5 minutes. Put the cream, caster sugar and vanilla seeds into a pan, and slowly bring up to the boil, whisking continuously. Take the pan off the heat. Take the gelatine out of the water, gently squeeze out the excess water and add to the cream mixture, whisking continuously until it has dissolved. Strain the mixture through a sieve into a measuring jug.

Divide the mixture equally between 4 x 200ml dariole moulds or ramekins, place them on a baking tray and leave them to set in the fridge for at least 3 hours or up to 2 days.

Choose the 4 nicest strawberries for decoration, then cut them in half with the stems intact. Remove the stalks from the remainder, then add to a blender with a squeeze of lemon juice and icing sugar to taste – the amount will depend on how sweet the strawberries are. Blitz to a smooth purée, then pass through a sieve into a jug.

To serve, leave at room temperature for 15 minutes, then turn each panna cotta upside down on to a serving plate. If it won't drop out, carefully dip the mould briefly into a bowl of warm water to loosen it. Serve with a drizzle of the strawberry compote and the sliced fresh strawberries.

SERVE AFTER …
Panna cotta is a brilliant stand-by dessert because it's quick and simple enough to make in the morning. I leave it to set in the fridge and serve after **Fragrant Butterflied Lamb** (p.69) with a large bowl of the best strawberries in Ireland. Pat Clarke has been delivering me strawberries for years, and their flavour is sensational.

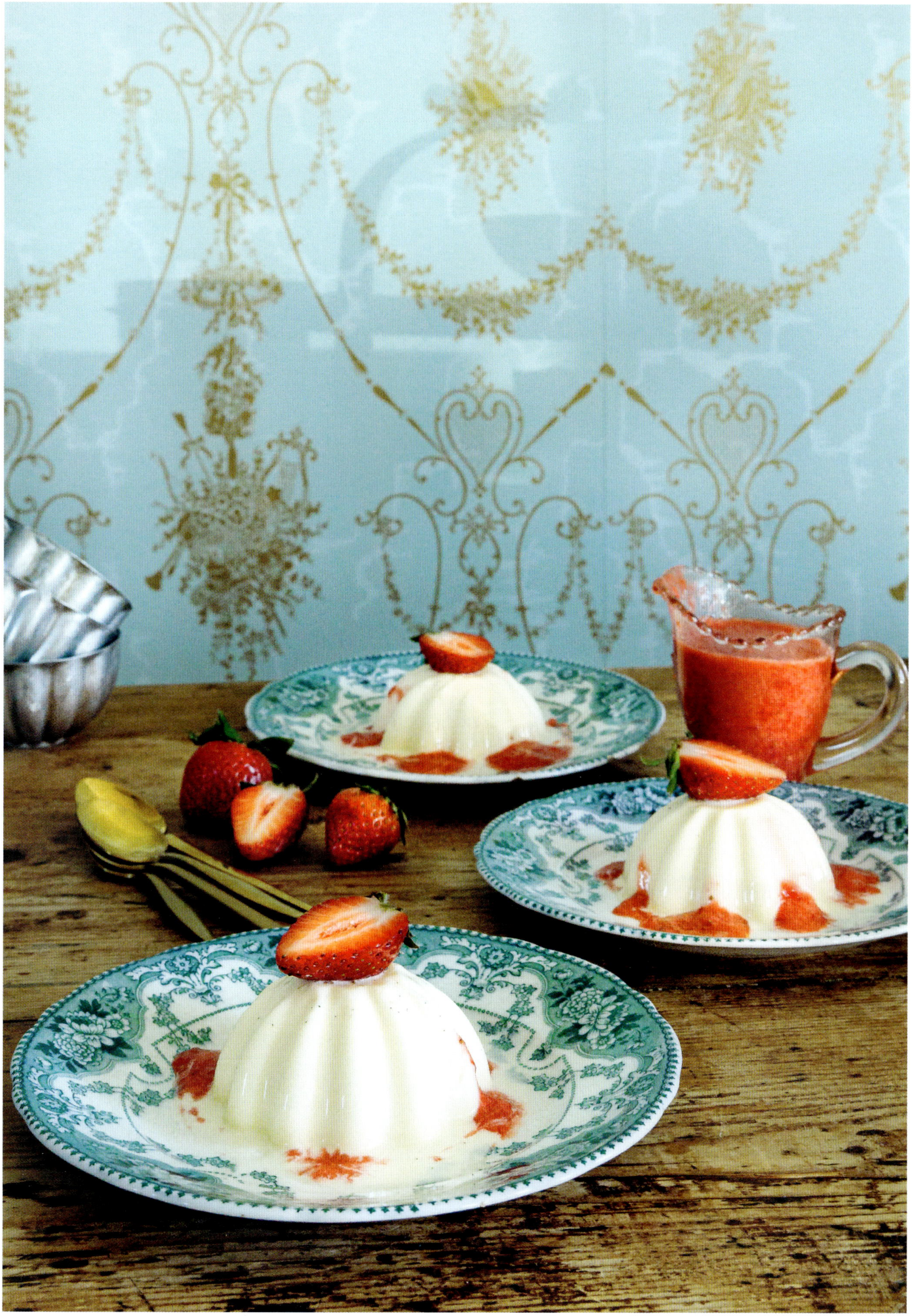

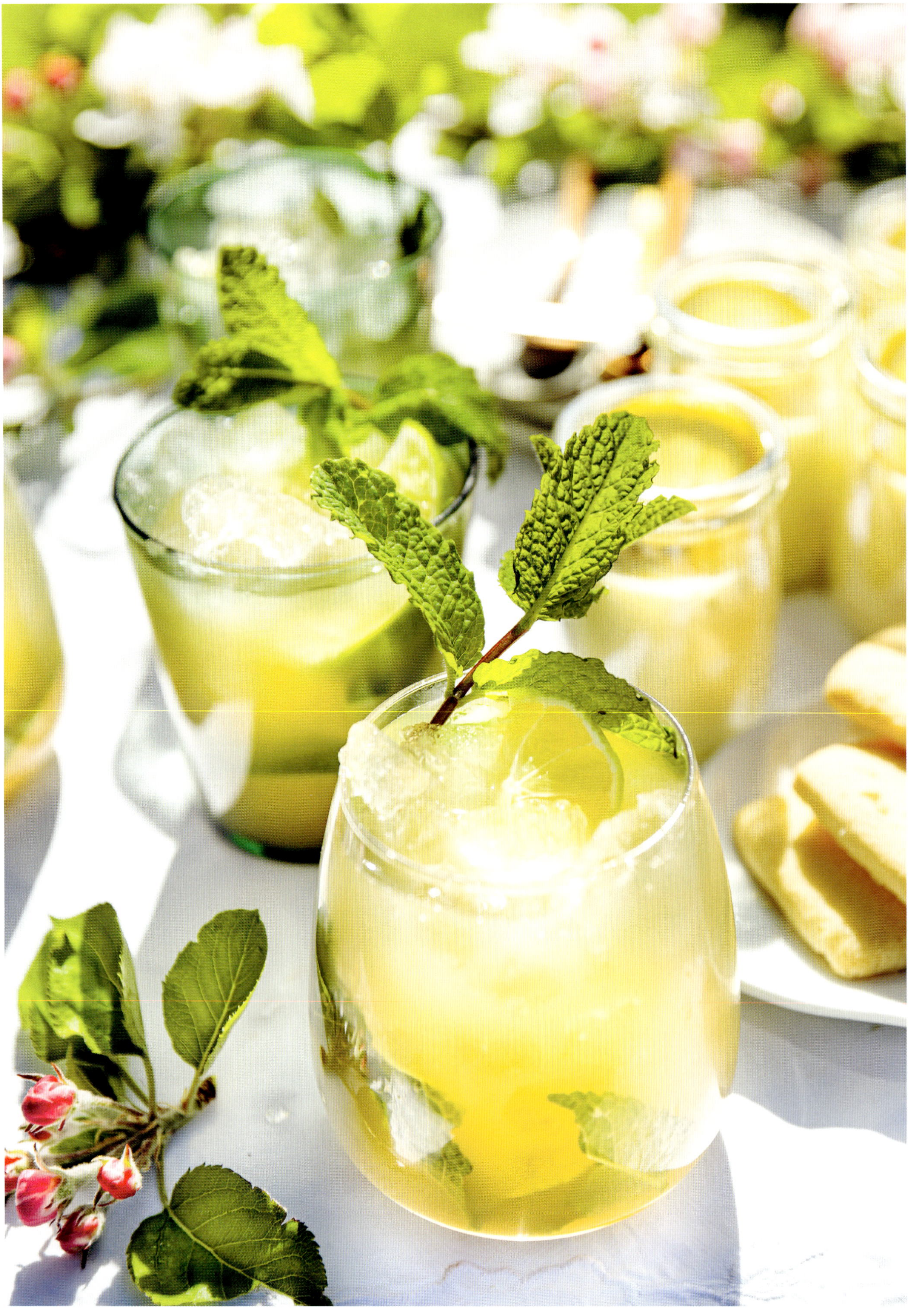

Apple Mojito

If you are serving this to large numbers, make a batch ahead of time in clean glass or plastic bottles – without the ice and muddling. Then, as your guests arrive, fill jugs with ice and plenty of mint and add the apple mojito. Give everything a good stir, and no one will be any the wiser! Master the knack, and your friends will be queuing up to get this one.

—

Serves 4
20g fresh mint
225g ice cubes
200ml dark or white rum (whatever you prefer)
600ml Tipperary apple juice (or similar)
juice from 2 limes, plus 4 extra wedges for the glasses

Strip all the mint leaves off the stems, put 5–6 into the bottom of each highball glass, then top up with plenty of ice.

Put the rum in a cocktail shaker with the apple and lime juice, and add another 10–12 mint leaves with a good handful of ice cubes. Shake well together, then strain into the highball glasses, adding a wedge of lime with an extra couple of mint leaves for decoration.

SERVE WITH ...
This Apple Mojito is hands down the most popular cocktail I've ever made for guests at home. It's easy to make, completely delicious, and it contains no added sugar – the tangy Irish apple juice gives the cocktail natural sweetness. Serve before a party as an aperitif, or as a cheeky thirst-quencher on a lazy summer's day in the garden with whatever nibbles you can rustle up and jars of **Lemon Posset** (p.180).

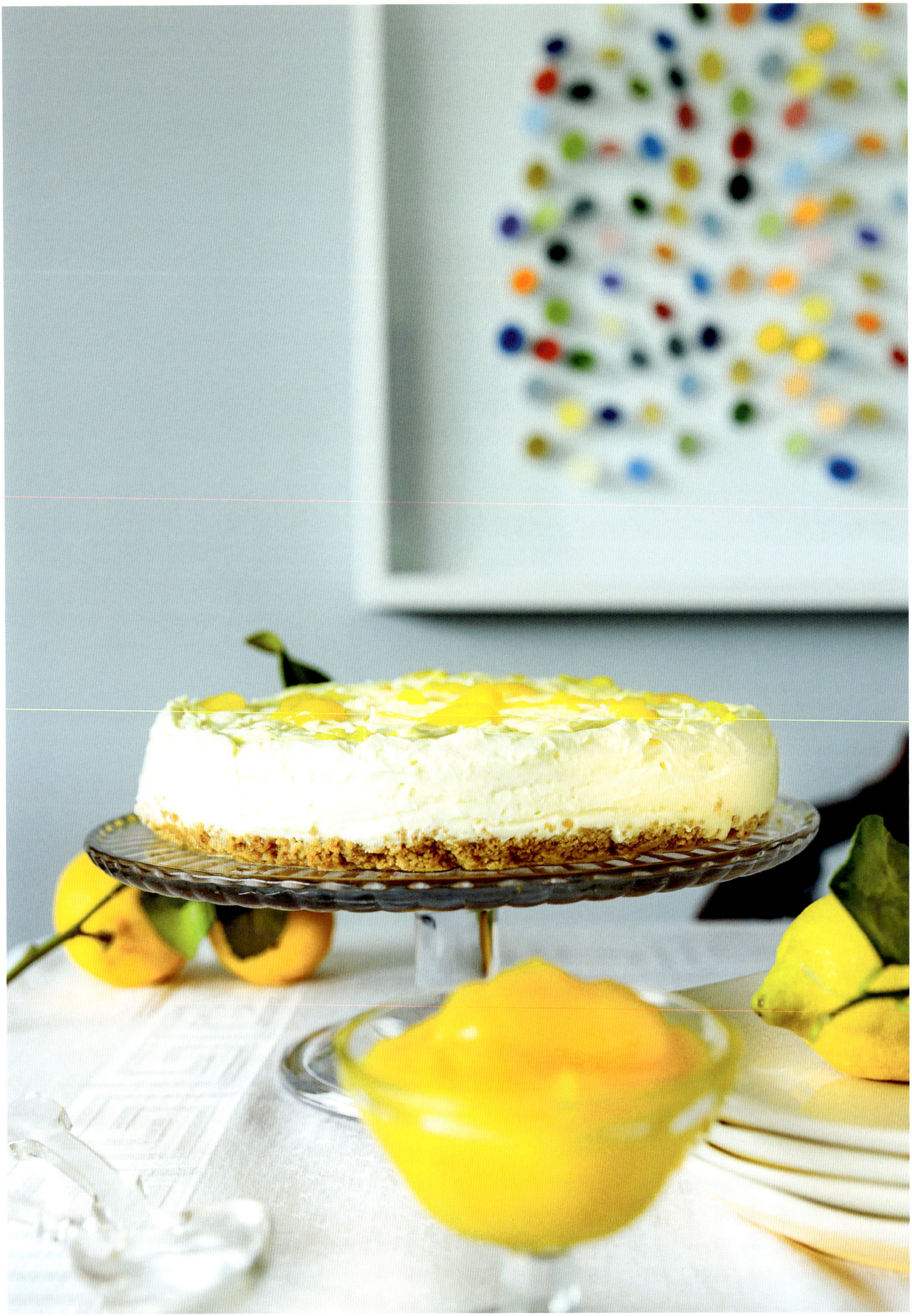

Lemon Curd Cheesecake

This cheesecake is packed full of tart, zesty flavours thanks to the incredible Sicilian lemon curd I've used. It can easily be made for a large gathering; in this case, instead of decorating while it's still whole, you can also add the berries to the slices after they have been plated for a pop of colour.

—

Serves 6–8
200g ginger biscuits
100g butter
325g jar Sicilian lemon curd
500g mascarpone cheese
2 x 500g cartons authentic Greek yogurt (10% fat)
juice of 2 lemons
icing sugar, to dust (optional)

Put the biscuits in a food processor and blend to crumbs. Melt the butter and put in a bowl with the biscuit crumbs. Mix well and use to line a springform tin, pressing down well with the back of a spoon.

Take out 2 tablespoons of the lemon curd and reserve, then put the rest in a bowl. Add the mascarpone, yogurt and lemon juice, then whisk until smooth. Using a spatula, cover the biscuit base, swirling around the top so it's not too smooth. Add small bloops of the reserved lemon curd and swirl into spirals with a toothpick. Chill for at least 2 hours – overnight is perfect.

Remove the cheesecake from the tin and, using a palette knife, put it on a cake stand. Give it a light dusting of icing sugar, if liked, just before bringing it to the table, and cut it into slices in front of your guests.

SERVE AFTER ...
This is great if you are feeding a larger crowd. Although it looks extravagant, it is very easy to prepare and can be made the day before. It's perfect after a summer garden feast of **Aromatic Poached Salmon with Avocado & Cucumber Salad** (p.83) and perhaps a **Warm Potato Salad** (p.146).

Basque Cheesecake with Cherry Compote

I first tasted this crustless cheesecake in I was in La Viva in San Sebastián, and I knew it was something I needed in my life! Easy to make and luscious to eat, this is a total joy. It is baked at such a high temperature, it has a signature 'burnt' surface, which helps hold it together. When lining the tin, don't worry about creases in the parchment paper – they give this cheesecake its unique look.

—

Serves 8–10

butter, for greasing
800g soft cream cheese (at room temperature)
225g caster sugar
4 eggs (at room temperature)
200g soured cream (at room temperature)
2 tsp vanilla extract
½ tsp sea salt flakes
2 tbsp plain flour

For the compote
500g packet frozen pitted dark cherries
50g caster sugar

Preheat the oven to 240°C (475°F/Gas Mark 9). Butter a 20cm springform cake tin. Lay 2 large squares of parchment on top of the other, one sheet turned 45 degrees, so that all the corners point in different directions. Put the parchment into the tin, pressing into the corners and up the sides so that the tin is well lined with plenty of room for the cheesecake to rise.

Put the cream cheese and sugar into a large bowl and beat for 4–5 minutes with an electric mixer until the grains of sugar have dissolved (or use a standalone mixer with a whisk attachment). Rub a little of the mixture between your fingertips: if it feels grainy, mix for another minute.

Add the eggs one at a time, beating until each one is incorporated. Scrape around the sides and add the soured cream, vanilla and salt, and mix again. Sieve the flour evenly on top and beat on a low speed until just incorporated. Scrape down the sides one last time, and give it another brief beating until very smooth and silky. Using a spatula, transfer into the lined cake tin, then give it a sharp bang on the worktop to remove any air bubbles. Bake for 30 minutes until deeply caramelised on the outside and puffed up like a soufflé. It should still have a wobble when you shake the tin. Leave to cool completely in the tin, then chill for at least 1 hour or up to 2 days.

To make the cherry compote, put the cherries into a heavy-based pan with the sugar over a medium heat. Cover and cook for 10 minutes, stirring occasionally. Leave to cool before serving – the juices will thicken as the compote sits. Remove the cheesecake from the tin and carefully peel back the parchment paper, then cut into slices and serve on plates with the cherry compote.

SERVE WITH…

While this dessert also works with any fresh berries or a rhubarb compote, this is the ultimate version for me, the cherry compote providing an intense, fruity sauce over the cut cheesecake. You could serve it after **Crispy Spatchcock Chicken** (p.60), and it is great for a large party as a little goes a long way.

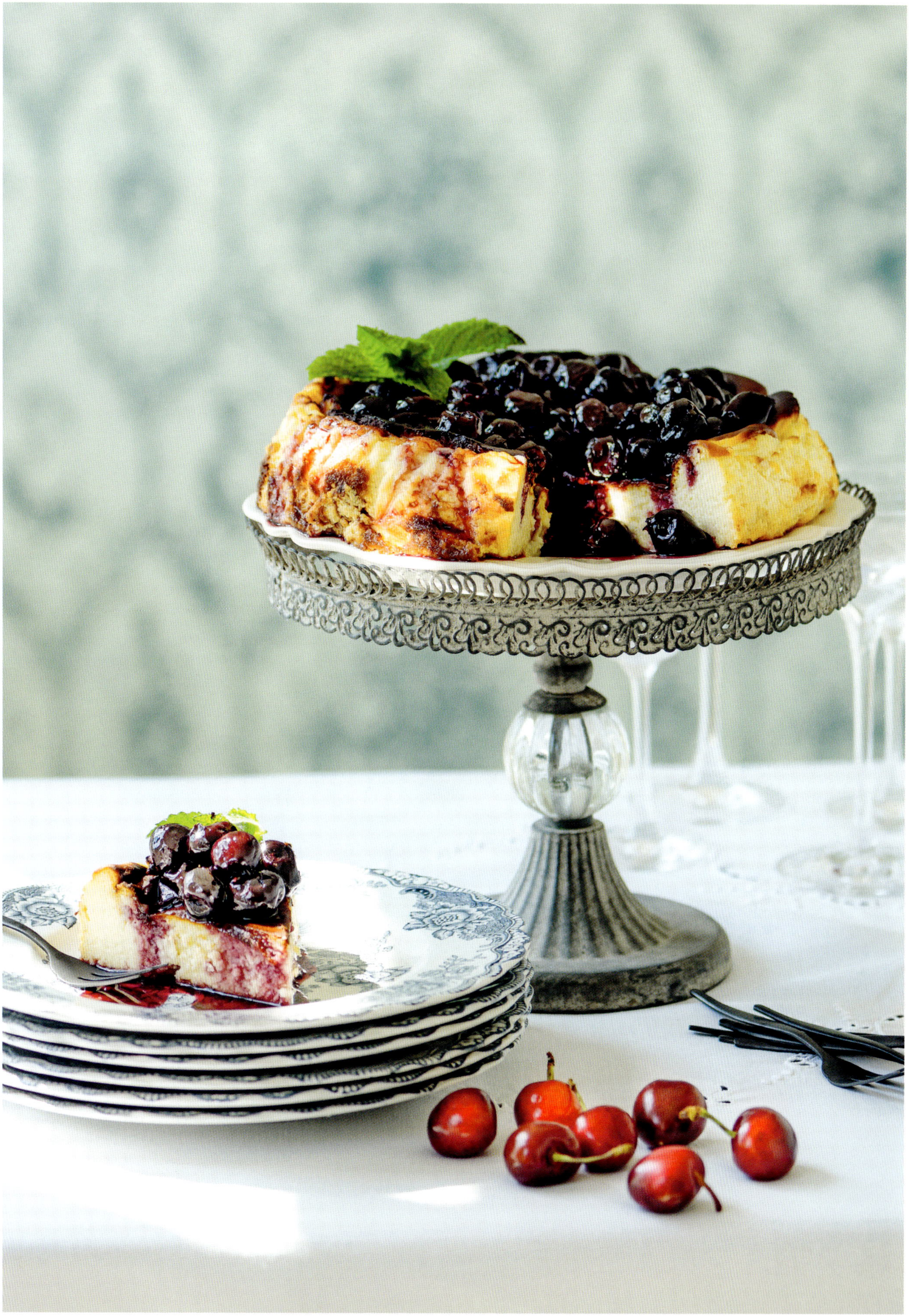

Cinnamon Swirl Apple Cake

This is a cross between two of my favourite things: cinnamon rolls and apple cake. The soured cream is what helps to give this dessert a deliciously moist crumb, while the glaze oozes down into any cracks.

—

Serves 8–12
240g butter, plus extra for greasing
2 apples
3 tbsp granulated sugar
2 tbsp ground cinnamon
150g light brown sugar
350g plain flour
4 tsp baking powder
½ tsp sea salt flakes
200g caster sugar
2 large eggs, lightly beaten
100ml milk
200g soured cream
1 tsp vanilla extract
pouring custard, to serve

For the glaze
200g icing sugar, sifted
3 tbsp milk
1 tsp vanilla extract
edible flowers and mint, to serve (optional)

Preheat the oven to 180°C (350°F/Gas Mark 4). Butter a 23cm baking tin and line with parchment paper. Peel, core and dice the apples, and mix in a bowl with the granulated sugar and 1 teaspoon of the cinnamon. Put the rest of the cinnamon in a bowl with the light brown sugar. Melt the butter in a small pan or in the microwave and, once cooled, stir half into the sugar mix.

Sieve the flour and baking powder into a bowl, and stir in the salt and caster sugar. Beat in the eggs, milk, soured cream and vanilla. Using a spatula, stir in the remaining butter, then gently fold in the apples. Transfer the cake batter into the prepared tin, spreading it out evenly. Add small dollops of the sugar-and-cinnamon butter, and quickly swirl this through the batter using a knife. Bake for 35–40 minutes until the cake is well risen and lightly golden – the apples will still be moist, and the cinnamon swirl should be gooey.

While the cake is in the oven, make the glaze. Mix the icing sugar, milk and vanilla together in a bowl until smooth. Pour this glaze over the warm cake, spreading it out evenly. Set aside for 30 minutes to cool in the tin, then cut into slices and serve warm or cold on plates with some custard, and decorate with edible flowers and mint, if you like.

SERVE WITH …
This cake is ideal for autumn or winter. It would make a lovely brunch option after something like the **Crab Gratin** (p.35) or the **Slow-Cooked Onion & Goat's Cheese Tart** (p.86) with a fresh green salad alongside.

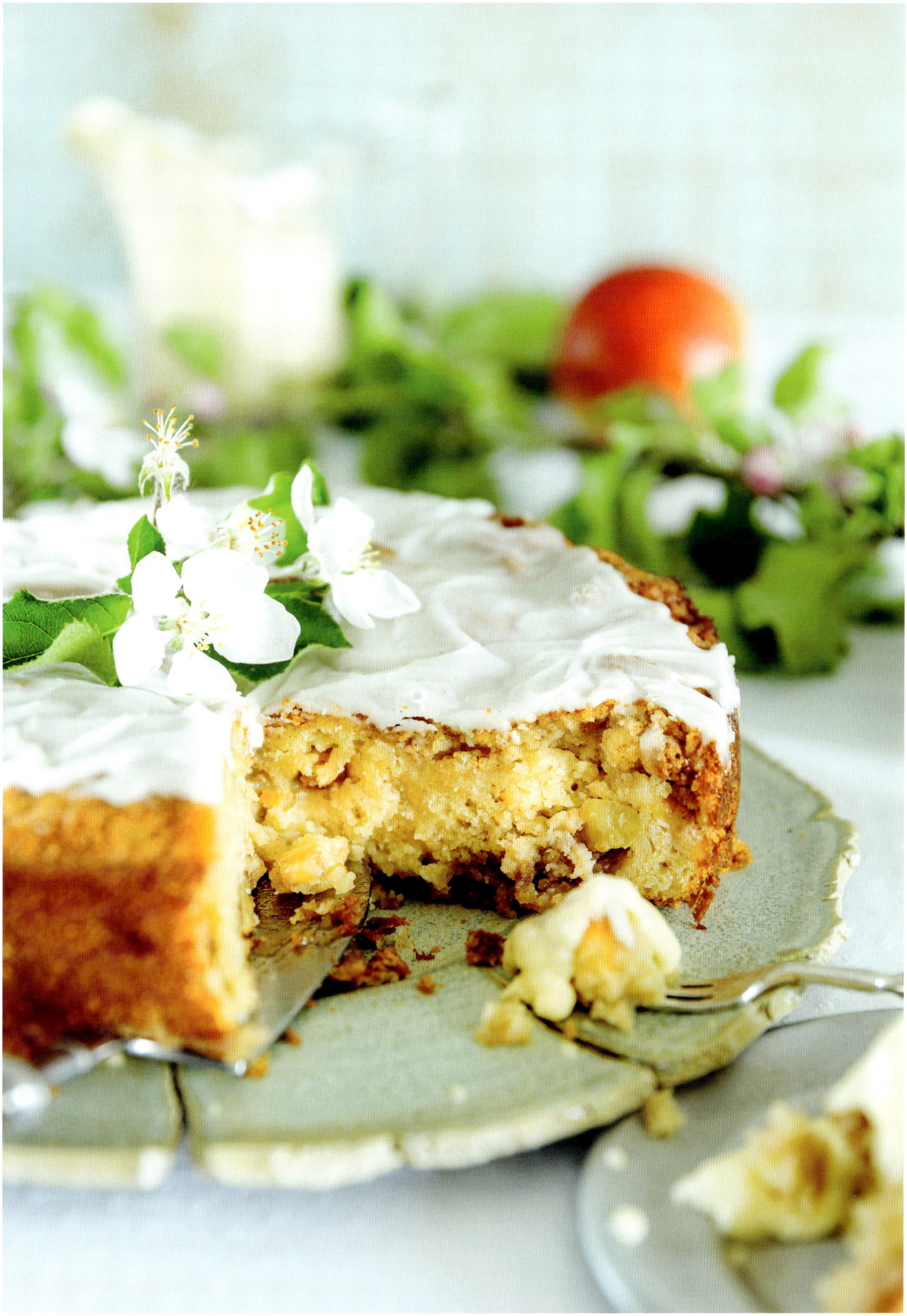

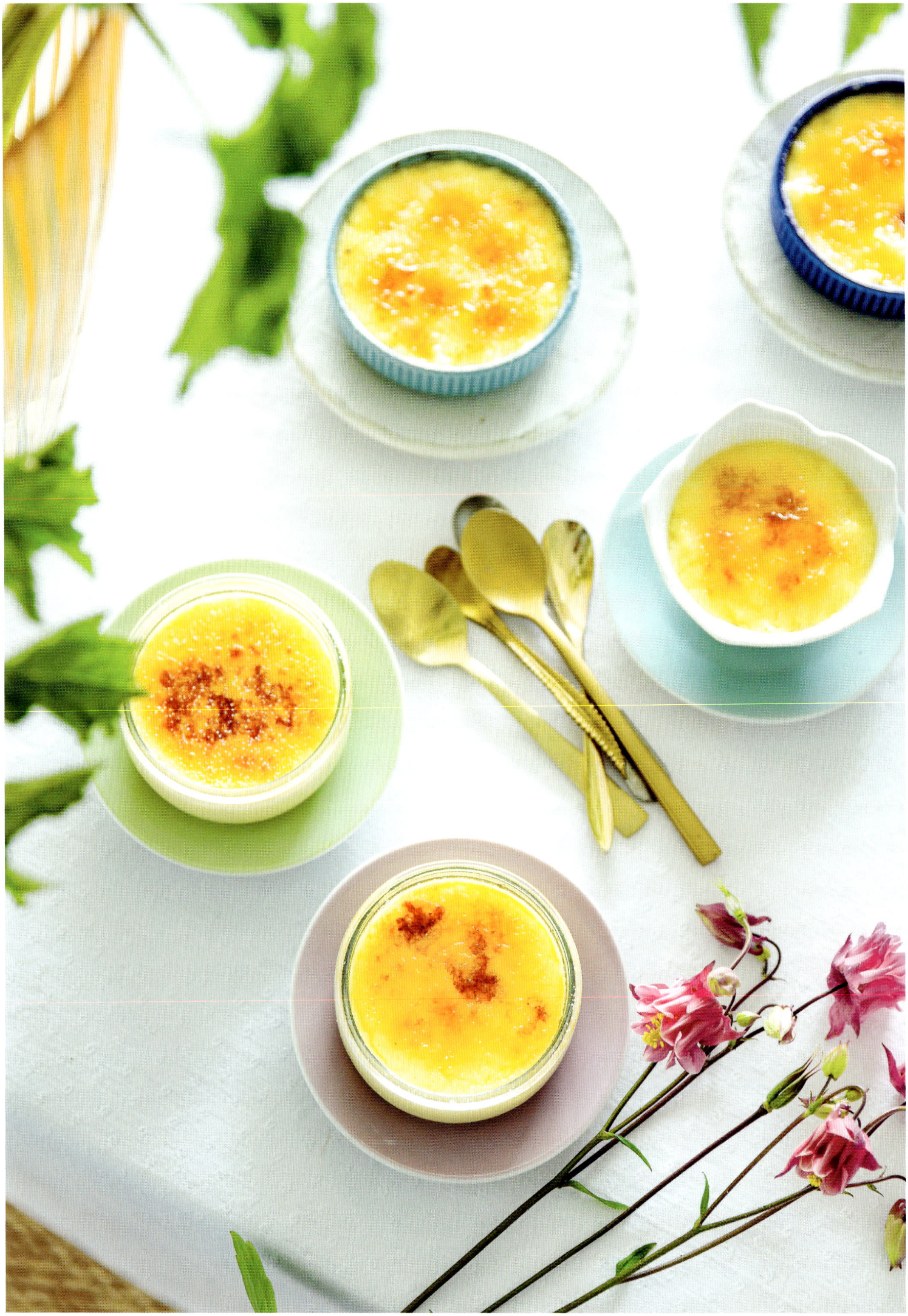

Coconut Crème Brûlée

With its perfectly caramelised sugar topping (and decadent custard with a tropical twist), this coconut crème brûlée is very beautiful to look at. Crack the sweet glaze, and it is also incredibly light and wonderfully smooth. I often serve it for large numbers – everyone can enjoy their own individual dessert, so it's easy to do the maths!

—

Serves 6–8
8 egg yolks
120g caster sugar
1 vanilla pod, split in half and seeds scraped out
400ml cream
400ml coconut milk

Preheat the oven to 110°C (225°F/Gas Mark ¼). Place the egg yolks in a large bowl with 125g of the sugar and the vanilla seeds. Whisk for about 5 minutes, until the mixture is pale and fluffy and holds the trail of a figure 8.

Meanwhile, place the cream and coconut milk in a pan with the scraped-out vanilla pod, and simmer gently until the mixture just comes to the boil. Remove the vanilla pod, then slowly pour the hot cream into the yolk mixture, whisking continuously. Pass through a sieve into a clean bowl.

Using a ladle, divide the mixture into 8 x 125ml small dishes or ramekins set in a baking tin filled with enough boiling water to come halfway up the sides of the ramekins (this is called a bain-marie). Bake in the oven for 1 hour, until just set but still with a slight wobble in the middle. Remove from the oven and leave in the bain-marie for another 30 minutes before removing and allowing to cool completely. Transfer to the fridge and allow to set for at least 6 hours, or preferably overnight.

To finish the brûlées, sprinkle each one with about 2 teaspoons of sugar in an even layer and use a blow torch to melt and glaze the sugar until caramelised. Arrange on plates.

SERVE AFTER...
This delicately flavoured pudding is dreamy after any spicy dinner, such as **Butter Chicken** (p.85) with **Pilau Rice** (p.131).

Coole Swan Chocolate Truffles

This features on the petits fours section in our restaurant, and we tend to change the flavour on a weekly basis, much to the delight of our regular customers. If you too would like to experiment with different flavours, try adding two tablespoons of Cointreau or crème de menthe instead of Coole Swan.

—

Makes about 30

125ml cream
50g butter, diced
250g plain chocolate, broken into squares (at least 70% cocoa solids)
4 tbsp Coole Swan Irish cream liqueur

For the coating
225g plain chocolate, broken into squares (at least 70% cocoa solids)
cocoa powder, for dusting

Place the cream in a pan and bring to the boil. Reduce the heat, then whisk in the butter and then the chocolate until smooth and melted. Stir in the Coole Swan and transfer to a bowl. Cover with cling film and chill for 3–4 hours or overnight. Whisk occasionally to prevent it from separating.

When the mixture is cold and set, use a melon baller to scoop it into 1.75cm balls. Make sure to dip the melon baller in hot water to get perfectly shaped truffles. Arrange the truffles on a baking sheet lined with parchment paper.

To make the coating, melt the chocolate in a heatproof bowl set over a pan of simmering water or in the microwave. Leave to cool a little, then dip the truffles in the melted chocolate and quickly roll in the cocoa powder. Chill to set.

To serve, arrange the truffles on a plate to hand around to your guests while they are enjoying their coffee. These truffles will keep well in an airtight container in the fridge for up to 1 week. They can also be frozen very successfully, but they should always be left at room temperature to thaw out completely.

SERVE AFTER ...
It always pays to have a load of these tucked away in the fridge! They are a perfect mouthful when you fancy something sweet to finish a meal, especially alongside a strong espresso.

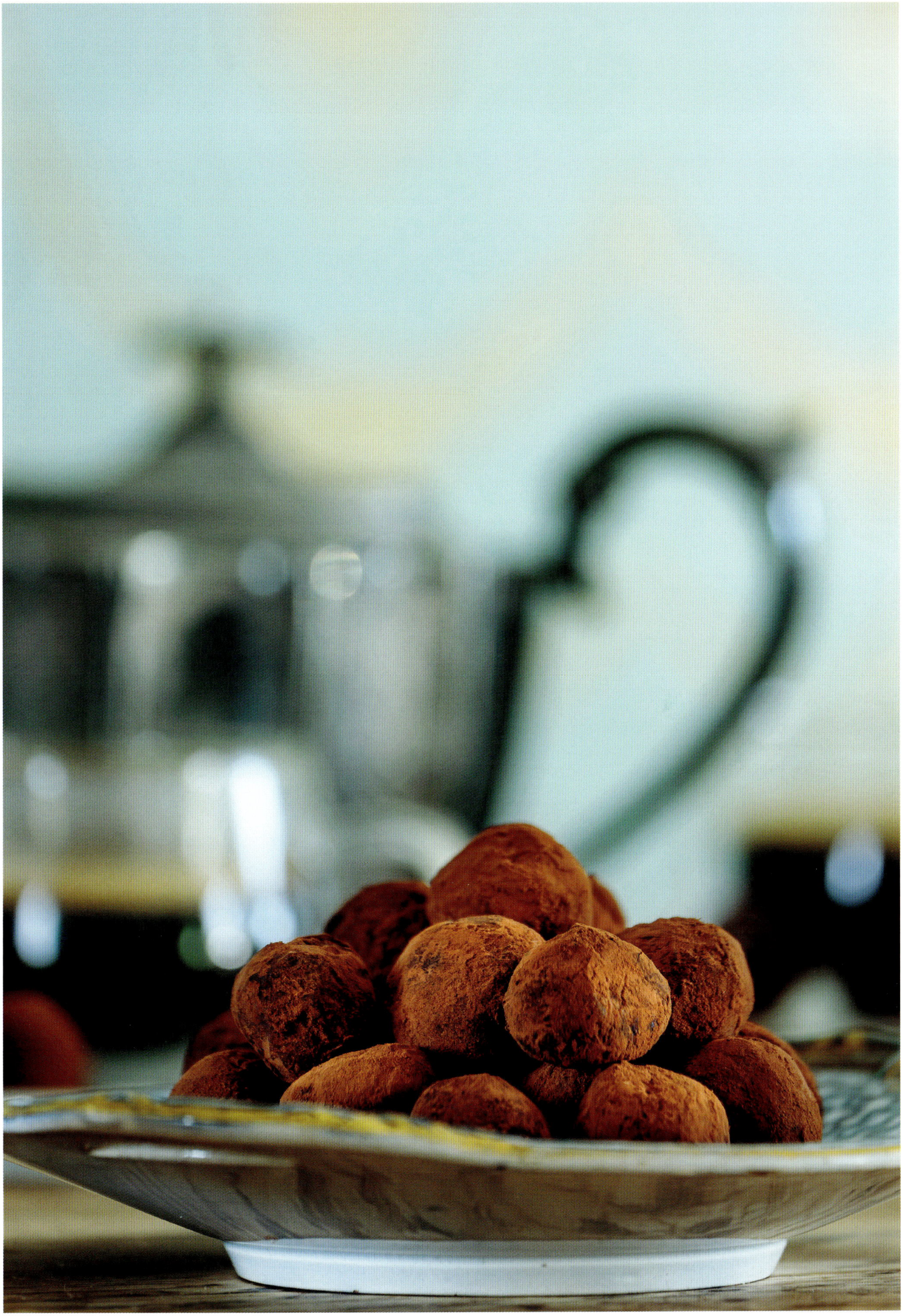

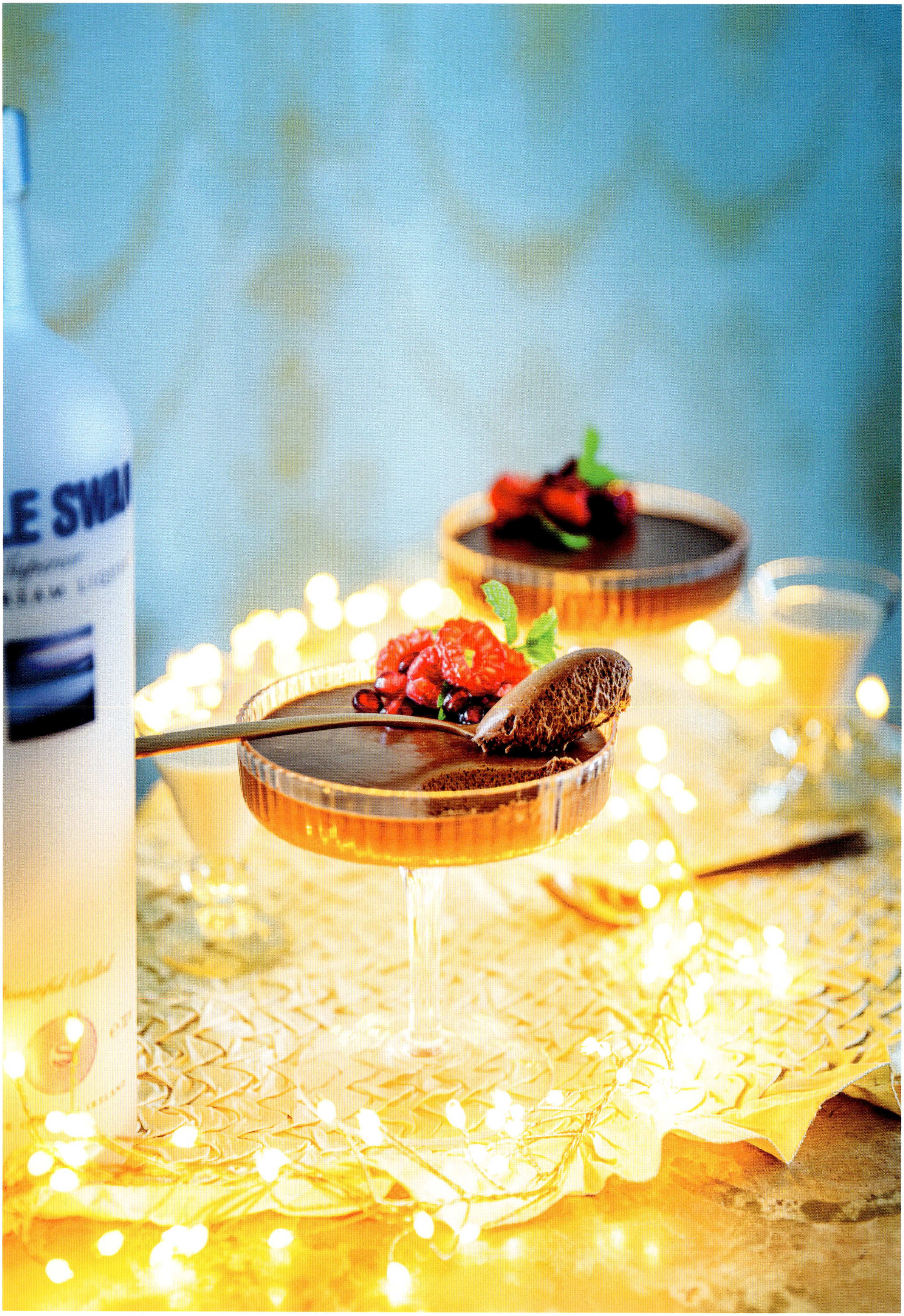

Chocolate Mousse Cups

Who doesn't like a good chocolate mousse? Light yet delicious, this classic can be made in minutes with just a few ingredients – and it's perfect for easy entertaining after a long, luxurious meal. Top with whipped cream and chocolate shavings or, for a pretty spectacle, with summer berries and fresh mint leaves.

—

Serves 4

225g plain chocolate, broken into squares (minimum 55% cocoa solids)
3 eggs
2 tbsp Coole Swan Irish cream liqueur (or use Grand Marnier, whiskey, Malibu or crème de menthe)
300ml cream
a selection of berries (such as raspberries, strawberries and pomegranate seeds), to decorate
a few sprigs of mint, to decorate

Melt the chocolate in a heatproof bowl set over a pan of simmering water. Whisk the eggs with the liqueur in a separate bowl over a pan of simmering water until double in size. It is very important to ensure the water does not boil or it will cook the eggs. Fold the melted chocolate into the egg mixture, then leave to cool for 5 minutes.

Meanwhile, whisk the cream in a bowl, fold into the chocolate mixture, then put into stemmed glasses or teacups using a spatula. Cover with cling film and refrigerate for 2–3 hours or overnight. Spoon over the berries and add a sprig of mint to serve.

SERVE WITH ...
This rich, intensely chocolatey dessert not only looks great in glasses but also vintage teacups. It can also be scooped into quenelles. Sometimes I'll serve it with a couple of thin buttery biscuits for dipping, or perhaps an ice-cold glass of the liqueur I've used to flavour the mousse.

Warm Blondies with Sea Salt Toffee Sauce

When baked, these blondies should still have some gooeyness, so don't be tempted to leave them in the oven for any extra time, or they will turn into cake. I just love them warm, with a shop-bought sea salt toffee sauce and some ice cream that immediately starts to melt a little in the bowl.

—

Serves 6–9
150g butter
150g white chocolate, roughly chopped
3 eggs, plus 2 egg yolks
150g light brown sugar
½ tsp vanilla extract
4 tbsp self-raising flour
pinch of sea salt flakes
100g pecan nuts, chopped
sea salt toffee sauce and ice cream, to serve

Preheat the oven to 190°C (375°F/Gas Mark 5) and line a 20cm square baking tin with parchment paper. Melt the butter in a pan over a low heat or in the microwave. Add the white chocolate, then remove it from the heat and leave the white chocolate to melt.

Put the eggs, egg yolks, sugar and vanilla in a bowl, and whisk with an electric beater until pale and frothy. Add the flour and salt, then gently beat this all together. Then, using a spatula, fold in the white-chocolate-and-butter mixture with the pecan nuts until well combined. Transfer to the prepared tin.

Bake for 22–25 minutes until the blondies are nicely crusted. Once baked, remove from the oven and leave to cool down a little before cutting into 6–9 even-sized squares – they will crack as you cut them. Serve warm in bowls with plenty of the sea salt toffee sauce and a scoop of ice cream.

SERVE AFTER …
These blondies, laced with buttery pecan nuts, are ideal for a midweek supper when something sweet is needed to save the day.

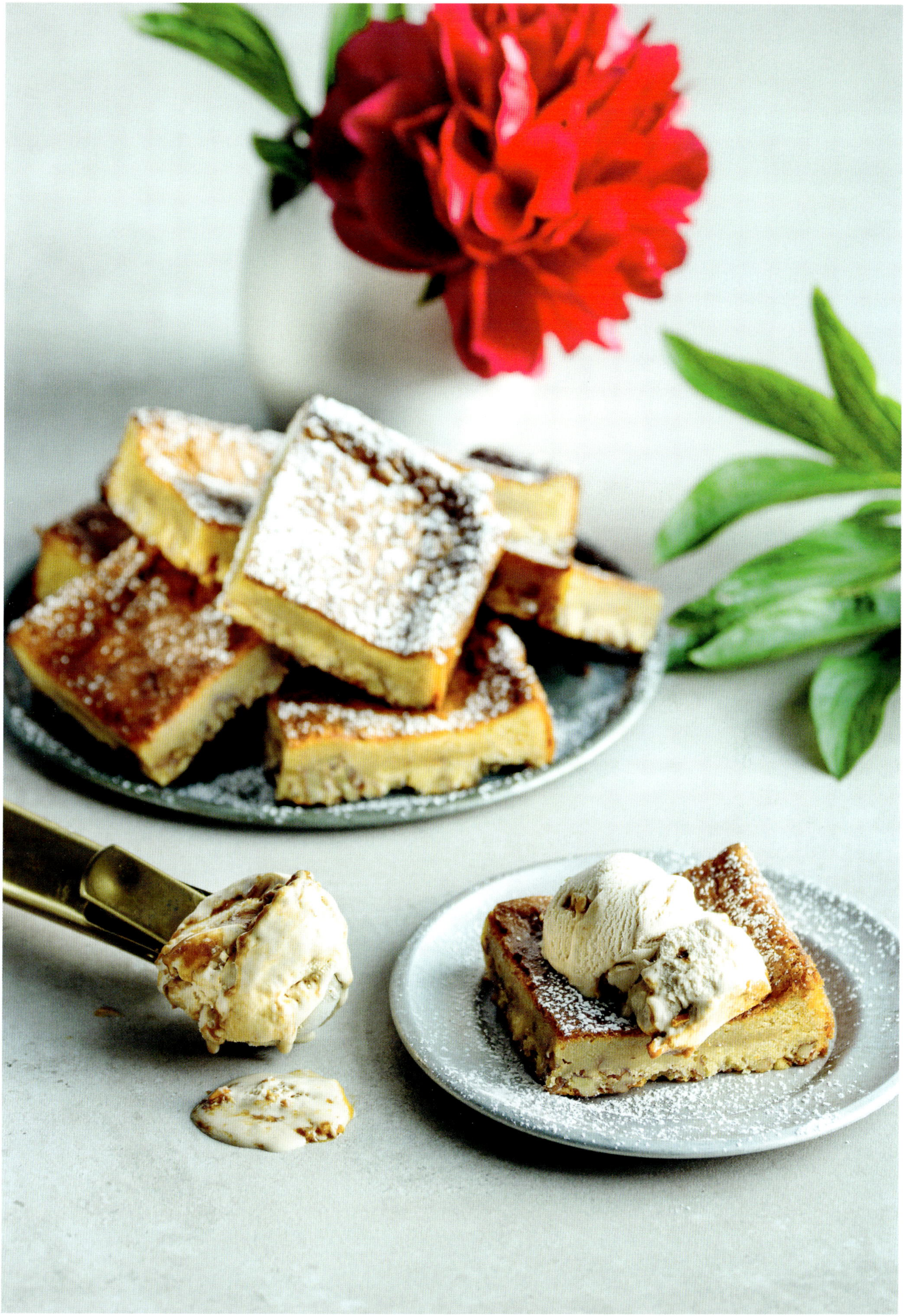

Walnut & Espresso Slice

Sweet coffee icing and the slightly bitter crunch of the walnuts makes for a lovely combination. This wonderfully light sponge brings back memories of visiting relatives as a child – all the adults would be chatting away, while I eyed up the coffee cake sitting on the table, next to the tray of sandwiches and a pot of tea ...

—

Serves 6–8
180g butter, softened
50g crème fraîche
180g soft light brown sugar
3 medium eggs
180g wholemeal or regular self-raising flour
½ tsp baking powder
2 tsp instant coffee mixed with 2 tsp hot water and left to cool
120g shelled walnuts, chopped

For the coffee buttercream
100g butter, softened
200g icing sugar
1 tsp instant coffee mixed with 1 tsp hot water and left to cool

Preheat the oven to 180°C (350°F/Gas Mark 4). Line a 20cm square tin with baking parchment. Put the butter and crème fraîche into a bowl, add the sugar, then cream them together using an electric mixer until light and fluffy. Beat in 2 of the eggs with half of the flour and the baking powder.

Add the other egg with the rest of the flour and the coffee mixture, and continue to beat until well combined, then fold in 80g of the walnuts. Tip this mixture into the prepared tin and smooth the top down with the back of a spoon. Bake for 30–35 minutes; to test if it is cooked, insert a skewer into the centre – it should come out clean. Leave to cool down completely in the tin.

Once the traybake has cooled down, make the coffee buttercream. Put the butter in a bowl and add the icing sugar, then beat it well until light and fluffy. Add the coffee mixture and beat again until smooth. Using a palette knife, spread the icing all over the traybake. Sprinkle the remaining walnuts on top and cut into slices to serve.

SERVE WITH ...
Sometimes I'll cut this into bite-sized pieces to serve with coffee if friends or family pop in during the day. The slices also would look lovely on a plate with some **Coole Swan Chocolate Truffles** (p.194) or served as petits fours after a dinner party.

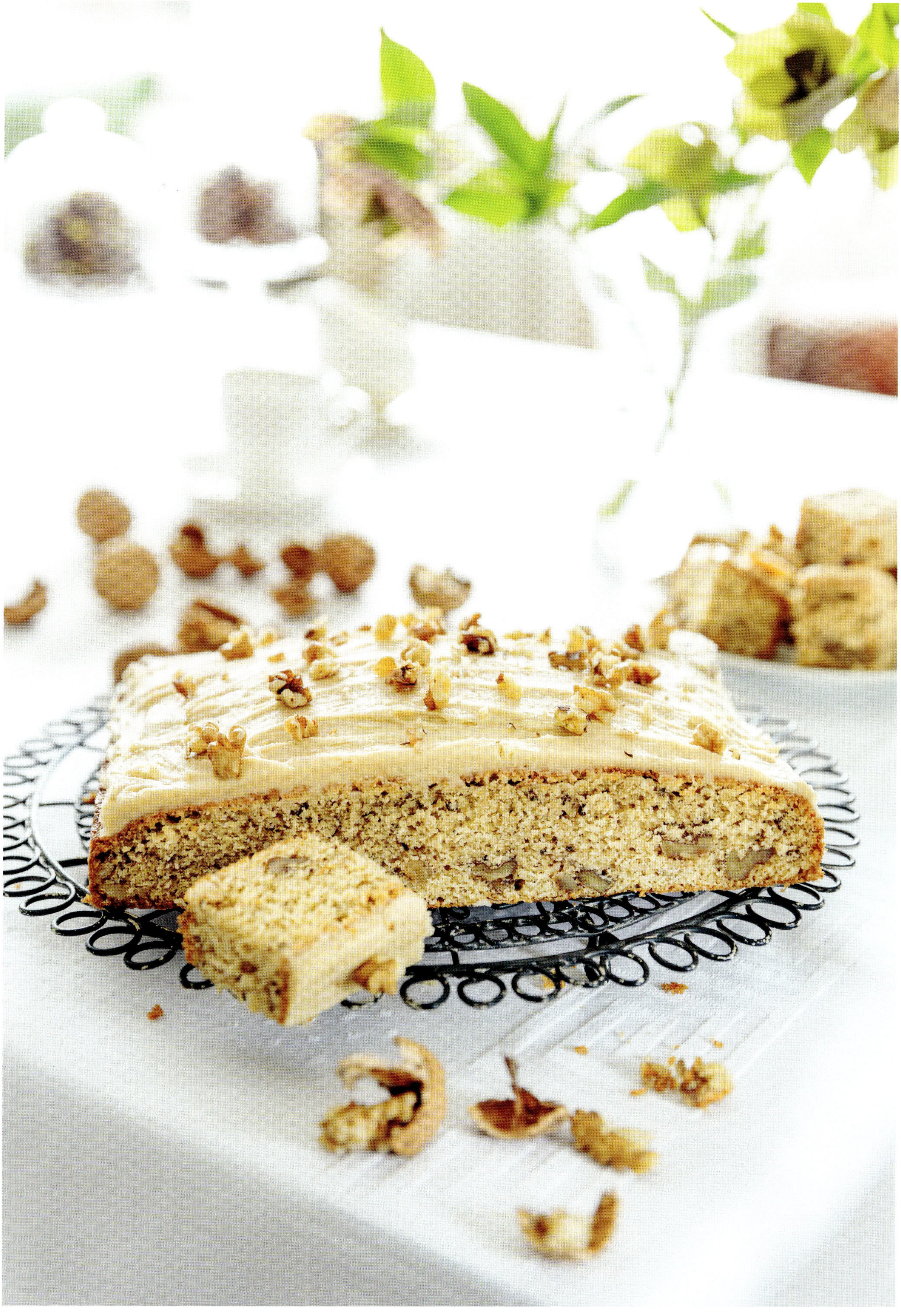

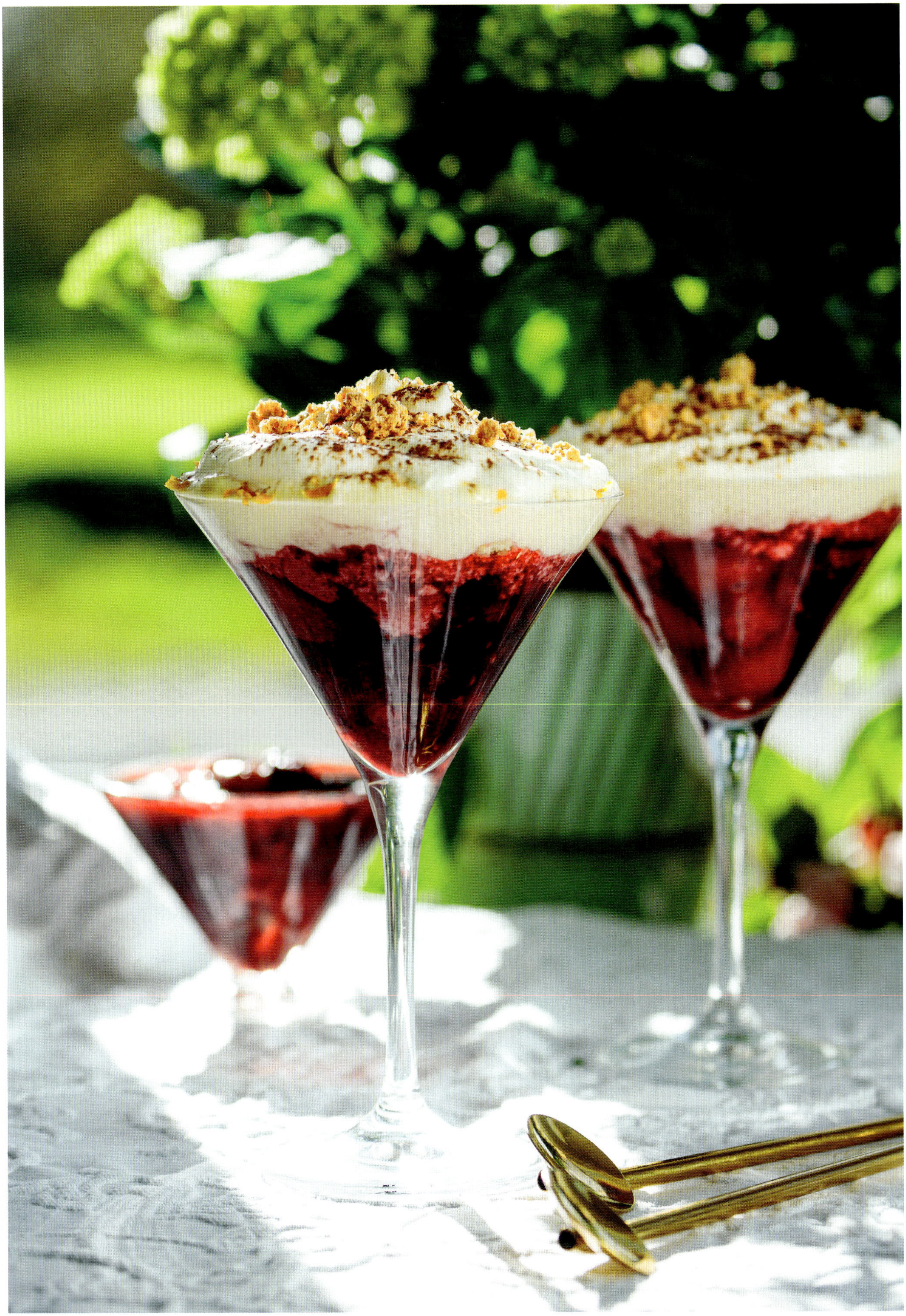

Summer Fruit Trifle

Summer in a glass! This is one of my favourite desserts, and I've been making it for as long as I can remember. My mum, Vera, always made a fabulous traditional Sherry trifle when we were growing up, and this variation has all the classic elements, but it takes no time at all to whip up.

—

Serves 4–6

300ml raspberry & Wexford rhubarb cordial
1 cinnamon stick
300g mixed summer berries (such as strawberries, blackberries, blueberries and raspberries)
1 tsp vanilla extract
150ml cream
finely grated rind of 1 orange
450g carton fresh vanilla bean custard
195g packet shortbread biscuits
cocoa powder, to dust
2–3 amaretti biscuits

Put the cordial into a pan with the cinnamon stick. Bring to the boil, then reduce the heat and simmer for 15 minutes until reduced by half and slightly thickened. Place the mixed berries in a heatproof bowl and pour over the cordial mixture, and add the vanilla. Stir to combine and leave to cool.

Remove the cinnamon stick from the marinated berries, and spoon into Martini glasses, reserving the liquid. Whip the cream in a bowl until it forms soft peaks and set aside until needed. In a separate bowl, fold the orange rind into the custard until evenly combined.

Crumble the shortbread biscuits over the marinated berries, then pour over a little of the reserved liquid. Spoon over the custard mixture and dollop or pipe the whipped cream on top. Chill for 1 hour, then add a light dusting of cocoa powder and crumble the amaretti biscuits on top to serve. These will keep in the fridge covered with cling film for up to 3 days.

SERVE AFTER ...
A celebration of summer berries, this trifle looks very fancy served in Martini glasses, and it can be made in the morning, so all you need to do at the last minute is a little decorating. It's a lovely thing in which to get the kids involved for the next generation of memories. With its orange custard and shortbread-biscuit crunch, it is the perfect end to a Sunday roast or barbecue.

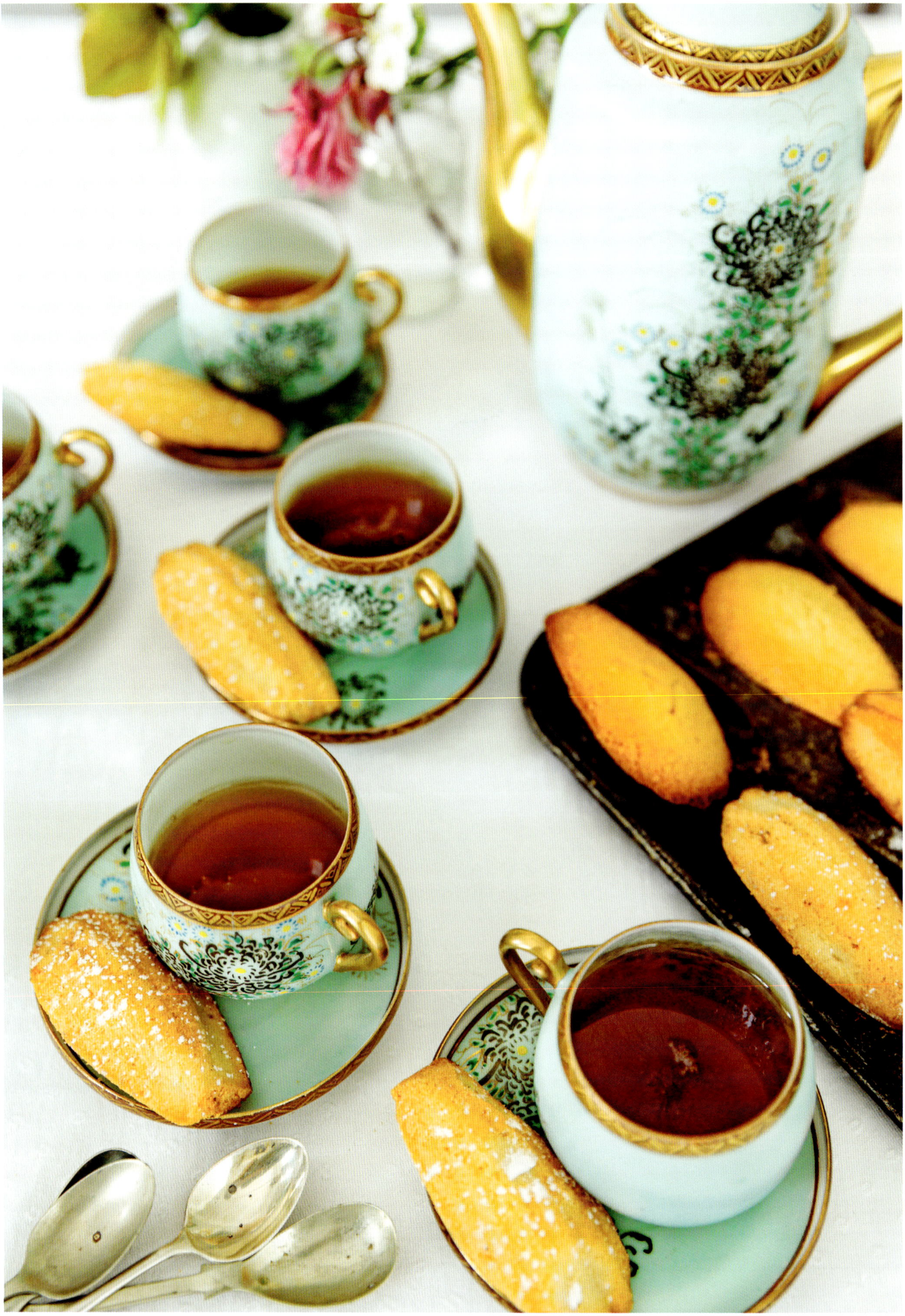

Brown Butter Madeleines

I have my good friend Léa Linster to thank for this recipe. Léa is the only female chef to win the Bocuse d'Or (a competition to crown the best chef in the world), and people travel from far and wide to taste her madeleines. Of course, they can also be made as mini cupcakes if you don't have the special tins.

—

Makes 24

160g butter, plus extra melted for greasing
50g plain flour, plus extra for dusting
70g ground almonds
160g icing sugar, plus extra for dusting
5 egg whites (at room temperature)

Lightly grease 2 x 12-shell madeleine trays or mini cupcake tins with melted butter, then dust with flour, shaking off any excess. Place in the fridge for at least 2 hours, but overnight is best.

Preheat the oven to 180°C (350°F/Gas Mark 4). Place the butter in a small pan and allow to brown slightly. Remove from the heat and leave to cool, but not set.

Place the flour, ground almonds and icing sugar into a large bowl. Add the egg whites and cooled brown butter. Using an electric mixer, beat until well combined and smooth. Spoon the mixture into a piping bag, then pipe into the prepared madeleine trays, being careful not to overfill. Bake for 12 minutes until well risen, golden and springy to the touch.

Remove the madeleines from the oven. Leave to rest in the tray for 2 minutes, then ease out of the tray with a spoon and leave to cool slightly on a wire rack. To serve, dust with a little icing sugar, arrange on plates and enjoy with a cup of tea or coffee.

SERVE WITH ...

Madeleines don't keep well, so they should be eaten on the day they are made. However, the raw mixture will keep in the fridge for one week, so you can make them as you need them. The final course after a rich meal like **Greek Beef & Macaroni Pie** (p.79) should be light and only a couple of mouthfuls, making these madeleines a great option.

Tiramisu

The name of this simple dessert comes from the Italian tirami su, *meaning 'pick me up' (or 'cheer me up'). Tiramisu has been subjected to many variations over the years, but this is the original recipe and – in my opinion – the best! This is a dessert that actually benefits from being made ahead, allowing the lovely flavours to mingle. As a result, it is perfect for a large gathering.*

—

Serves 8–10
4 large eggs
100g caster sugar
250g mascarpone cheese
250ml cream
250ml freshly brewed strong espresso coffee (left to cool completely)
150ml Tia Maria or Kahlúa liqueur
40 sponge fingers
50g bar plain chocolate
2 tsp cocoa powder

Separate the eggs, putting the yolks in one bowl with 80g of the sugar, and the egg whites in another. Using an electric beater, whisk the egg yolks and sugar until pale and creamy, then mix in the mascarpone cheese until well combined. Whip the cream in a separate bowl until soft peaks form, then fold into the egg yolk and mascarpone mixture. Using spotlessly clean beaters, whisk the egg whites with 20g of sugar until soft peaks form, then fold this into the mascarpone cream. Spoon a third of this mixture into a suitable dish that is at least 2cm deep.

Pour the coffee into a shallow dish and stir in the Tia Maria or Kahlúa. Dip in enough of the sponge fingers to make an even layer on top of the mascarpone mixture. Only dip the sponge fingers in as you go along, so they don't soak for too long and become difficult to handle. Cover the layer of soaked sponge fingers with another third of the mascarpone mixture, then grate most of the chocolate bar on top using the coarse side of a grater. Add another layer with the rest of the soaked sponge fingers, then spoon over the remaining mascarpone mixture and spread evenly with a back of a spoon. Cover with cling film and chill overnight to allow the flavours to develop and the dessert to settle.

To serve, give the tiramisu a good dusting of cocoa powder, then grate over the rest of the chocolate. Place in the middle of the table so that everyone can help themselves.

SERVE AFTER ...
A go-to dessert if you like spoiling your guests after a long Italian-inspired meal. Tiramisu is ideal for the warmer months since it can be made well in advance and kept in the fridge until needed.

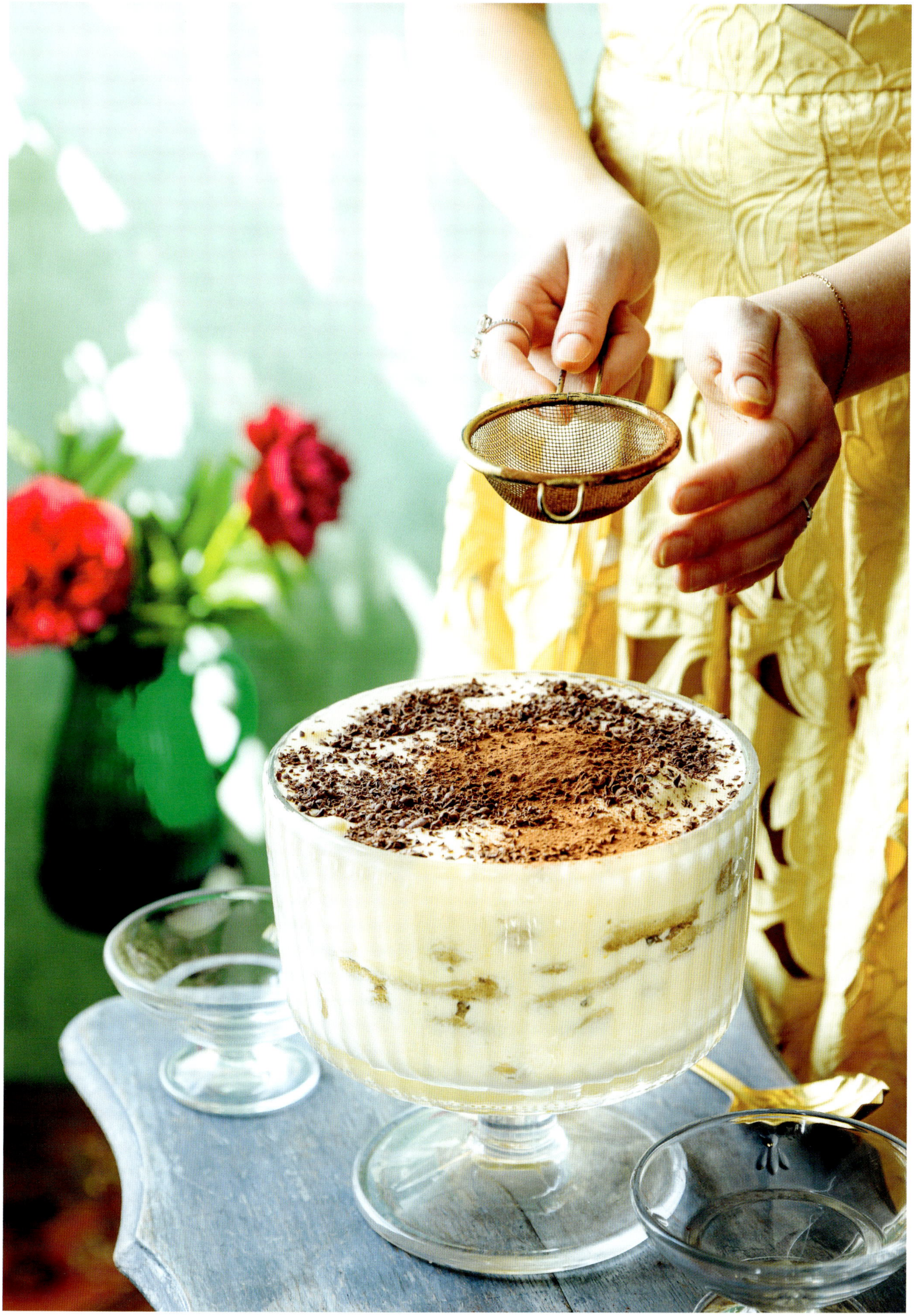

Victoria Sponge with Rhubarb, Lemon Curd & Cream

Buttery, light sponge with tart rhubarb jam, whipped cream and a layer of lip-smacking lemon curd ... Not only is this very simple to make, it is also quite possibly one of the best cakes there is! My version tinkers only a little with the traditional recipe: I use some rhubarb yogurt, which creates the most subtle flavour through the sponge and ensures a moist bake, while reducing the fat content.

—

Serves 8–10

150g butter, plus extra for greasing (at room temperature)
75g rhubarb yogurt
225g caster sugar
1 tsp vanilla extract
4 large eggs, at room temperature
225g self-raising flour
½ tsp sea salt
icing sugar, to dust

For the filling
300g rhubarb, cut into small chunks
275g caster sugar
300ml cream
4 tbsp Sicilian lemon curd

Preheat the oven to 180°C (350°F/Gas Mark 4). Lightly grease 2 x 20cm sandwich tins with butter and line with parchment paper.

Cream the butter, yogurt, sugar and vanilla together until well mixed. Add the eggs and beat in – don't worry if they curdle: all will be fine. Sift over the flour and salt, and fold in to make a smooth cake batter.

Divide the batter between the prepared cake tins and bake for 20–25 minutes until a skewer inserted into the centre comes out clean. Remove from the oven and leave to cool in the tins for 5 minutes, then turn out on to wire racks and leave to cool completely.

To make the filling, put the rhubarb and sugar into a pan with 1 tablespoon of water. Bring to the boil, stirring, then reduce to a simmer and cook down gently for about 15 minutes until thickened and jam-like, stirring frequently. Pour into a bowl and leave to cool completely. Whip the cream in a bowl to soft peaks. Place one of the cooled cakes on a cake stand and spread over the rhubarb jam. Dollop over the cream. Spread the second cake with the lemon curd and place on top of the cream. Dust with icing sugar and eat within a couple of hours.

SERVE AFTER ...
Everyone loves a Victoria sponge, which is also a perfect birthday cake. I don't advise making it in advance, as it stales quickly – this is best enjoyed within a few hours of baking. You can't go wrong with what you serve before this.

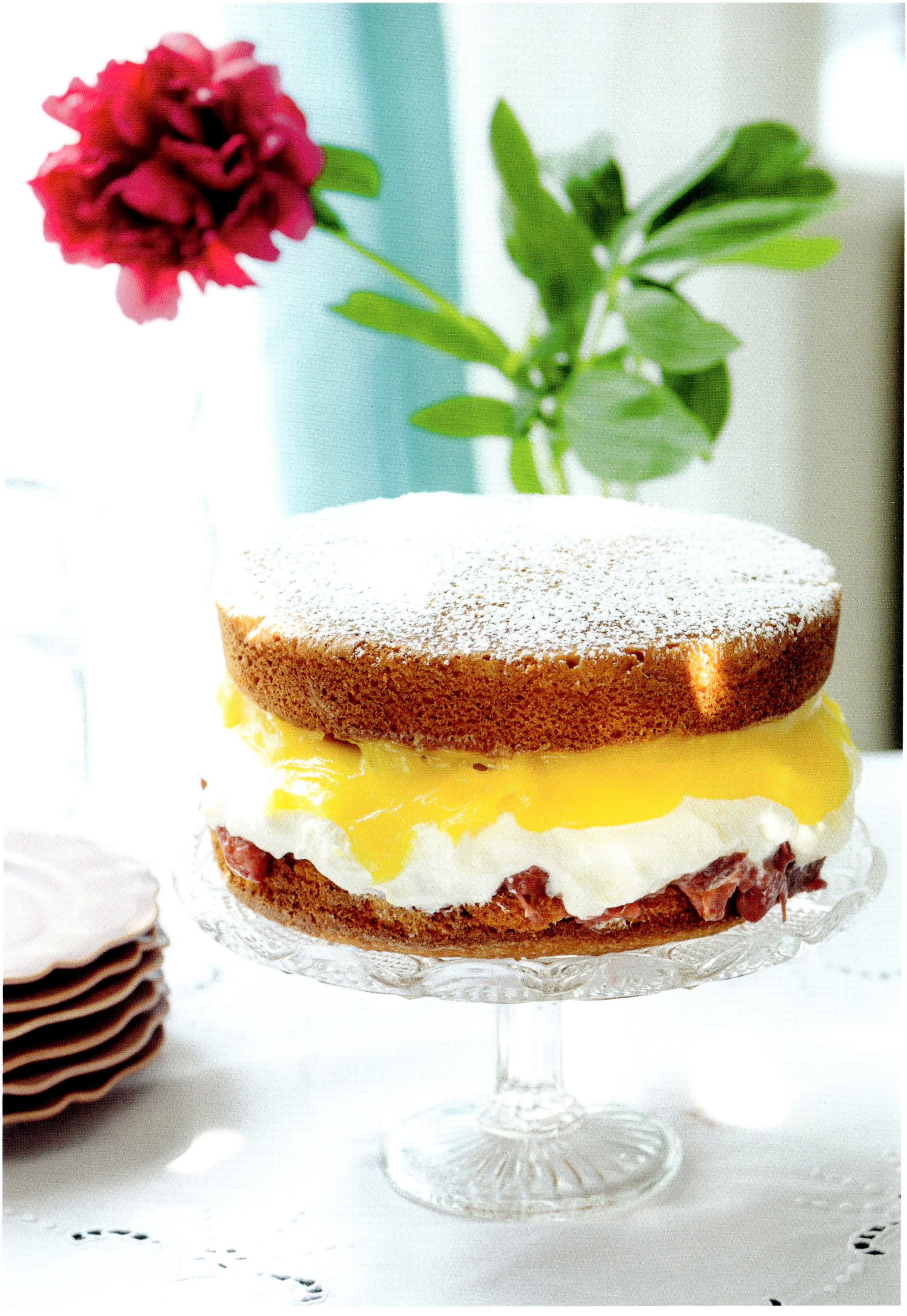

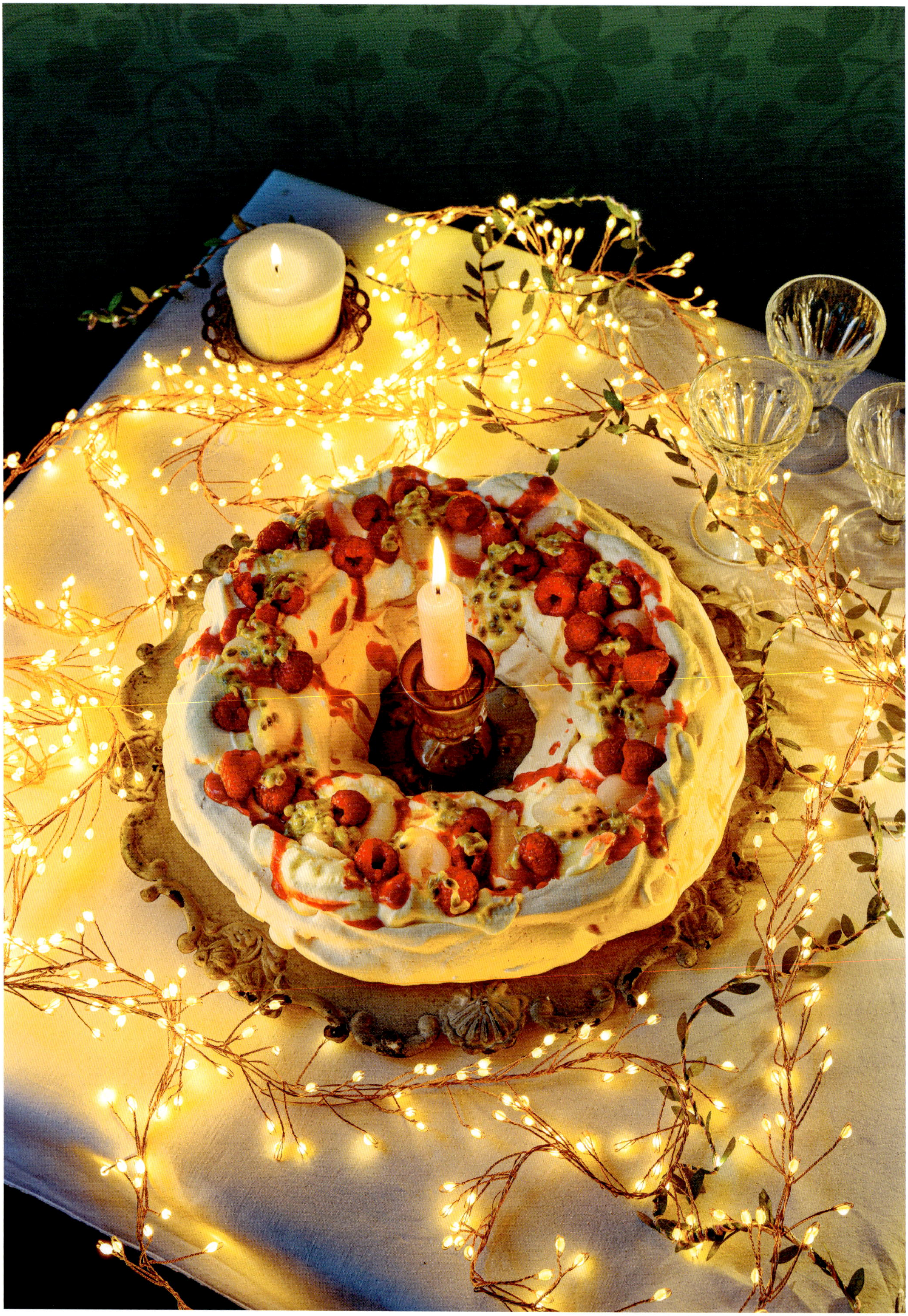

Pavlova Wreath with Exotic Fruit

Cakes are always the sweet option of choice for birthdays and anniversaries. However, I would like to introduce to you the Pavlova Wreath – it is very pretty and easy to make, and it delivers an incredible flavour. As always, feel free to use your own favourite combination of flavours to personalise it. Be sure to produce it with a flourish for that 'ta-da' moment!

—

Serves 10–12
For the meringue
5 egg whites
250g caster sugar
50g icing sugar
2 tsp cornflour

For the raspberry sauce
200g raspberries
2 tbsp icing sugar
1 tbsp lime juice
2 tsp cornflour or arrowroot

For the crème Chantilly
200ml cream (well chilled)
1 tsp vanilla extract
40g icing sugar

To decorate
200g raspberries
400g tin lychees, well drained and cut in half
2 passion fruit, halved and seeds scooped out

Preheat the oven to 140°C (275°F/Gas Mark 1). Put the egg whites into the bowl of a stand mixer. Turn on to a medium speed and whisk until they begin to go frothy and hold their shape a little. Mix the caster and icing sugar together, then add about one third to the eggs in a steady stream, whisking all the time on medium to high. The mixture will now begin to thicken a little. Make sure that all the sugar has dissolved before you add any more. Add the next third and repeat the process, whisking it all up well. Then add the final third of the sugar. Whisk on high now, since the egg mixture will be much more stable. Keep whisking until you reach the stiff-peak stage. Add the cornflour and fold in with a spoon.

Draw a 25cm circle on a piece of parchment paper and use it to line a large baking sheet, then draw a 10cm circle in the middle. This is your stencil. Put dollops of the meringue mixture on to the wreath stencil, keeping it within the edges. Bake for 55–60 minutes until the meringue has just a little colour. Remove it from the oven and leave to cool.

Meanwhile, make the raspberry sauce. Blitz the raspberries in a food processor with the icing sugar and lime juice, then pass through a sieve into a small pan using a plastic spatula. Mix the cornflour or arrowroot with one tablespoon of water until smooth, then add this to the raspberries. Bring to the boil over medium to high heat, then simmer gently for a few minutes until thickened, stirring occasionally. Set aside to cool.

For the crème Chantilly, whisk up the cream, vanilla and sugar in a bowl until it is just beginning to hold soft peaks. Cover with cling film and chill until needed.

Carefully slide your Pavlova wreath on to a large, flat serving plate. Place dollops of the crème Chantilly around the top of the wreath, then drizzle over some of the raspberry sauce; the rest can be served in a jug at the table. Decorate the wreath with the raspberries, lychees and passion fruit pulp. Serve straight away.

Peanut Butter Fudge with Goji Berries & Pistachios

This chewy fudge is so pretty and delicious, it's hard to believe it contains no refined sugar or dairy – indeed, it is actually packed full of good nutrients and antioxidants. It is perfect for vegans and anyone following a gluten-free diet. Cacao is the raw unadulterated form of the chocolate bean, whereas cocoa powder has been heat-treated and roasted to give it a longer shelf life.

—

Serves 10–20

4 tbsp extra virgin coconut oil
380g crunchy peanut butter
120g date or maple syrup
4 tbsp raw cacao powder
100g ground almonds
2 tsp vanilla extract
1 tsp sea salt flakes
100g pistachio nuts
100g goji berries
50g raw cacao nibs

Melt the coconut oil in a pan over a low heat and pour into a bowl. Add the peanut butter, date or maple syrup, cacao powder, ground almonds, vanilla and half of the sea salt, then mix well to combine. Transfer to a parchment-lined 23cm square baking tin.

Put the pistachio nuts into a frying pan over a medium heat and lightly toast, tossing regularly. Tip on to a chopping board and leave to cool, then roughly chop and scatter over the fudge with the goji berries and cacao nibs. Sprinkle with the remaining salt and press everything down gently so that it sticks into the fudge.

Place in the fridge for a couple of hours to set. Cut into even-sized squares. Store in the fridge and use as required. This keeps well in the fridge for 1 week and can also be frozen – just be sure to keep it in a sealed container.

SERVE AFTER ...
This fudge is so delicious and is a great petit four combination with the **Coole Swan Truffles** (p.194). It is hard to eat just one square! It is an excellent option after a meze meal over which you've had the luxury to take your time, but really it goes with absolutely everything.

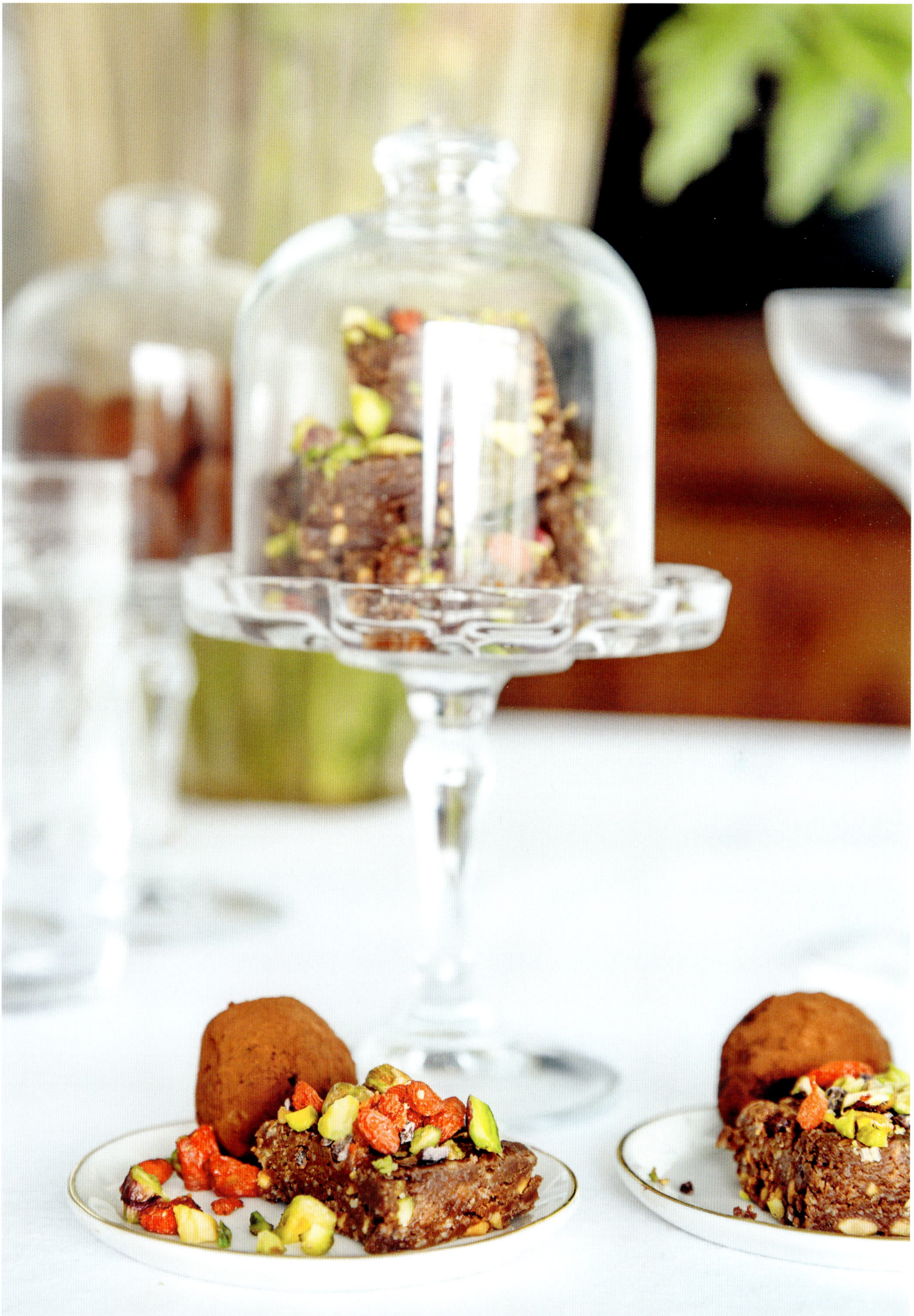

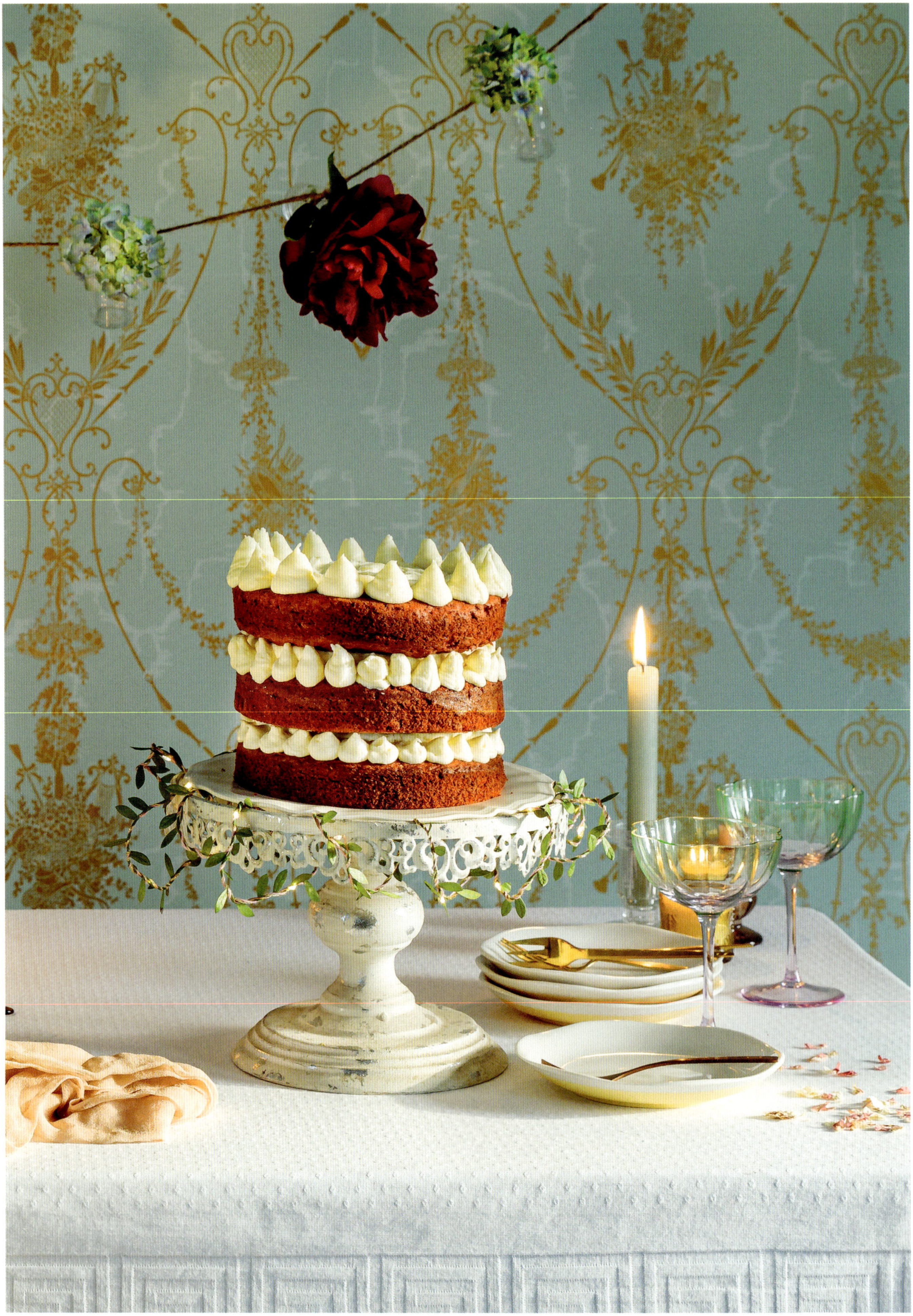

Red Velvet Cake

Smothered in cream cheese-frosting kisses, this cake is great at Christmas time. Just imagining it now immediately brings back joyful, celebratory family memories, such as Connor and Lucia, piping bag in hand, practising their craft. If the occasion demands, add some candles to complete the spectacle.

—

Serves 12–20
350g butter, softened
350g caster sugar
7 eggs, lightly beaten
325g self-raising flour, sifted
2 tbsp cocoa powder, sifted
1 tbsp red food colouring gel

For the frosting
175g butter, softened
400g icing sugar
175g soft cream cheese

Preheat the oven to 180°C (350°F/Gas Mark 4). Line the base of 3 x 20cm loose-bottomed cake tins with parchment paper. Cream together the butter and caster sugar until light and fluffy; this should take a good 5 minutes using a handheld electric beater, a bit less with a stand mixer and about twice that time if using a hand whisk. Add half of the eggs with half of the flour, and beat well together. Add the remaining eggs with the rest of the flour and the cocoa powder, and beat well until evenly combined. Add enough red food colouring until the sponge is the colour that you want it and beat again.

Divide the mixture evenly between the prepared cake tins and smooth the tops with the back of a spoon. Bake for 25–30 minutes or until a skewer inserted into the centre of each cake comes out clean.

To make the frosting, put the butter in a stand mixer or use a hand-held one and beat well until very soft and light. Add the icing sugar in four stages, beating well between each addition. Add the cream cheese and beat until just combined. Chill to firm up a little, so that you can pipe it. Once the cakes are cold, put them on the work surface, flat sides up. Fit a piping bag with a 1cm plain nozzle and half-fill it with the frosting, then pipe kisses over the three cakes and layer them up. Once the cakes are stacked together, carefully transfer the whole cake on to a serving plate or cake stand to serve.

SERVE WITH ...
A well-made cake is one of life's great pleasures, and this one is a real showstopper! I would also serve it as part of an afternoon tea with a nice selection of dainty sandwiches. The colours work brilliantly during the festive season, and no one will be able to resist a little slice.

Cookies & Cream Birthday Cake

The perfect cake for a birthday party – and you don't even need to turn on the oven for it. It looks and tastes so good, no one will believe it took so little effort to put together. And if you don't have the patience for intricate decorating, this is definitely the cake for you. It's super sweet, so you'll find that a little goes a long way.

—

Serves 12–14

sunflower oil, for greasing
600ml cream
250g mascarpone cheese
1 tsp vanilla extract
3 tbsp icing sugar
4 x 154g packets chocolate cream-filled sandwich cookies (such as Oreo)
200g plain chocolate, broken into squares

Lightly oil a 20cm springform cake tin and line with parchment paper. Whisk the cream, mascarpone, vanilla and icing sugar in a large bowl until smooth and soft peaks have formed.

Line the base of the tin with a single layer of the cookies – don't worry about the gaps: these will be filled up with the cream mixture. Spoon over a third of the cream mixture and smooth down with a spatula, spreading right to the edges. Set aside a handful of cookies for decoration, then repeat these layers twice with the rest of the cookies and the cream mixture. Cover with cling film and chill for at least 24 hours or up to 2 days.

Melt the chocolate in a heatproof bowl set over a pan of simmering water or in the microwave. Set aside for 10 minutes to cool down completely. Meanwhile, remove the cake from the tin, peel off the parchment paper and transfer to a flat plate. Once the chocolate has cooled down, drizzle it over the top, allowing it to dribble down the sides. Crumble over the reserved cookies and either serve immediately or chill for up to 2 hours before cutting into slices.

SERVE AFTER ...

A special cake brings excitement to any occasion, especially a birthday. This one never fails to impress at a tea party or after a formal dinner. Whatever the occasion, go all out and cover it with candles and sparklers, then dim the lights and get everyone singing as loud as they can.

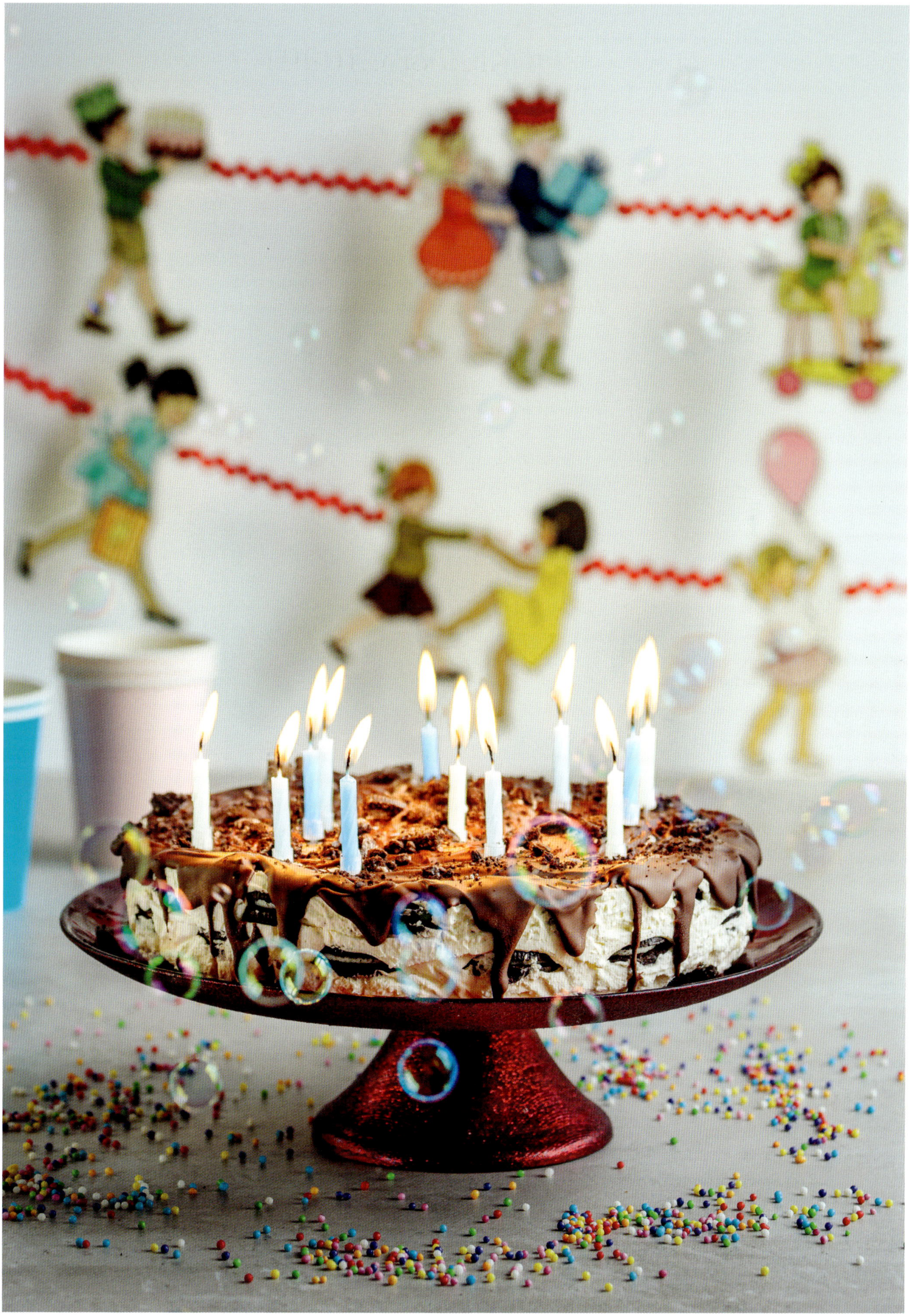

Cooking by numbers

For an intimate gathering

SMALL PLATES

Crispy Squid with Smoked Paprika Mayonnaise (p.8)
Carlingford Oysters with Shallot & Tarragon Dressing (p.11)
Mussels in Spiced Cream (p.12)
Beetroot & Hazelnut Salad with Whipped Goat's Cheese (p.16)
Spiced Cauliflower Bites (p.21)
Crispy Duck Confit Salad (p.23)
Crab Gratin (p.35)
Baba Ghanoush Salad (p.39)
Artichoke & Parma Ham Salad (p.40)
Tunisian Carrot Salad (p.42)
Spanish Tapas (p.45)
Sizzling Garlic & Chilli Prawns (p.46)
Fully Loaded Nachos (p.49)
Crispy Lamb-Stuffed Flatbreads (p.54)

BIG PLATES

Crispy Spatchcock Chicken with Lemon & Herbs (p.60)
Beef Ragu Lasagne (p.64)
Italian Stuffed Conchiglioni (p.67)
Fragrant Butterflied Lamb (p.69)
Cottage Pie (p.71)
Aubergines Stuffed with Onions, Tomatoes, Chilli & Parsley (p.76)
Aromatic Poached Salmon with Avocado & Cucumber Salad (p.83)
Slow-Cooked Onion & Goat's Cheese Tart (p.86)
Iberico Pork with Red Gooseberry Relish (p.92)
Macaroni Cheese with 'Nduja Crumbs (p.95)
Chateaubriand with Béarnaise Sauce (p.96)
Large Plaice with Garlic Butter Sauce (p.101)
Stuffed Beef Rolls with Tomato Ragu (p.102)
Hake with Red Pepper Sauce (p.104)
Spiced Roast Cauliflower (p.106)

SIDE PLATES

Homemade Flatbreads (p.114)
Chargrilled Tenderstem Broccoli with Caesar Dressing (p.117)
Green Couscous (p.118)
Chargrilled Aubergine with Tahini Dressing (p.120)
Frites (p.123)
Smashed Roast Potatoes (p.124)
Grilled Corn Salad (p.127)
Pilau Rice (p.131)
House Salad with Amelda's Dressing (p.132)
Lemon Roast Potato Wedges (p.137)
Braised Petits Pois with Bacon (p.138)
Potato Gratin (p.143)
Grilled Courgettes with Green Chimichurri Sauce (p.144)
Slow-Roast Tomatoes with Puy Lentils (p.148)
Creamy Butter Beans with Leeks (p.153)
Chargrilled Cabbage with Kimchi Dressing (p.155)
Steamed Asparagus with Hollandaise (p.156)
Tomato & Cucumber Salad with Whipped Feta (p.158)
Honey-Glazed Spiced Carrots with Pistachio & Dill (p.160)
Summer Slaw (p.163)
Apple & Fennel Salad (p.164)

SWEET THINGS

Affogato (p.168)
Moroccan Orange Salad with Pomegranate (p.170)
Aperol Spritz Sorbet (p.173)
Hot Chocolate with Cinnamon Churros (p.175)
Mango with Lime, Chilli & Star Anise (p.178)
Lemon Posset with Passion Fruit (p.180)
Vanilla Panna Cotta with Clarke's Strawberries (p.182)
Apple Mojito (p.185)
Coconut Crème Brûlée (p.193)
Chocolate Mousse Cups (p.197)
Summer Fruit Trifle (p.203)

For larger groups

SMALL PLATES
Caponata with Burrata (p.6)
Two Bruschettas: Tomato & Basil, Broad Bean (p.15)
Spanakopita (p.18)
Ham Hock Terrine (p.24)
Mushroom Risotto (p.31)
Sweet Potato & Cáis Óir Fritters (p.32)
Smoked Salmon Wreath (p.37)
Pickled Mixed Vegetables (p.53)

BIG PLATES
Sticky Damson Ham with Star Anise (p.58)
One-Pot Fish Pie (p.62)
Roast Picanha & Chargrilled Pepper Salad (p.72)
Greek Beef & Macaroni Pie (p.79)
Crispy Porchetta with Fennel & Herbs (p.80)
Chicken Shawarma (p.89)
Turkey Roulade with Maple Glaze (p.98)
Beef & Medjool Date Tagine (p.108)

SIDE PLATES
Focaccia with Rosemary & Sea Salt (p.112)
Pickled Red Onions (p.140)

SWEET THINGS
Lemon Curd Cheesecake (p.187)
Basque Cheesecake with Cherry Compote (p.188)
Cinnamon Swirl Apple Cake (p.190)
Coole Swan Chocolate Truffles (p.194)
Warm Blondies with Sea Salt Toffee Sauce (p.198)
Walnut & Espresso Slice (p.200)
Brown Butter Madeleines (p.205)
Tiramisu (p.206)
Victoria Sponge with Rhubarb, Lemon Curd & Cream (p.208)
Pavlova Wreath with Exotic Fruit (p.211)
Peanut Butter Fudge with Goji Berries & Pistachios (p.212)
Red Velvet Cake (p.215)
Cookies & Cream Birthday Cake (p.216)

Suggested menus for larger groups

Many of the recipes in this book can be sized up or down, and much of the preparation (and even cooking) can be done in advance of your guests arriving.

AN ITALIAN AFFAIR
Caponata with Burrata (p.6)
Beef Ragu Lasagne (p.62)
Focaccia with Rosemary & Sea Salt (p.112)
House Salad with Amelda's Dressing (p.132)
Tiramisu (p.206)

A CELEBRATION OF VEGETABLES
Spanakopita (p.18)
Aubergines Stuffed with Onions, Tomato, Chilli & Parsley (p.76)
Spiced Roast Cauliflower (p.106)
Green Couscous (p.118)
Peanut Butter Fudge with Goji Berries & Pistachios (p.212)

LONG LEISURELY LUNCH
Beetroot & Hazelnut Salad with Whipped Goat's Cheese (p.16)
Crispy Porchetta with Fennel & Herbs (p.80)
House Salad with Amelda's Dressing (p.132)
Lemon Roast Potato Wedges (p.137)
Affogato (p.168)

EASTER SUNDAY LUNCH
Crab Gratin (p.35)
Fragrant Butterflied Lamb (p.69)
House Salad with Amelda's Dressing (p.132)
Slow-Roast Tomatoes with Puy Lentils (p.148)
Lemon Posset with Passion Fruit (p.180)

CHRISTMAS DAY
Ham Hock Terrine (p.24)
Turkey Roulade with Maple Glaze (p.98)
Smashed Roast Potatoes (p.124)
Braised Petits Pois with Bacon (p.138)
Honey-Glazed Spiced Carrots with Pistachio & Dill (p.160)
Pavlova Wreath with Exotic Fruit (p.211)

BIRTHDAY CELEBRATION
Fully Loaded Nachos (p.49)
Tacos with Chicken Tinga (p.74)
Grilled Corn Salad (p.127)
Summer Slaw (p.163)
Cookies & Cream Birthday Cake (p.216)

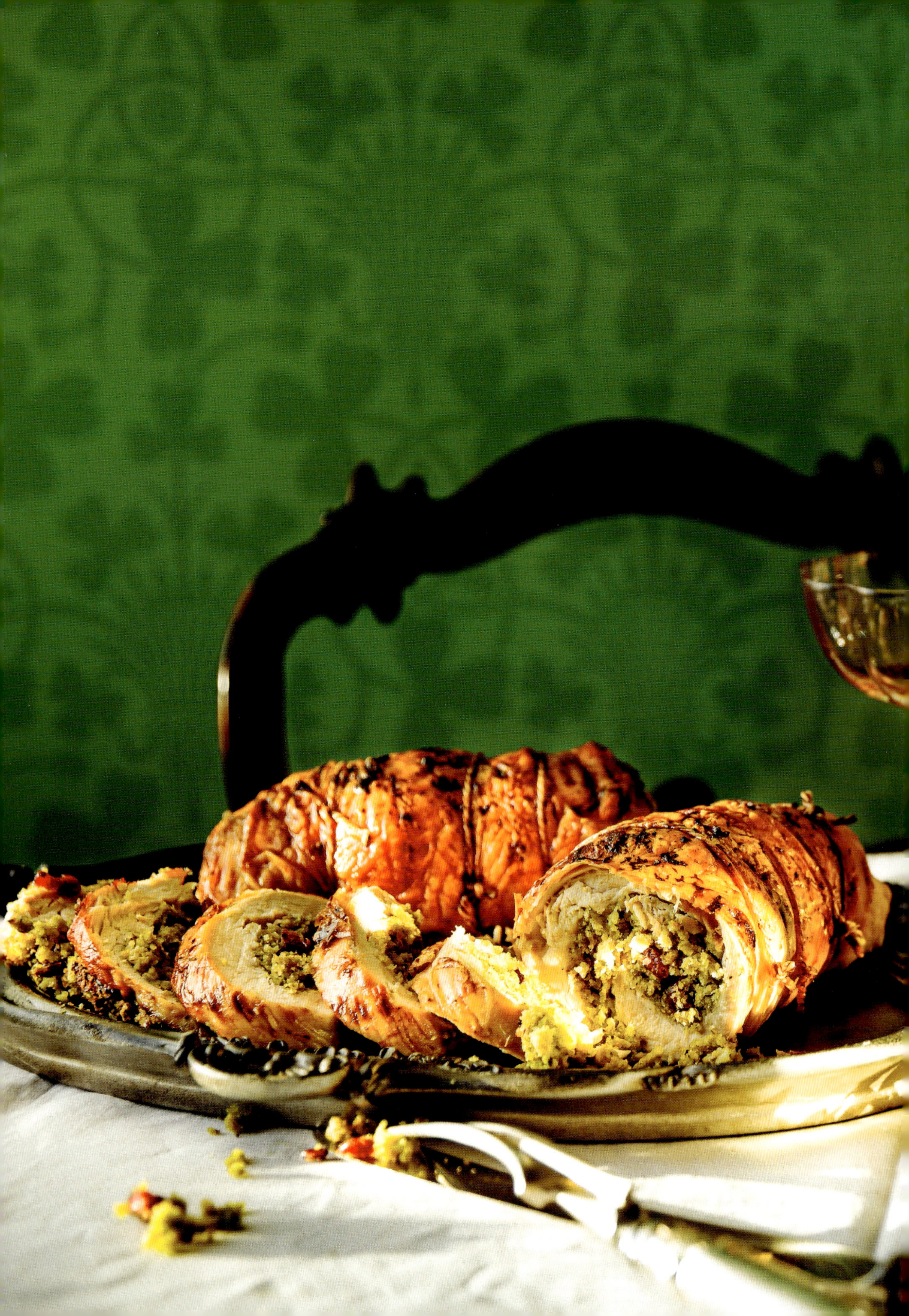

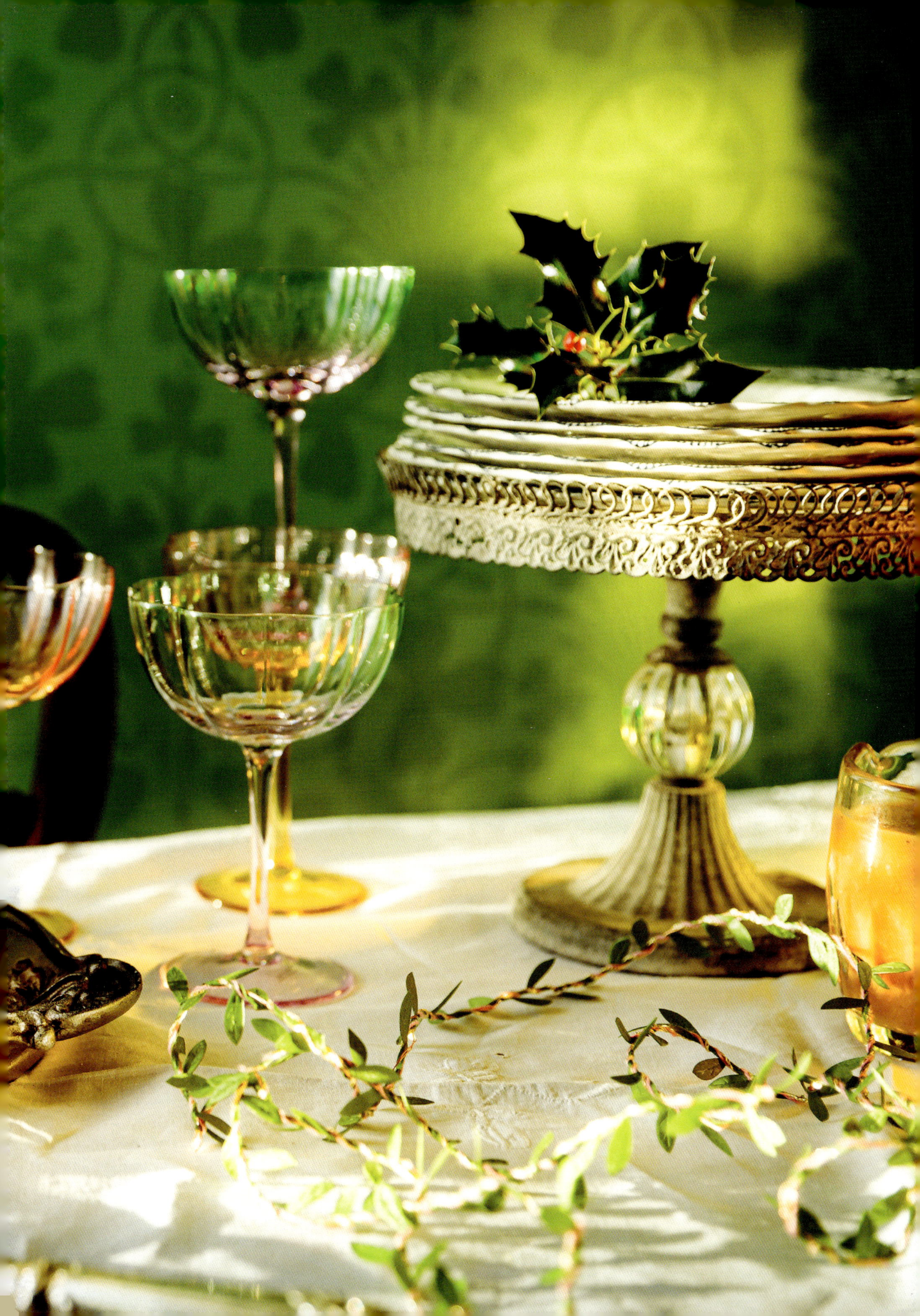

Cooking by season

Spring

SMALL PLATES
Beetroot & Hazelnut Salad with Whipped Goat's Cheese (p.16)
Chicken Potstickers (p.28)
Sweet Potato & Cáis Óir Fritters (p.32)
Crab Gratin (p.35)
Spanish Tapas (p.45)
Crispy Lamb-Stuffed Flatbreads (p.54)

BIG PLATES
Italian Stuffed Conchiglioni (p.67)
Roast Picanha & Chargrilled Pepper Salad (p.72)
Chicken Shawarma (p.89)
Large Plaice with Garlic Butter Sauce (p.101)
Hake with Red Pepper Sauce (p.104)
Spiced Roast Cauliflower (p.106)

SIDE PLATES
Focaccia with Rosemary & Sea Salt (p.112)
Lemon Roast Potato Wedges (p.137)
Braised Petits Pois with Bacon (p.138)
Warm Potato Salad (p.146)
Creamy Butter Beans with Leeks (p.153)
Steamed Asparagus with Hollandaise (p.156)

SWEET THINGS
Mango with Lime, Chilli & Star Anise (p.178)
Lemon Curd Cheesecake (p.187)
Brown Butter Madeleines (p.205)
Tiramisu (p.206)
Victoria Sponge with Rhubarb, Lemon Curd & Cream (p.208)
Red Velvet Cake (p.215)

Summer

SMALL PLATES
Caponata with Burrata (p.6)
Crispy Squid with Smoked Paprika Mayonnaise (p.8)
Carlingford Oysters with Shallot & Tarragon Dressing (p.11)
Two Bruschettas: Tomato & Basil, Broad Bean (p.15)
Sizzling Garlic & Chilli Prawns (p.46)
Pickled Mixed Vegetables (p.53)

BIG PLATES
Crispy Spatchcock Chicken with Lemon & Herbs (p.60)
Tacos with Chicken Tinga (p.74)
Aubergines Stuffed with Onions, Tomato, Chilli & Parsley (p.76)
Aromatic Poached Salmon with Avocado & Cucumber Salad (p.83)
Slow-Cooked Onion & Goat's Cheese Tart (p.86)
Iberico Pork with Red Gooseberry Relish (p.92)

SIDE PLATES
Chargrilled Aubergine with Tahini Dressing (p.120)
Grilled Corn Salad (p.127)
House Salad with Amelda's Dressing (p.132)
Green Beans with Goat's Cheese (p.134)
Grilled Courgettes with Green Chimichurri Sauce (p.144)
Summer Slaw (p.163)

SWEET THINGS
Affogato (p.168)
Moroccan Orange Salad with Pomegranate (p.170)
Aperol Spritz Sorbet (p.173)
Summer Blush (p.176)
Lemon Posset with Passion Fruit (p.180)
Vanilla Panna Cotta with Clarke's Strawberries (p.182)
Summer Fruit Trifle (p.203)
Cookies & Cream Birthday Cake (p.216)

Autumn

SMALL PLATES

Mussels in Spiced Cream (p.12)
Mushroom Risotto (p.31)
Baba Ghanoush Salad (p.39)
Artichoke & Parma Ham Salad (p.40)
Tunisian Carrot Salad (p.42)
Fully Loaded Nachos (p.49)

BIG PLATES

Beef Ragu Lasagne (p.64)
Fragrant Butterflied Lamb (p.69)
Greek Beef & Macaroni Pie (p.79)
Crispy Porchetta with Fennel & Herbs (p.80)
Butter Chicken (p.85)
Chateaubriand with Béarnaise Sauce (p.96)
Stuffed Beef Rolls with Tomato Ragu (p.102)

SIDE PLATES

Homemade Flatbreads (p.114)
Green Couscous (p.118)
Pilau Rice (p.131)
Potato Gratin (p.143)
Tomato & Cucumber Salad with Whipped Feta (p.158)
Honey-Glazed Spiced Carrots with Pistachio & Dill (p.160)

SWEET THINGS

Apple Mojito (p.185)
Coconut Crème Brûlée (p.193)
Warm Blondies with Sea Salt Toffee Sauce (p.198)
Walnut & Espresso Slice (p.200)
Peanut Butter Fudge with Goji Berries & Pistachios (p.212)

Winter

SMALL PLATES

Spanakopita (p.18)
Spiced Cauliflower Bites (p.21)
Crispy Duck Confit Salad (p.23)
Ham Hock Terrine (p.24)
Celeriac Remoulade with Smoked Trout (p.26)
Smoked Salmon Wreath (p.37)
Bubbling Cheese with Roasted Grapes (p.50)

BIG PLATES

Sticky Damson Ham with Star Anise (p.58)
One-Pot Fish Pie (p.62)
Cottage Pie (p.71)
Macaroni Cheese with 'Nduja Crumbs (p.95)
Turkey Roulade with Maple Glaze (p.98)
Beef & Medjool Date Tagine (p.108)

SIDE PLATES

Chargrilled Tenderstem Broccoli with Caesar Dressing (p.117)
Frites (p.123)
Smashed Roast Potatoes (p.124)
Pickled Red Onions (p.140)
Slow-Roast Tomatoes with Puy Lentils (p.148)
Chargrilled Cabbage with Kimchi Dressing (p.155)
Apple & Fennel Salad (p.164)

SWEET THINGS

Hot Chocolate with Cinnamon Churros (p.175)
Basque Cheesecake with Cherry Compote (p.188)
Cinnamon Swirl Apple Cake (p.190)
Coole Swan Chocolate Truffles (p.194)
Chocolate Mousse Cups (p.197)
Pavlova Wreath with Exotic Fruit (p.211)

Cooking by timings

Can be prepared well in advance

SMALL PLATES
Caponata with Burrata (p.6)
Spanakopita (p.18)
Ham Hock Terrine (p.24)
Chicken Potstickers (p.28)
Baba Ghanoush Salad (p.39)
Tunisian Carrot Salad (p.42)
Pickled Mixed Vegetables (p.53)

BIG PLATES
Sticky Damson Ham with Star Anise (p.58)
Crispy Spatchcock Chicken with Lemon & Herbs (p.60)
One-Pot Fish Pie (p.62)
Beef Ragu Lasagne (p.64)
Italian Stuffed Conchiglioni (p.67)
Fragrant Butterflied Lamb (p.69)
Greek Beef & Macaroni Pie (p.79)
Butter Chicken (p.85)
Slow-Cooked Onion & Goat's Cheese Tart (p.86)
Chicken Shawarma (p.89)
Iberico Pork with Red Gooseberry Relish (p.92)
Macaroni Cheese with 'Nduja Crumbs (p.95)
Turkey Roulade with Maple Glaze (p.98)
Stuffed Beef Rolls with Tomato Ragu (p.102)
Beef & Medjool Date Tagine (p.108)

SIDE PLATES
Focaccia with Rosemary & Sea Salt (p.112)
Chargrilled Aubergine with Tahini Dressing (p.120)
Pickled Red Onions (p.140)
Potato Gratin (p.143)
Slow-Roast Tomatoes with Puy Lentils (p.148)
Creamy Butter Beans with Leeks (p.153)

SWEET THINGS
Aperol Spritz Sorbet (p.173)
Lemon Posset with Passion Fruit (p.180)
Vanilla Panna Cotta with Clarke's Strawberries (p.182)
Lemon Curd Cheesecake (p.187)
Basque Cheesecake with Cherry Compote (p.188)
Coconut Crème Brûlée (p.193)
Coole Swan Chocolate Truffles (p.194)
Chocolate Mousse Cups (p.197)
Walnut & Espresso Slice (p.200)
Tiramisu (p.206)
Pavlova Wreath with Exotic Fruit (p.211)
Peanut Butter Fudge with Goji Berries & Pistachios (p.212)
Red Velvet Cake (p.215)
Cookies & Cream Birthday Cake (p.216)

Can be prepared a few hours before

SMALL PLATES
Caponata with Burrata (p.6)
Beetroot & Hazelnut Salad with Whipped Goat's Cheese (p.16)
Spanakopita (p.18)
Ham Hock Terrine (p.24)
Celeriac Remoulade with Smoked Trout (p.26)
Chicken Potstickers (p.28)
Sweet Potato & Cáis Óir Fritters (p.32)
Crab Gratin (p.35)
Baba Ghanoush Salad (p.39)
Tunisian Carrot Salad (p.42)
Pickled Mixed Vegetables (p.53)
Crispy Lamb-Stuffed Flatbreads (p.54)

BIG PLATES
Sticky Damson Ham with Star Anise (p.58)
Crispy Spatchcock Chicken with Lemon & Herbs (p.60)
One-Pot Fish Pie (p.62)
Beef Ragu Lasagne (p.64)
Italian Stuffed Conchiglioni (p.67)
Fragrant Butterflied Lamb (p.69)
Tacos with Chicken Tinga (p.74)
Aubergines Stuffed with Onions, Tomato, Chilli & Parsley (p.76)
Greek Beef & Macaroni Pie (p.79)
Butter Chicken (p.85)
Slow-Cooked Onion & Goat's Cheese Tart (p.86)
Chicken Shawarma (p.89)
Iberico Pork with Red Gooseberry Relish (p.92)
Macaroni Cheese with 'Nduja Crumbs (p.95)
Turkey Roulade with Maple Glaze (p.98)
Stuffed Beef Rolls with Tomato Ragu (p.102)
Spiced Roast Cauliflower (p.106)
Beef & Medjool Date Tagine (p.108)

SIDE PLATES
Focaccia with Rosemary & Sea Salt (p.112)
Green Couscous (p.118)
Chargrilled Aubergine with Tahini Dressing (p.120)
Grilled Corn Salad (p.127)
Pickled Red Onions (p.140)
Potato Gratin (p.143)
Grilled Courgettes with Green Chimichurri Sauce (p.144)

Warm Potato Salad (p.146)
Slow-Roast Tomatoes with Puy Lentils (p.148)
Creamy Butter Beans with Leeks (p.153)
Tomato & Cucumber Salad with Whipped Feta (p.158)
Summer Slaw (p.163)

SWEET THINGS
Moroccan Orange Salad with Pomegranate (p.170)
Aperol Spritz Sorbet (p.173)
Mango with Lime, Chilli & Star Anise (p.178)
Lemon Posset with Passion Fruit (p.180)
Vanilla Panna Cotta with Clarke's Strawberries (p.182)
Lemon Curd Cheesecake (p.187)
Basque Cheesecake with Cherry Compote (p.188)
Cinnamon Swirl Apple Cake (p.190)
Coconut Crème Brûlée (p.193)
Coole Swan Chocolate Truffles (p.194)
Chocolate Mousse Cups (p.197)
Warm Blondies with Sea Salt Toffee Sauce (p.198)
Walnut & Espresso Slice (p.200)
Summer Fruit Trifle (p.203)
Brown Butter Madeleines (p.205)
Tiramisu (p.206)
Victoria Sponge with Rhubarb, Lemon Curd & Cream (p.208)
Pavlova Wreath with Exotic Fruit (p.211)
Peanut Butter Fudge with Goji Berries & Pistachios (p.212)
Red Velvet Cake (p.215)
Cookies & Cream Birthday Cake (p.216)

Serve straight away

SMALL PLATES
Crispy Squid with Smoked Paprika Mayonnaise (p.8)
Carlingford Oysters with Shallot & Tarragon Dressing (p.11)
Mussels in Spiced Cream (p.12)
Two Bruschettas: Tomato & Basil, Broad Bean (p.15)
Spiced Cauliflower Bites (p.21)
Crispy Duck Confit Salad (p.23)
Mushroom Risotto (p.31)
Smoked Salmon Wreath (p.37)
Artichoke & Parma Ham Salad (p.40)
Spanish Tapas (p.45)
Sizzling Garlic & Chilli Prawns (p.46)
Fully Loaded Nachos (p.49)
Bubbling Cheese with Roasted Grapes (p.50)

BIG PLATES
Roast Picanha & Chargrilled Pepper Salad (p.72)
Aromatic Poached Salmon with Avocado & Cucumber Salad (p.83)
Chateaubriand with Béarnaise Sauce (p.96)
Large Plaice with Garlic Butter Sauce (p.101)
Stuffed Beef Rolls with Tomato Ragu (p.102)
Hake with Red Pepper Sauce (p.104)
Beef & Medjool Date Tagine (p.108)

SIDE PLATES
Homemade Flatbreads (p.114)
Chargrilled Tenderstem Broccoli with Caesar Dressing (p.117)
Frites (p.123)
House Salad with Amelda's Dressing (p.132)
Green Beans with Goat's Cheese (p.134)
Lemon Roast Potato Wedges (p.137)
Braised Petits Pois with Bacon (p.138)
Chargrilled Cabbage with Kimchi Dressing (p.155)
Steamed Asparagus with Hollandaise (p.156)
Tomato & Cucumber Salad with Whipped Feta (p.158)
Honey-Glazed Spiced Carrots with Pistachio & Dill (p.160)
Apple & Fennel Salad (p.164)

SWEET THINGS
Affogato (p.168)
Hot Chocolate with Cinnamon Churros (p.175)
Summer Blush (p.176)

Can be thrown together in a hurry

SMALL PLATES
Two Bruschettas: Tomato & Basil, Broad Bean (p.15)
Artichoke & Parma Ham Salad (p.40)
Spanish Tapas (p.45)
Sizzling Garlic & Chilli Prawns (p.46)
Fully Loaded Nachos (p.49)

BIG PLATES
Crispy Spatchcock Chicken with Lemon & Herbs (p.60)
Aromatic Poached Salmon with Avocado & Cucumber Salad (p.83)
Chateaubriand with Béarnaise Sauce (p.96)
Large Plaice with Garlic Butter Sauce (p.101)
Hake with Red Pepper Sauce (p.104)

SIDE PLATES
Homemade Flatbreads (p.114)
House Salad with Amelda's Dressing (p.132)
Green Beans with Goat's Cheese (p.134)
Braised Petits Pois with Bacon (p.138)
Grilled Courgettes with Green Chimichurri Sauce (p.144)
Tomato & Cucumber Salad with Whipped Feta (p.158)
Apple & Fennel Salad (p.164)

SWEET THINGS
Affogato (p.168)
Moroccan Orange Salad with Pomegranate (p.170)
Summer Blush (p.176)
Mango with Lime, Chilli & Star Anise (p.178)
Apple Mojito (p.185)
Warm Blondies with Sea Salt & Toffee Sauce (p.198)

Vegetarian listing

SMALL PLATES

Caponata with Burrata (p.6)
Two Bruschettas: Tomato & Basil, Broad Bean (p.15)
Beetroot & Hazelnut Salad with Whipped Goat's Cheese (p.16)
Spanakopita (p.18)
Spiced Cauliflower Bites (p.20)
Mushroom Risotto (p.31)
Sweet Potato & Cáis Óir Fritters (p.32)
Baba Ghanoush Salad (p.39)
Tunisian Carrot Salad (p.42)
Fully Loaded Nachos (p.49)
Bubbling Cheese with Roasted Grapes (p.50)
Pickled Mixed Vegetables (p.53)

BIG PLATES

Italian Stuffed Conchiglioni (p.67)
Fragrant Butterflied Lamb (p.69)
Aubergines Stuffed with Onions, Tomato, Chilli & Parsley (p.76)
Slow-Cooked Onion & Goat's Cheese Tart (p.86)
Spiced Roast Cauliflower (p.106)

SIDE PLATES

Focaccia with Rosemary & Sea Salt (p.112)
Homemade Flatbreads (p.114)
Chargrilled Tenderstem Broccoli with Caesar Dressing (p.117)
Green Couscous (p.118)
Chargrilled Aubergine with Tahini Dressing (p.120)
Frites (p.123)
Smashed Roast Potatoes (p.124)
Grilled Corn Salad (p.131)
Pilau Rice (p.131)
House Salad with Amelda's Dressing (p.132)
Green Beans with Goat's Cheese (p.134)
Lemon Roast Potato Wedges (p.137)
Pickled Red Onions (p.140)
Potato Gratin (p.143)
Grilled Courgettes with Green Chimichurri Sauce (p.144)
Slow-Roast Tomatoes with Puy Lentils (p.148)
Creamy Butter Beans with Leeks (p.153)
Chargrilled Cabbage with Kimchi Dressing (p.155)
Steamed Asparagus with Hollandaise (p.156)

Tomato & Cucumber Salad with Whipped Feta (p.158)
Honey-Glazed Spiced Carrots with Pistachio & Dill (p.160)
Summer Slaw (p.163)
Apple & Fennel Salad (p.164)

SWEET THINGS
Affogato (p.168)
Moroccan Orange Salad with Pomegranate (p.170)
Aperol Spritz Sorbet (p.173)
Hot Chocolate with Cinnamon Churros (p.175)
Summer Blush (p.176)
Mango with Lime, Chilli & Star Anise (p.178)
Lemon Posset with Passion Fruit (p.180)
Apple Mojito (p.185)
Lemon Curd Cheesecake (p.187)
Basque Cheesecake with Cherry Compote (p.188)
Cinnamon Swirl Apple Cake (p.190)
Coconut Crème Brûlée (p.193)
Coole Swan Chocolate Truffles (p.194)
Chocolate Mousse Cups (p.197)
Warm Blondies with Sea Salt Toffee Sauce (p.198)
Walnut & Espresso Slice (p.200)
Summer Fruit Trifle (p.203)
Brown Butter Madeleines (p.205)
Tiramisu (p.206)
Victoria Sponge with Rhubarb, Lemon Curd & Cream (p.208)
Pavlova Wreath with Exotic Fruit (p.211)
Peanut Butter Fudge with Goji Berries & Pistachios (p.212)
Red Velvet Cake (p.215)
Cookies & Cream Birthday Cake (p.216)

Acknowledgements

First of all I would like to thank my readers, many of whom I have had the pleasure of meeting over the years. They often have questions, observations and comments that find their way into my books. I enjoy listening to people at demos, and without these people I am sure I would not have reached this milestone of publishing my 20th book. And a big thank you to the bookshops, who have always been so supportive.

A lot has changed in terms of the Irish palate over these years, and in the superb quality of food produced at home and the huge range available on shelves today. I hope that this is well reflected in *Eat Out at Home*.

My thanks to Gill for having faith in me once again. Nicki Howard worked closely with me on this book. Her creativity is inspiring. I am thrilled with the work of food stylist Sally Dunne and her assistant extraordinaire, Tilly Brennan; photographer Gillian Buckley for her stunning food photography; and Mike O'Dwyer who did all the retouching. Thank you to David Skinners for the use of his stunning wallpapers, designer Graham Thew and editor Isabelle Hanrahan. Together they have given this book a look that I am thrilled with. Once again, Orla Broderick was marvellous to collaborate with in developing and testing the recipes. Her attention to detail is second to none.

Most of the people who have supported me in my career have been with me for many years now, and I hugely appreciate it. A big thank you to Bord Bia. Flogas and John Rooney, Eoin O'Flynn and my brother Kenneth have worked with me on demos and on our television programmes. Thank you to the TV team of David Hare and crew, and Claire Beasley from MacNean Restaurant. RTÉ's Brian Walsh is also great to work with.

Over the years I have enjoyed working with the media and met so many great people – too many to mention – but Marty Whelan has been there from day one on *Open Lyric*. He has still never cooked for me. Thank you Marty.

Every week I work with the *Irish Farmers Journal*, with the Simply Better team at Dunnes Stores, and with the many excellent Irish producers who supply us at the restaurant. Thank you for your support and inspiration.

The centre of my life is always Blacklion, family, and the restaurant. My team at MacNean, led by head chef Carmel McGirr, are a fabulous group of hard-working, talented people who love food and hospitality. I always enjoy working with them – as I do with my right-hand woman, Andrea Doherty, and of course, Amelda.

I hope readers get enjoyment from these recipes and the pleasure of cooking for and eating with family and friends. Nothing beats it.

Index

A

Affogato 168
agave syrup, Mango with Lime, Chilli & Star Anise 178
almonds
    Beef & Medjool Date Tagine 108
    Spanish Tapas 45
almonds (ground)
    Brown Butter Madeleines 205
    Peanut Butter Fudge with Goji Berries & Pistachios 212
anchovies
    Caponata with Burrata 6
    Chargrilled Tenderstem Broccoli with Caesar Dressing 117
    Slow-Cooked Onion & Goat's Cheese Tart 86
Aperol Spritz Sorbet 173
apple cider vinegar
    Celeriac Remoulade with Smoked Trout 26
    Ham Hock Terrine 24
    House Salad with Amelda's Dressing 132
    Pickled Red Onions 140
    Tunisian Carrot Salad 42
Apple Mojito 185
apples
    Apple & Fennel Salad 164
    Celeriac Remoulade with Smoked Trout 26
    Cinnamon Swirl Apple Cake 190
Aromatic Poached Salmon with Avocado & Cucumber Salad 83
Artichoke & Parma Ham Salad 40
asparagus, Steamed Asparagus with Hollandaise 156
aubergines
    Aubergines Stuffed with Onions, Tomato, Chilli & Parsley 76
    Baba Ghanoush Salad 39
    Caponata with Burrata 6
    Chargrilled Aubergine with Tahini Dressing 120
avocados
    Aromatic Poached Salmon with Avocado & Cucumber Salad 83
    Fully Loaded Nachos 49
    Smoked Salmon Wreath 37

B

Baba Ghanoush Salad 39
bacon
    Braised Petits Pois with Bacon 138
    see also ham; pork
Basque Cheesecake with Cherry Compote 188
beans
    Creamy Butter Beans with Leeks 153
    Green Beans with Goat's Cheese 134
    Two Bruschettas: Tomato & Basil, Broad Bean 15
beef
    Beef & Medjool Date Tagine 108
    Beef Ragu Lasagne 64
    Chateaubriand with Béarnaise Sauce 96
    Cottage Pie 71
    Greek Beef & Macaroni Pie 79
    Roast Picanha & Chargrilled Pepper Salad 72
    Stuffed Beef Rolls with Tomato Ragu 102
Beetroot & Hazelnut Salad with Whipped Goat's Cheese 16
berries
    Chocolate Mousse Cups 197
    Iberico Pork with Red Gooseberry Relish 92
    Pavlova Wreath with Exotic Fruit 211
    Peanut Butter Fudge with Goji Berries & Pistachios 212
    Summer Fruit Trifle 203
    Vanilla Panna Cotta with Clarke's Strawberries 182
biscuits
    Cookies & Cream Birthday Cake 216
    Lemon Curd Cheesecake 187
    Summer Fruit Trifle 203
bok choy, Chicken Potstickers 28
Braised Petits Pois with Bacon 138
bread
    Focaccia with Rosemary & Sea Salt 112
    Homemade Flatbreads 114
    see also flatbreads
breadcrumbs
    Crab Gratin 35
    Macaroni Cheese with 'Nduja Crumbs 95
    Turkey Roulade with Maple Glaze 98
broccoli, Chargrilled Tenderstem Broccoli with Caesar Dressing 117
Brown Butter Madeleines 205
Bubbling Cheese with Roasted Grapes 50
burrata cheese
    Beef Ragu Lasagne 64
    Caponata with Burrata 6
Butter Chicken 85
buttermilk
    Spiced Cauliflower Bites 21
    Sweet Potato & Cáis Óir Fritters 32

C

cabbage
    Chargrilled Cabbage with Kimchi Dressing 155
    Summer Slaw 163
cacao nibs, Peanut Butter Fudge with Goji Berries & Pistachios 212
Cáis Óir
    Greek Beef & Macaroni Pie 79
    Sweet Potato & Cáis Óir Fritters 32
cakes
    Brown Butter Madeleines 205
    Cinnamon Swirl Apple Cake 190
    Cookies & Cream Birthday Cake 216
    Red Velvet Cake 215
    Victoria Sponge with Rhubarb, Lemon Curd & Cream 208
    Walnut & Espresso Slice 200
    Warm Blondies with Sea Salt Toffee Sauce 198
capers
    Caponata with Burrata 6
    Celeriac Remoulade with Smoked Trout 26
    House Salad with Amelda's Dressing 132
Caponata with Burrata 6
Carlingford Oysters with Shallot & Tarragon Dressing 11
carrots
    Cottage Pie 71
    Ham Hock Terrine 24
    Honey-Glazed Spiced Carrots with Pistachio & Dill 160
    Pickled Mixed Vegetables 53

Summer Slaw 163
Tunisian Carrot Salad 42
cauliflower
   Pickled Mixed Vegetables 53
   Spiced Cauliflower Bites 21
   Spiced Roast Cauliflower 106
Celeriac Remoulade with Smoked Trout 26
celery
   Apple & Fennel Salad 164
   Beef Ragu Lasagne 64
   Caponata with Burrata 6
   Cottage Pie 71
   Greek Beef & Macaroni Pie 79
   Ham Hock Terrine 24
   Sticky Damson Ham with Star Anise 58
   Stuffed Beef Rolls with Tomato Ragu 102
Chargrilled Aubergine with Tahini Dressing 120
Chargrilled Cabbage with Kimchi Dressing 155
Chargrilled Tenderstem Broccoli with Caesar Dressing 117
Chateaubriand with Béarnaise Sauce 96
Cheddar cheese
   Cottage Pie 71
   Crispy Lamb-Stuffed Flatbreads 54
   Fully Loaded Nachos 49
   Macaroni Cheese with 'Nduja Crumbs 95
cheese
   Artichoke & Parma Ham Salad 40
   Bubbling Cheese with Roasted Grapes 50
   Creamy Butter Beans with Leeks 153
   Italian Stuffed Conchiglioni 67
   Mushroom Risotto 31
   Spanish Tapas 45
   see also burrata cheese; Cáis Óir; Cheddar cheese; cream cheese; feta cheese; goat's cheese; mascarpone; Parmesan
cheesecake
   Basque Cheesecake with Cherry Compote 188
   Lemon Curd Cheesecake 187
cherries, Basque Cheesecake with Cherry Compote 188

chicken
   Butter Chicken 85
   Chicken Potstickers 28
   Chicken Shawarma 89
   Crispy Spatchcock Chicken with Lemon & Herbs 61
   Tacos with Chicken Tinga 74
chimichurri sauce, Grilled Courgettes with Green Chimichurri Sauce 144
chocolate
   Affogato 168
   Chocolate Mousse Cups 197
   Cookies & Cream Birthday Cake 216
   Coole Swan Chocolate Truffles 194
   Hot Chocolate with Cinnamon Churros 175
   Tiramisu 206
   Warm Blondies with Sea Salt Toffee Sauce 198
chorizo, Spanish Tapas 45
cider vinegar, Pickled Mixed Vegetables 53
Cinnamon Swirl Apple Cake 190
cocoa powder
   Coole Swan Chocolate Truffles 194
   Red Velvet Cake 215
   Summer Fruit Trifle 203
   Tiramisu 206
Coconut Crème Brûlée 193
coffee
   Affogato 168
   Tiramisu 206
   Walnut & Espresso Slice 200
Cookies & Cream Birthday Cake 216
cooking by numbers 218–21
cooking by season 224–7
cooking by timings 228–33
   prepared a few hours before 230–1
   prepared well in advance 228–9
   serve straight away 232
   thrown together in a hurry 233
Coole Swan Chocolate Truffles 194
cordial
   Summer Blush 176
   Summer Fruit Trifle 203
corn, Grilled Corn Salad 127
cornichons, Celeriac Remoulade with Smoked Trout 26
Cottage Pie 71

courgettes, Grilled Courgettes with Green Chimichurri Sauce 144
couscous, Green Couscous 118
Crab Gratin 35
cranberries, Turkey Roulade with Maple Glaze 98
cream
   Butter Chicken 85
   Chocolate Mousse Cups 197
   Coconut Crème Brûlée 193
   Cookies & Cream Birthday Cake 216
   Coole Swan Chocolate Truffles 194
   Cottage Pie 71
   Hot Chocolate with Cinnamon Churros 175
   Lemon Posset with Passion Fruit 180
   Mussels in Spiced Cream 12
   One-Pot Fish Pie 62
   Pavlova Wreath with Exotic Fruit 211
   Potato Gratin 143
   Summer Fruit Trifle 203
   Tiramisu 206
   Vanilla Panna Cotta with Clarke's Strawberries 182
   Victoria Sponge with Rhubarb, Lemon Curd & Cream 208
cream cheese
   Basque Cheesecake with Cherry Compote 188
   Beetroot & Hazelnut Salad with Whipped Goat's Cheese 16
   Red Velvet Cake 215
cream (sour)
   Basque Cheesecake with Cherry Compote 188
   Cinnamon Swirl Apple Cake 190
   Fully Loaded Nachos 49
   Summer Slaw 163
   Sweet Potato & Cáis Óir Fritters 32
   Tacos with Chicken Tinga 74
Creamy Butter Beans with Leeks 153
crème fraîche
   Crab Gratin 35
   Creamy Butter Beans with Leeks 153
   Walnut & Espresso Slice 200
Crispy Duck Confit Salad 23

Crispy Lamb-Stuffed Flatbreads 54
Crispy Porchetta with Fennel & Herbs 80
Crispy Spatchcock Chicken with Lemon & Herbs 61
Crispy Squid with Smoked Paprika Mayonnaise 8
cucumbers
    Aromatic Poached Salmon with Avocado & Cucumber Salad 83
    Baba Ghanoush Salad 39
    Crispy Duck Confit Salad 23
    House Salad with Amelda's Dressing 132
    Smoked Salmon Wreath 37
    Tomato & Cucumber Salad with Whipped Feta 158
curry, Butter Chicken 85
custard, Summer Fruit Trifle 203

D
damson jam, Sticky Damson Ham with Star Anise 58
dates, Beef & Medjool Date Tagine 108
drinks
    Apple Mojito 185
    Summer Blush 176
duck, Crispy Duck Confit Salad 23
dumpling wrappers, Chicken Potstickers 28

E
eggs (savoury recipes)
    Chargrilled Tenderstem Broccoli with Caesar Dressing 117
    Chateaubriand with Béarnaise Sauce 96
    Chicken Potstickers 28
    Cottage Pie 71
    Italian Stuffed Conchiglioni 67
    One-Pot Fish Pie 62
    Slow-Cooked Onion & Goat's Cheese Tart 86
    Spanokopita 18
    Steamed Asparagus with Hollandaise 156
    Sweet Potato & Cáis Óir Fritters 32
eggs (sweet recipes)
    Basque Cheesecake with Cherry Compote 188
    Brown Butter Madeleines 205
    Chocolate Mousse Cups 197
    Cinnamon Swirl Apple Cake 190
    Coconut Crème Brûlée 193
    Hot Chocolate with Cinnamon Churros 175
    Pavlova Wreath with Exotic Fruit 211
    Red Velvet Cake 215
    Tiramisu 206
    Victoria Sponge with Rhubarb, Lemon Curd & Cream 208
    Walnut & Espresso Slice 200
    Warm Blondies with Sea Salt Toffee Sauce 198

F
fennel bulbs
    Apple & Fennel Salad 164
    Smoked Salmon Wreath 37
feta cheese
    Grilled Corn Salad 127
    Spanokopita 18
    Tomato & Cucumber Salad with Whipped Feta 158
fish
    Celeriac Remoulade with Smoked Trout 26
    Hake with Red Pepper Sauce 104
    Large Plaice with Garlic Butter Sauce 101
    One-Pot Fish Pie 62
    Smoked Salmon Wreath 37
    see also shellfish; squid
flatbreads
    Chicken Shawarma 89
    Crispy Lamb-Stuffed Flatbreads 54
    Homemade Flatbreads 114
Focaccia with Rosemary & Sea Salt 112
Fragrant Butterflied Lamb 69
Frites 123
fudge, Peanut Butter Fudge with Goji Berries & Pistachios 212
Fully Loaded Nachos 49

G
goat's cheese
    Beetroot & Hazelnut Salad with Whipped Goat's Cheese 16
    Green Beans with Goat's Cheese 134
    Slow-Cooked Onion & Goat's Cheese Tart 86
grapes, Bubbling Cheese with Roasted Grapes 50
gravy, Turkey Roulade with Maple Glaze 98
Greek Beef & Macaroni Pie 79
Green Beans with Goat's Cheese 134
Green Couscous 118
Grilled Corn Salad 127
Grilled Courgettes with Green Chimichurri Sauce 144

H
Hake with Red Pepper Sauce 104
ham
    Artichoke & Parma Ham Salad 40
    Ham Hock Terrine 24
    Spanish Tapas 45
    Sticky Damson Ham with Star Anise 58
    Stuffed Beef Rolls with Tomato Ragu 102
    see also bacon; pork
hazelnuts
    Beetroot & Hazelnut Salad with Whipped Goat's Cheese 16
    Spiced Roast Cauliflower 106
hollandaise, Steamed Asparagus with Hollandaise 156
Homemade Flatbreads 114
Honey-Glazed Spiced Carrots with Pistachio & Dill 160
Hot Chocolate with Cinnamon Churros 175
House Salad with Amelda's Dressing 132

I
Iberico Pork with Red Gooseberry Relish 92
ice cream
    Affogato 168
    Mango with Lime, Chilli & Star Anise 178
Italian Stuffed Conchiglioni 67

K
kimchi, Chargrilled Cabbage with Kimchi Dressing 155

L

lamb
  Crispy Lamb-Stuffed Flatbreads 54
  Fragrant Butterflied Lamb 69
  Large Plaice with Garlic Butter Sauce 101
leeks
  Creamy Butter Beans with Leeks 153
  One-Pot Fish Pie 62
lemon curd, Victoria Sponge with Rhubarb, Lemon Curd & Cream 208
lemons
  Apple & Fennel Salad 164
  Artichoke & Parma Ham Salad 40
  Baba Ghanoush Salad 39
  Beetroot & Hazelnut Salad with Whipped Goat's Cheese 16
  Butter Chicken 85
  Celeriac Remoulade with Smoked Trout 26
  Chargrilled Aubergine with Tahini Dressing 120
  Chargrilled Tenderstem Broccoli with Caesar Dressing 117
  Chateaubriand with Béarnaise Sauce 96
  Crab Gratin 35
  Crispy Porchetta with Fennel & Herbs 80
  Crispy Spatchcock Chicken with Lemon & Herbs 61
  Hot Chocolate with Cinnamon Churros 175
  Large Plaice with Garlic Butter Sauce 101
  Lemon Curd Cheesecake 187
  Lemon Posset with Passion Fruit 180
  Lemon Roast Potato Wedges 137
  Mussels in Spiced Cream 12
  Sizzling Garlic & Chilli Prawns 46
  Smoked Salmon Wreath 37
  Steamed Asparagus with Hollandaise 156
  Vanilla Panna Cotta with Clarke's Strawberries 182
lentils, Slow-Roast Tomatoes with Puy Lentils 148

lettuce
  Braised Petits Pois with Bacon 138
  Chicken Shawarma 89
  House Salad with Amelda's Dressing 132
  Summer Slaw 163
limes
  Apple Mojito 185
  Aromatic Poached Salmon with Avocado & Cucumber Salad 83
  Crispy Duck Confit Salad 23
  Fully Loaded Nachos 49
  Grilled Corn Salad 127
  Mango with Lime, Chilli & Star Anise 178
liqueurs
  Affogato 168
  Aperol Spritz Sorbet 173
  Chocolate Mousse Cups 197
  Coole Swan Chocolate Truffles 194
  Tiramisu 206
lychees, Pavlova Wreath with Exotic Fruit 211

M

Macaroni Cheese with 'Nduja Crumbs 95
mangoes
  Crispy Duck Confit Salad 23
  Mango with Lime, Chilli & Star Anise 178
maple syrup
  Peanut Butter Fudge with Goji Berries & Pistachios 212
  Spiced Cauliflower Bites 21
  Turkey Roulade with Maple Glaze 98
mascarpone
  Cookies & Cream Birthday Cake 216
  Lemon Curd Cheesecake 187
  Tiramisu 206
mayonnaise
  Crispy Squid with Smoked Paprika Mayonnaise 8
  Summer Slaw 163
menus for larger groups 221
Moroccan Orange Salad with Pomegranate 170
Mushroom Risotto 31
Mussels in Spiced Cream 12

N

'nduja, Macaroni Cheese with 'Nduja Crumbs 95
nuts
  Spiced Roast Cauliflower 106
  Warm Blondies with Sea Salt Toffee Sauce 198
  see also almonds; hazelnuts; pine nuts; pistachios; walnuts

O

olives
  Baba Ghanoush Salad 39
  Caponata with Burrata 6
  Slow-Cooked Onion & Goat's Cheese Tart 86
  Spanish Tapas 45
  Tomato & Cucumber Salad with Whipped Feta 158
One-Pot Fish Pie 62
oranges
  Aperol Spritz Sorbet 173
  Moroccan Orange Salad with Pomegranate 170
  Sticky Damson Ham with Star Anise 58
  Summer Fruit Trifle 203

P

Padrón peppers, Spanish Tapas 45
panna cotta, Vanilla Panna Cotta with Clarke's Strawberries 182
Parmesan
  Beef Ragu Lasagne 64
  Chargrilled Tenderstem Broccoli with Caesar Dressing 117
  Crab Gratin 35
  Italian Stuffed Conchiglioni 67
  Macaroni Cheese with 'Nduja Crumbs 95
  Mushroom Risotto 31
  Two Bruschettas: Tomato & Basil, Broad Bean 15
passata
  Aubergines Stuffed with Onions, Tomato, Chilli & Parsley 76
  Beef Ragu Lasagne 64
  Butter Chicken 85
  Italian Stuffed Conchiglioni 67
passion fruit
  Lemon Posset with Passion Fruit 180

Pavlova Wreath with Exotic Fruit 211
pasta
   Beef Ragu Lasagne 64
   Greek Beef & Macaroni Pie 79
   Italian Stuffed Conchiglioni 67
   Macaroni Cheese with 'Nduja Crumbs 95
   Stuffed Beef Rolls with Tomato Ragu 102
pastry
   One-Pot Fish Pie 62
   Slow-Cooked Onion & Goat's Cheese Tart 86
   Spanokopita 18
Pavlova Wreath with Exotic Fruit 211
pea shoots, Smoked Salmon Wreath 37
Peanut Butter Fudge with Goji Berries & Pistachios 212
peanut and chilli rayu
   Chargrilled Cabbage with Kimchi Dressing 155
   Chicken Potstickers 28
pears, Artichoke & Parma Ham Salad 40
peas, Braised Petits Pois with Bacon 138
peppers
   Caponata with Burrata 6
   Hake with Red Pepper Sauce 104
   Roast Picanha & Chargrilled Pepper Salad 72
   Spanish Tapas 45
   Tacos with Chicken Tinga 74
Pickled Mixed Vegetables 53
Pickled Red Onions 140
Pilau Rice 131
pine nuts, Baba Ghanoush Salad 39
pistachios
   Green Couscous 118
   Honey-Glazed Spiced Carrots with Pistachio & Dill 160
   Peanut Butter Fudge with Goji Berries & Pistachios 212
pomegranate seeds
   Beef & Medjool Date Tagine 108
   Moroccan Orange Salad with Pomegranate 170
   Spiced Roast Cauliflower 106
   Summer Blush 176
pork
   Crispy Porchetta with Fennel & Herbs 80
   Iberico Pork with Red Gooseberry Relish 92
   see also bacon; ham
potatoes
   Cottage Pie 71
   Frites 123
   Lemon Roast Potato Wedges 137
   One-Pot Fish Pie 62
   Potato Gratin 143
   Smashed Roast Potatoes 124
   Warm Potato Salad 146
Prosecco, Summer Blush 176

R

radishes
   House Salad with Amelda's Dressing 132
   Pickled Mixed Vegetables 53
   Smoked Salmon Wreath 37
   Summer Slaw 163
raisins, Caponata with Burrata 6
red onions
   Butter Chicken 85
   Fully Loaded Nachos 49
   Iberico Pork with Red Gooseberry Relish 92
   Pickled Mixed Vegetables 53
   Pickled Red Onions 140
   Slow-Cooked Onion & Goat's Cheese Tart 86
   Spanokopita 18
   Summer Slaw 163
Red Velvet Cake 215
rhubarb, Victoria Sponge with Rhubarb, Lemon Curd & Cream 208
rice
   Mushroom Risotto 31
   Pilau Rice 131
rice vinegar
   Aromatic Poached Salmon with Avocado & Cucumber Salad 83
   Carlingford Oysters with Shallot & Tarragon Dressing 11
ricotta, Italian Stuffed Conchiglioni 67
Roast Picanha & Chargrilled Pepper Salad 72
rocket
   Artichoke & Parma Ham Salad 40
   Celeriac Remoulade with Smoked Trout 26
   Crispy Duck Confit Salad 23
   Green Couscous 118
   Slow-Roast Tomatoes with Puy Lentils 148
rum, Apple Mojito 185

S

scallions
   Aromatic Poached Salmon with Avocado & Cucumber Salad 83
   Braised Petits Pois with Bacon 138
   Chargrilled Cabbage with Kimchi Dressing 155
   Chicken Potstickers 28
   Green Couscous 118
   Grilled Corn Salad 127
   Smoked Salmon Wreath 37
   Spanokopita 18
   Sweet Potato & Cáis Óir Fritters 32
   Warm Potato Salad 146
semolina, Crispy Squid with Smoked Paprika Mayonnaise 8
shallots
   Carlingford Oysters with Shallot & Tarragon Dressing 11
   Chateaubriand with Béarnaise Sauce 96
   Crab Gratin 35
   Green Beans with Goat's Cheese 134
   Grilled Courgettes with Green Chimichurri Sauce 144
   Hake with Red Pepper Sauce 104
   Mussels in Spiced Cream 12
   One-Pot Fish Pie 62
   Slow-Roast Tomatoes with Puy Lentils 148
shellfish
   Carlingford Oysters with Shallot & Tarragon Dressing 11
   Crab Gratin 35
   Mussels in Spiced Cream 12
   Sizzling Garlic & Chilli Prawns 46
   see also fish; squid
Sizzling Garlic & Chilli Prawns 46
Slow-Cooked Onion & Goat's Cheese Tart 86
Slow-Roast Tomatoes with Puy Lentils 148
Smashed Roast Potatoes 124
Smoked Salmon Wreath 37
sorbet, Aperol Spritz Sorbet 173

Spanish Tapas 45
Spanokopita 18
Spiced Cauliflower Bites 21
Spiced Roast Cauliflower 106
spinach
    Crispy Duck Confit Salad 23
    Italian Stuffed Conchiglioni 67
    Spanokopita 18
sponge fingers, Tiramisu 206
squid, Crispy Squid with Smoked Paprika Mayonnaise 8
star anise
    Hake with Red Pepper Sauce 104
    Mango with Lime, Chilli & Star Anise 178
    Pickled Red Onions 140
    Sticky Damson Ham with Star Anise 58
Steamed Asparagus with Hollandaise 156
Sticky Damson Ham with Star Anise 58
Stuffed Beef Rolls with Tomato Ragu 102
Summer Blush 176
Summer Fruit Trifle 203
Summer Slaw 163
Sweet Potato & Cáis Óir Fritters 32

T
Tacos with Chicken Tinga 74
tahini
    Baba Ghanoush Salad 39
    Chargrilled Aubergine with Tahini Dressing 120
    Chicken Shawarma 89
tequila, Mango with Lime, Chilli & Star Anise 178
Tiramisu 206
tomato purée
    Greek Beef & Macaroni Pie 79
    Stuffed Beef Rolls with Tomato Ragu 102
tomatoes
    Aubergines Stuffed with Onions, Tomato, Chilli & Parsley 76
    Baba Ghanoush Salad 39
    Fully Loaded Nachos 49
    Greek Beef & Macaroni Pie 79
    House Salad with Amelda's Dressing 132
    Slow-Roast Tomatoes with Puy Lentils 148
    Spanish Tapas 45
    Tacos with Chicken Tinga 74
    Tomato & Cucumber Salad with Whipped Feta 158
    Two Bruschettas: Tomato & Basil, Broad Bean 15
tomatoes (tinned)
    Beef & Medjool Date Tagine 108
    Stuffed Beef Rolls with Tomato Ragu 102
tortilla chips, Fully Loaded Nachos 49
tortillas, Tacos with Chicken Tinga 74
trout/trout roe
    Celeriac Remoulade with Smoked Trout 26
    Smoked Salmon Wreath 37
Tunisian Carrot Salad 42
Turkey Roulade with Maple Glaze 98
Two Bruschettas: Tomato & Basil, Broad Bean 15

V
Vanilla Panna Cotta with Clarke's Strawberries 182
vegetarian listing 234–5
Victoria Sponge with Rhubarb, Lemon Curd & Cream 208

W
walnuts
    Apple & Fennel Salad 164
    Artichoke & Parma Ham Salad 40
    Bubbling Cheese with Roasted Grapes 50
    Green Beans with Goat's Cheese 134
    Walnut & Espresso Slice 200
Warm Blondies with Sea Salt Toffee Sauce 198
Warm Potato Salad 146
watercress, Crispy Duck Confit Salad 23
white-wine vinegar
    Beetroot & Hazelnut Salad with Whipped Goat's Cheese 16
    Caponata with Burrata 6
    Hake with Red Pepper Sauce 104
wine (red)
    Cottage Pie 71
    Greek Beef & Macaroni Pie 79
    Stuffed Beef Rolls with Tomato Ragu 102
wine (white)
    Braised Petits Pois with Bacon 138
    Chateaubriand with Béarnaise Sauce 96
    Crab Gratin 35
    Creamy Butter Beans with Leeks 153
    Mushroom Risotto 31
    Mussels in Spiced Cream 12

Y
yogurt
    Beef & Medjool Date Tagine 108
    Butter Chicken 85
    Chicken Shawarma 89
    Homemade Flatbreads 114
    Lemon Curd Cheesecake 187
    Spiced Roast Cauliflower 106
    Tomato & Cucumber Salad with Whipped Feta 158
    Victoria Sponge with Rhubarb, Lemon Curd & Cream 208

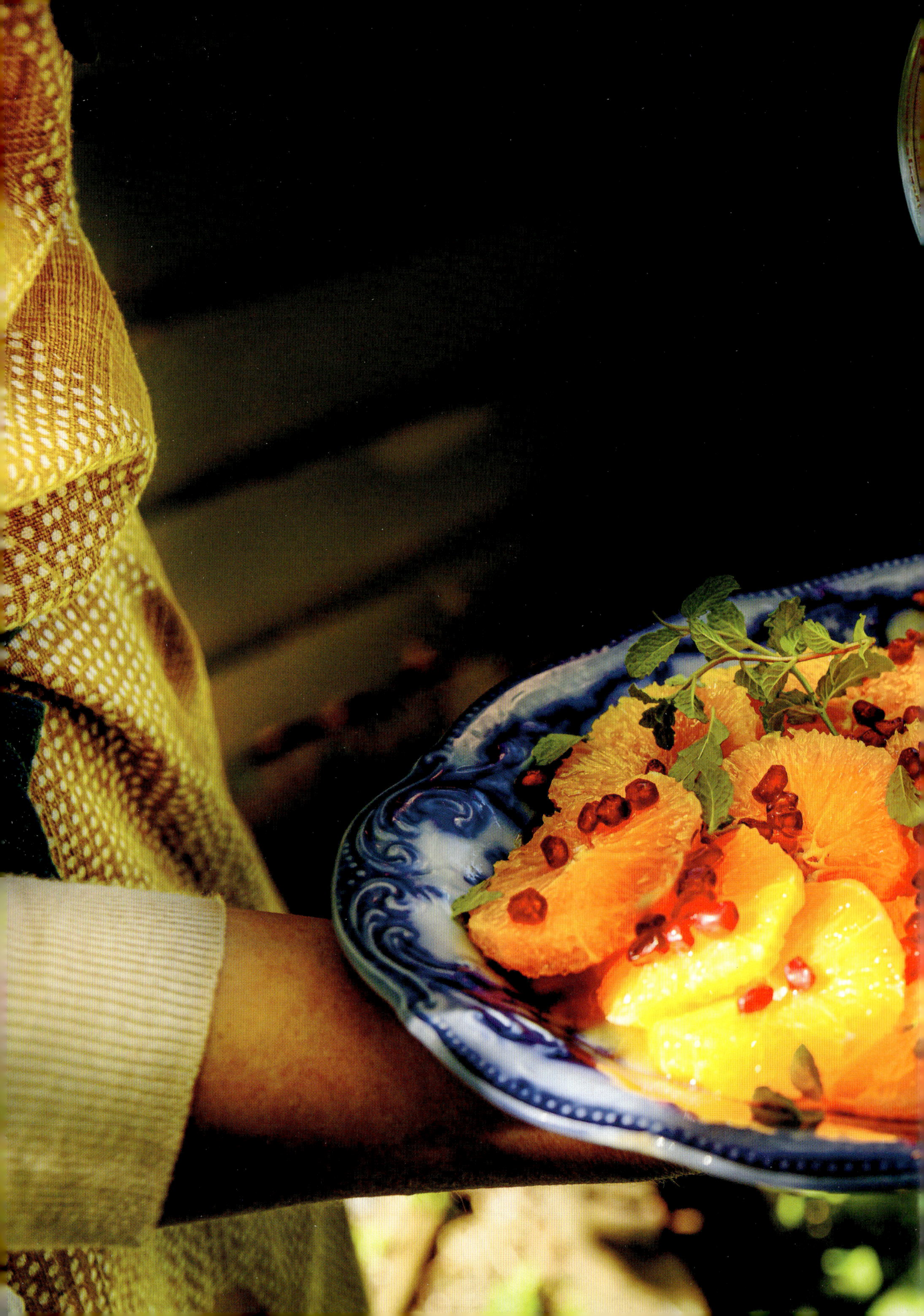